THE HORSE AND PONY Gift Book

THE HORSE AND PONY Gift Book

edited by

Robert Owen

and

John Bullock

Hamlyn

London · New York · Toronto · Sydney

Acknowledgments

The editors and publishers gratefully acknowledge the following sources of illustrations in this book: John Alexander, Animal Photography Ltd, Apollo Photography, Australian News & Information Bureau, Barnaby's Picture Library, British Tourist Authority, the Trustees of the British Museum, Burrell Collection (Glasgow Art Galleries), Canadian Government Travel Bureau, Colorsport, Colour Library International, Commissioner of Police of the Metropolis, Findlay Davidson, Equestrian Services Ltd, Hamlyn Group Picture Library, Clive Hiles, Riccardo Jucker Collection (Milan), Keystone Press Agency, E. D. Lacey, Leslie Lane, Mansell Collection, the Mellon Collection, Musée d'Art Moderne (Paris), Musée du Louvre (Paris), the Trustees of the National Gallery, Northern Ireland Tourist Board, Orbis Publishing Ltd, Photonews, Peter Roberts, Mike Slingsby, Syndication International Ltd, Walker Art Gallery (Liverpool), Wallace Collection, Watney Mann & Truman Brewers Ltd, Windsor, Slough & Eton Express.

Published by The Hamlyn Publishing Group Limited
London · New York · Sydney · Toronto
Astronaut House, Feltham, Middlesex, England
Originated, designed and produced by
Trewin Copplestone Publishing Ltd London
© Trewin Copplestone Publishing Ltd 1975
Filmsetting by Tradespools Ltd, Frome
Origination by Hilo Offset Ltd, Chelmsford
Printed in Spain by Mateu Cromo Artes Gráficas

SBN 600 34487 8

Contents

A History Of The Horse

by E. Hartley Edwards

The history of the horse is really a part of the history of the development of mankind, or perhaps you could put it the other way round. What is certain is that the greater part of human progress up to the end of the nineteenth century depended upon the strength and mobility of the horse.

In the course of some 5000 years the horse provided men with a means of transport and communication. Horses helped men to clear and cultivate land and, most importantly if rather sadly, they enabled men to wage war against each other. It was because of the horse that empires were won and lost and the spread of civilisation was made possible. Indeed, without horses it would have taken very much longer for the world to develop in the way that it has.

Think, for example, of the vast continent of America. The first white men to arrive there in force were the sixteenth-century Spanish *conquistadores* (conquerors). They landed in a huge, sparsely populated country in which, for some reason, perhaps because of some violent climatic change thousands of years before, or possibly because of some unknown disease, there were no horses at all. Much of the success of the *conquistadores* in conquering the native tribes was due to the horses they took with them. Never having seen such animals before, the people were terrified, thinking that the mounted soldiers were not men but monstrous gods.

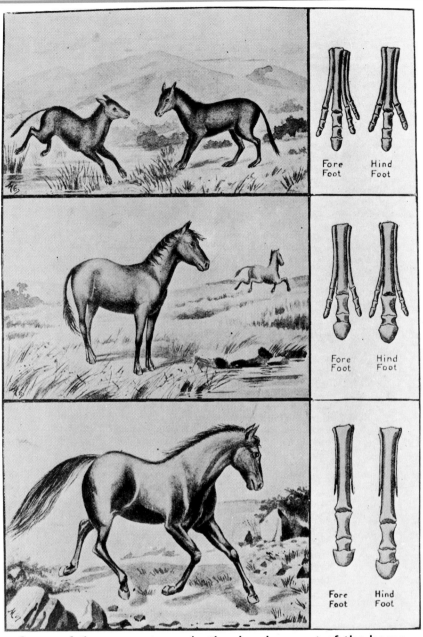

Some of the many stages in the development of the horse

These horses re-established the species in America, and it was their descendants that changed the lives of the American Indians who became horse-people, able to range far and wide in search of hunting grounds, whereas before they had been confined to the immediate surroundings of their settlements. As more white colonists poured into America they took more horses with them, and by the year 1900 America was a big, powerful nation. Most of that huge accomplishment was made in not much more than 200 years, and it was made possible, to a very large degree, by the horse.

A French writer of the eighteenth century paid tribute to the horse in this way: 'The horse,' he wrote, 'was swifter than anything on the face of the earth: he could outrun the deer, leap higher than the goat, endure longer than the wolf. Man, encompassed by the elements which conspired to destroy him, by beasts faster and stronger than himself, would have been a slave, had not the horse made him a King.' That was a rather poetical way of putting it but he was quite right.

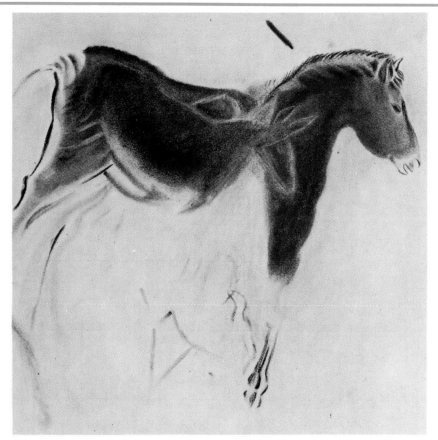

Above: Part of the well-known cave painting found at Altamira, Spain. Below: Sety I, who ruled in Ancient Egypt between 1326 and 1300 BC, is shown in his chariot on the walls of the Temple at Karnak

But, of course, while horses changed men's way of living, men also made some changes in the horse. The first horses that were tamed and used by the primitive people of 5000 years ago had developed from a little animal that was on the earth millions of years before. This animal, the first recognisable horse, we now call Eohippus. He was very small, about as big as a fox, and instead of hooves he had toes on his feet, four in front and three behind. Over the countless centuries he developed in size, shape and speed in order to survive in his changing surroundings.

At the time when horses started to be tamed and used for work his toes had long since disappeared and he looked very much like our horses of today, except that he was much smaller, In fact, we should think of him as a pony. Up to that time the horse's development was controlled only by his natural surroundings and by the amount of food they were able to provide. But when the partnership between men and horses came about changes in the size and appearance of the horse were more rapid.

It did not happen over night, but gradually men began to improve their horses, breeding them carefully for particular purposes, giving them artificial foods, dried grasses and grain, and crossing one strain with another, always with a view to producing bigger or faster or stronger horses. As a result of what began 5000 years ago there are now over 200 separate breeds of horses in the world. On one side we have the huge 'heavy' horses like the Shire who can weigh well over a ton and may stand 18 hands high, and on the other we have the light, very fast riding horses like the Thoroughbred racehorse and the Arab.

Mind you, man didn't do it all on his own. Nature produced horses that could survive in particular surroundings. The heavy horses (which we call the 'cold-bloods'), originating in the cold marshlands which covered Europe thousands of years ago and the lighter, faster horses (called 'hot-bloods') originating in the warm Eastern lands. All that man has really done is to improve upon what he found.

The first horses were tamed somewhere about 3000 BC, much later than dogs, for instance, who were living with men in domestic conditions about 6750 BC, or cattle which were domesticated 5–4000 BC. Sheep and goats, in fact, were probably domesticated even earlier. The first people we know of who used horses domestically were a tough breed of Indo-Europeans who lived in the steppes north of the mountain ranges bordering the Black and Caspian Seas, in the country we now know as Russia. But long before this time the horse was of use to man as a means of filling his larder. Primitive man hunted horses for food, often killing them in large numbers by driving them over cliffs.

Just how the horse was domesticated we don't know. Probably, since human beings have always had a soft spot for the very young, a foal was kept as a pet and gradually a herd of horses was built up with the mares being used for milk, a practice which continued for a very long time and which is still carried out today in places like Mongolia.

To start with horses do not seem to have been ridden, at any rate not seriously. They were used much more as pack animals and probably pulled a primitive form of sledge, very much like the *travois* used much later by the American Indians. This consisted of a pair of poles fastened on the horse like shafts at one end and trailing on the ground at the other. The poles were joined at the ground end and the space between them covered in such a way as to provide a platform to which articles could be secured.

The wheel, possibly man's greatest invention, did not arrive until about 1800 BC and thereafter it was the horse-drawn chariot that reigned supreme, although there is evidence of horses being ridden.

Among the early peoples to realise the use of mounted cavalry

were the Assyrians, mighty hunters and warriors, who so plagued the Israelites of the Old Testament. They were followed by Persians and Greeks and Scythians and a whole lot of others. By the time of Xenophon, a Greek general who lived between 430–355 BC, horses were very much a part of life and their management and training was well understood. Cavalry was used increasingly but it had its limitations because, as yet, riders were not entirely secure. Saddles were rough and ready or did not exist at all, and stirrups had not been invented.

If the wheel was the most important of man's inventions, the stirrup follows close behind. Somewhere about the 4th century AD the Huns from Mongolia stormed across the known world on shaggy ponies, riding short and using the stirrup.

That simple piece of equipment changed the role of the horseman and of cavalry tactics. It allowed cavalry to be used in mass formations against infantry. Because of the extra security it gave cavalry was able to charge the enemy without being unseated by the impact.

In AD 732 the French ruler Charles Martel and his knights, using the stirrup, charged and broke the Moorish invasion of Europe at Poitiers, and the pattern of cavalry action was established for the next 1600 years.

One of the most remarkable of the empires won and lost from the backs of horses was that created 800 years ago by an illiterate nomadic savage from the Gobi Desert. His name was Genghis Khan, and with his Mongol hordes, like Attila before him, he swept out of his own harsh world and within one lifetime made himself ruler of the world from the China Sea to the Baltic.

These Mongols were a race of horsemen brought up on mares milk and able to live on dried mare's curds. They used dung for their fires and when exhausted slit a vein in their horses' necks to drink the blood. On Mongol ponies of 13 hands or so, the *tumans* (a division of 10,000)

could cover eighty miles a day, each man having as many as three ponies and switching from one to another at the gallop.

Genghis Khan was also the inventor of the first 'pony-express', the Yam. Staging posts were set up through Asia and deep into Europe and along these routes messengers, changing horses at the posts, galloped 150 miles a day without rest.

The history of both horse and man tends to be dominated by warfare, but the horse played an equally important part in transport and communication and always he was used for sport.

The use of the horse for transport reached its height in nineteenth-century England, which had a postal and transport system that was the envy of the world. By 1845 the coming of the railways had largely killed the 'golden age' of the stage coach which was the pride of England. But horses continued to be employed in huge numbers up to and immediately following the First World War when the motor-car and the internal combustion engine finally took over the roles they had played so well for 5000 years.

For the horse the centuries of unremitting toil, the horrors of the battlefield and the all too frequent cruelties and abuses inflicted on him by the masters he had served for so long were over. He had no further part to play in the building of nations. In short, it looked as though his day was done.

However, although it might have been expected that in our century the horse would only be kept in small numbers for sport, in fact his popularity grew and grew. The history of the horse, instead of drawing gradually to its close, entered a new age after the Second World War.

Up till that time it was only the relatively well-to-do country dweller who could afford the cost of keeping horses for pleasure. But after the War, when everyone had more money and more leisure than ever before, horse-owning and riding were within the reach of many more people. Previously horses had been kept out of

From the Bayeux Tapestry

necessity for the purpose of work, now thousands upon thousands turned to them as an escape from their often dull town lives, keeping and riding horses purely for sport and recreation. Today some two million people in Britain alone ride for pleasure, and horses represent one of the most popular sports in the world.

Of course, right from the beginning, horses were used for sport as well as for war and work. The history of racing is probably as old as recorded time. Early man, once he had learnt to sit on a horse, must have matched one horse against another, and chariot racing was certainly popular for centuries before the birth of Christ. The Romans built huge amphitheatres for the purpose, and the ancient Greeks knew all about the sport, although horses took no part in their Olympic Games until the 25th Olympiad in 680 BC when chariot racing was one of the events. The early 'gold medallists' received the traditional and coveted olive wreaths, or rather the owners received them whilst the drivers were given more humble headbands made from sheep's wool.

The very wealthy Alcibiades of Athens entered no less than seven four-in-hand teams in the games of 416 BC. King Hieron of Syracuse was a winner in 476, 472 and 468 BC and in AD 67 the victor's wreath was awarded to the notorious Emperor-God Nero. Nero, in fact, tipped over when driving a 10-horse team and did not complete the course, but he still claimed the wreath – and not surprisingly, got it.

The modern counterparts of the chariot race are the trotting races which are almost as popular as flat racing on the Continent and in America, Australia and New Zealand. The chariots have been replaced by lightweight trotting 'sulkies' but many of the horses still wear a head plume that is extraordinarily like that worn by the chariot horses of the Romans.

Ridden races, considered socially inferior to chariot races, were not held at the Olympics until 647 BC, but by 256 BC, when stallions were raced, they had become popular.

The equine hero, or rather heroine, of the ancient Olympics was a mare belonging to Pheidolas of Corinth. She lost her jockey but passed the post first and of her own accord took up the winner's position in front of the judges. She was awarded the race and

was honoured by having her statue placed amongst those of other immortals in the Sacred Grove.

In Britain racing is a sport of long standing. There seems to have been an established breed of native 'running horse' long before the importation of the Arab sires in the seventeenth and eighteenth centuries which resulted in the eventual production of the super racehorse, the English Thoroughbred. There seems no doubt that the 'running horse' had already been improved by Oriental blood before the development of the Thoroughbred, which took place in the hundred years or so after the Restoration in 1660. None the less, three Arab horses can be considered as the founding fathers of the Thoroughbred breed. These three were the Darley Arabian, the Godolphin Arabian and the Byerley Turk. All modern Thoroughbreds are descended in the male line from these three horses.

Steeplechasing, or racing over fences, is not nearly so old a sport. It started in the eighteenth century and was given the name because it was originally a race across country from one church steeple to another.

One of the most famous of these early races was that which took place in County Cork, Ireland, in 1752 when Messrs O'Calaghan and Blake raced their hunters over four and a half miles from Buttevant Church to where the steeple of St Leger Church could be seen in the distance.

Almost as old as the sport of racing is that of hunting from horseback. The Assyrians hunted lions, using spears, which must have been quite a feat since they rode without saddles. In India the tiger was hunted as well as the fierce wild boar, and Genghis Khan's Mongols held each year 'The Great Hunt', which as much as anything was a military training exercise. An area of country was selected and the *tumans* stationed all round it in a huge ring. At a given time the ring began to close, involving everyone in some very hard cross-country riding which included the crossing of rivers and mountain ranges. The wild animals were driven remorselessly into the centre and then, when the Khan had made the first kill, the hordes drew their weapons and slaughtered every living thing.

In time hounds were introduced to hunting in both Europe and elsewhere, the quarry in the former part of the world being boar and stag.

This form of hunting continues today. There are still stag hunts but the most popular hunting is that of the fox, a sport which started in Britain some 100 years ago. Modern Britain is still the centre of the foxhunting world but the sport, although in some parts carried on with a different quarry, such as jackal, is popular in America, Australia and New Zealand as well as in India and South Africa.

Polo was brought to Europe in the nineteenth century by British officers who learnt the game in India. Just when the game started is not known but forms of the sport were certainly played in Persia, China and Mongolia as far back as the fourth and fifth centuries AD and probably even before that.

The three principal competitive sports, which we sometimes call the three disciplines, are show jumping, horse trials or eventing and dressage. We tend to think of them as modern sports, which in a sense they are. Assyrians, for instance, didn't jump horses over coloured poles in a ring. But, in fact these sports are all counterparts of games and exercises devised hundreds of years ago as forms of military training.

Show jumping, the most artificial of the three, is the most recent of the modern sports. It probably arose partly from the hunting field and partly from the cross-country training of cavalry. Centuries before, when cavalry consisted of heavily armoured knights, the sport played to fit the knight for the battlefield was the joust – a 'friendly' fight between two knights who charged towards each other, separated by a barrier, and tried to unhorse their opponent by a thrust from the lance. Even in those days there were professionals who journeyed from tourney to tourney just as today there are professional show jumpers on the show circuit.

The horse trial or three-day event is even more closely associated with military practice. In fact, it used to be called 'The Military'. The idea behind this supreme test of horse and rider was that of an *aide* carrying despatches across open country and jumping the obstacles as he came to them. The first Olympic 'Military' was held in 1912 in Sweden and comprised a thirty-three-mile long-distance ride which included a three-mile cross-country, a two-mile steeplechase, show jumping and a final dressage test to prove that the horse was still sound, supple and obedient. The word 'dressage' means nothing more than training, something which men have done with horses ever since they started to ride.

Nowadays, the three-day event starts with a dressage test which is followed by a speed and endurance phase which includes a section of roads and tracks, a steeplechase and a cross-country course over some thirty pretty formidable obstacles. The final day is devoted to a jumping test.

At its highest level dressage becomes the classical *haute école*, the High School, and is not so much a sport as an art, like music, painting or ballet. It began with the Greek general, Xenophon, who has already been mentioned. He wrote books which are still relevant today and his teachings were rediscovered by the men of the Renaissance period between about 1500 and 1600 AD. The Renaissance (which means 'rebirth') was a most important age in the history of the world and of the horse, and all the arts flowered and flourished, painting, poetry, music, architecture *and* riding, which was just as much a part of a gentleman's education as anything else. It started in Italy, but before long beautiful riding halls were built all over Europe in which riders showed off their skills, making their horses wheel and pirouette, perform the lofty cadenced trot called the passage, and leap high in the air in the 'schools above the ground'. What, in fact, these Renaissance riders were doing was to imitate the movements performed by the knights in battle. They, when hard-pressed by infantry, could escape by making their horses kick out behind or leap in the air and it was, of course, necessary for the knight to be able to manoeuvre his horse in order for him to use his weapons effectively.

It was during this period that the famous Spanish Riding School of Vienna was founded, in 1572. Today, over 400 years later, the school exists to preserve the traditions of classical riding and to delight thousands with the performances carried out by the legendary white Lipizzaner stallions.

For thousands of years the horse, hauling loads, cultivating the land, carrying messages and galloping over the world's battlefields, was the servant of man.

Now he is used for our recreation and pleasure and is much better treated. In a way he has the last horse laugh – we have become his servants'!

Learning to Ride

If you have a love of horses and ponies your biggest thrill will come when you 'climb aboard' for the first time. You may be one of those who have always looked upon horses as animals that bite at the front and kick at the rear. If so, you will have all the more reason for wanting to learn to sit happily and safely mid-way between the two ends, and where you can get the maximum enjoyment!

First of all you must learn to get on and off correctly. Although more advanced riders have to learn to mount and dismount from either side, the correct way to start is to learn to mount from the near side. When you are ready to mount-up make sure that the girths holding the saddle in place are tight, and

the stirrup irons are down and about the correct length. Then face the tail with your left shoulder alongside the pony's near shoulder and take the reins and stick in the left hand. The reins should be properly separated ready for riding, and short enough to prevent the horse from moving forward, with the near side rein the slightly longer of the two.

Put your left hand in front of the withers, and taking hold of the stirrup with the other hand, place your left foot into the stirrup iron. Then press your toe down under the girth and gently swing round to face the pony. By seizing the far side of the saddle, you will be able to spring lightly up until you are in a position to swing your right leg

gently over the pony's quarters. At the same time move your right hand to the front arch so that your body can sink gently down into the centre of the saddle, and you can slide your right foot into the stirrup iron.

After learning to mount properly it is as well to learn to dismount correctly and gracefully, and, what is also important, in your own time! First remove both feet from the stirrups, and lean forward placing your left hand, containing the stick, on to the pony's neck. By putting your right hand onto the pommel you will then find it easy to vault off, keeping your right leg well clear of the pony's quarters. Be sure to land gently on your toes and away from the pony's front

legs. Once you are on the ground, take the reins over the pony's head and, with the ends in your left hand, hold the reins close up to the bit with your right.

You must make sure that, unless you are using a western saddle, both feet are clear of the stirrups before you attempt to dismount. Although some riders like to show off by throwing their legs over the horse's withers, this is really rather foolish because to do so they have to let go of the reins and lose real control of their horse or pony.

Once you have learnt to mount you must learn to hold the reins correctly, and to develop what is known as a good seat. When we refer to 'the seat', we really mean the rider's position in the saddle to

have correct control of the pony.

The reins should normally be held in both hands. From the bit they pass below the little finger and across the palm, so that they can be held in position by the first finger and the thumb. The hands should be about four inches apart. Some riders also prefer to allow the reins to pass between the little finger and the third finger as shown in the photograph.

It is through the reins, and consequently the hands, that the rider can help to regulate the pace and direction of the pony. For this reason the hands must at all times be light and responsive, and able to 'give and take' very quickly and without effort.

A good seat depends upon a combination of balance, suppleness and grip. An experienced horseman rides by balance and poise and with a good sense of rhythm. He must also remain supple and always be in a position to grip instantly when necessary so as to preserve his balance before it is lost. A good general purpose saddle will assist the rider to sit properly and will make it easy for varying lengths of stirrup leathers to be used for either hacking or jumping. The rider must learn to maintain a good strong seat independent of any assistance from the reins. This can best be achieved by regular active riding and the help of exercises.

The rider's seat should be well down in the centre of the saddle, with the upper part of the body upright and free from any stiffness. The head should be erect so that his eyes can look straight between the pony's ears.

The knee and thigh should be

kept close to the saddle, with the knee and ankles supple. The lower part of the leg should be kept slightly back so that it can be applied close behind the girth when necessary. In other words, the lower part of the leg should be in a position to enable the stirrup leather to remain perpendicular to the ground. The rider's heels should be below the level of the toes to ensure that the muscles on the inside of the thigh are kept taught. The knees and the toes should be pointed towards the front, because

13

if the toes are pointed out the rider will tend to grip with the back of the calf. Holding the stirrups on the ball of the foot will also help the ankle to remain supple. The arms should hang naturally with the elbows close into the sides.

There are four main forward movements of the pony. The walk is a marching pace in which the four legs of the pony follow one another in four time. In other words there are four steps to a stride. When the four beats cease to be maintained regularly, the walk is said to have become disunited or broken. When doing the ordinary walk, the pony should move energetically with even and determined steps, and the rider should keep a light and steady contact with its mouth. There are also three other forms of walk. In the collected walk the pony moves resolutely forward with its neck raised and arched. Each step covers less ground and is higher than in the ordinary walk, with the hind feet touching the ground behind the foot prints of the fore feet. The extended walk is when a pony covers as much ground as possible without haste and without losing the regularity of its steps. The free walk is when the pony is allowed complete freedom of movement of its head and neck, and the reins can be stretched accordingly.

When trotting a pony takes two steps to a stride which is a pace referred to as two time. The trot must always be free, with the pony taking active and regular steps without undue hesitation. Experts judge the quality of the trot by the general impression given by the elasticity and regularity of the steps while keeping the same

cadence. There are three types of trot — ordinary, collected and extended. When trotting the rider either rises in time with the motion of the pony in what is known as the rising trot, or he sits down into the saddle for the sitting trot, used frequently in dressage movements. The ordinary trot and extended trot are usually ridden in the 'rising' position, and the collected trot is nearly always ridden in the 'sitting' position.

The canter is a pace of three time in which there are three steps to a stride. The rider sits down in the saddle and keeps a light but firm contact on the pony's mouth.

As in the trot there are three forms of canter, known by the terms ordinary, collected and extended. The ordinary canter is a pace between the extended canter and the collected canter where the pony is perfectly straight from head to tail and moves freely with a natural balance. The strides are

long and even and the pace is well modulated. With the collected canter the shoulders are free and supple and the quarters are very active, so that the pony's mobility is increased without any loss of impulsion.

In the extended canter the pony extends its neck with the tip of the nose pointing more or less forwards. The pony lengthens its stride without losing any appearance of calmness or lightness. The pony should always be cantered 'true' or 'united' which is when the leading foreleg and the leading hindleg appears to be on the same side. It will be said to be cantering 'disunited' when the leading hindleg appears to be on the opposite side to the leading foreleg.

Like the walk, the gallop has four steps to a stride. A rider can adopt two alternative positions when riding at the gallop. If the pony requires 'pushing', the rider should sit well down in the saddle

urging the pony forward with his seat and legs. A very common fault is too much movement of the hands. If they are continually working backwards and forwards, or up and down, with every movement of the rider's body, the pony's mouth will become hard. The gallop is a fast pace which shows how important it is for a rider to have a strong and independent seat, because the reins must never be used as a means of staying in the saddle. The reins are only there to guide and direct the movements of the pony.

When the pony appears happy to move freely, the rider should adopt a forward position, with the weight of the body taken on the knees and stirrups. The seat should be above the saddle with the body leant forward over the rider's hands. This position can be easily maintained so long as there is a firm and even contact between the rider and the bit. It is also a com-

fortable position for the pony because the rider's weight is poised over the centre of gravity.

Once you have learnt to control your pony properly at the walk, trot, canter and gallop, you will be ready to enjoy the fun of dressage and jumping.

The time spent on these preparatory stages is of tremendous importance particularly when the time comes for you to compete not only in the show jumping arena, but also in the very exacting and demanding cross-country courses found at One or Three-Day Events.

In other parts of this book we take a more detailed look at these specialised forms of equestrian sport and deal with them more fully.

Owning and Caring for a Pony

by John Allen

If you are to get real enjoyment from owning a pony, it is essential that your pony is sensible, safe and suited to the type of activity you want it to do. It is also important that the pony should be well and happy, and so the first essential must be to make sure that you have the necessary facilities for keeping it.

Too often people say, 'Oh I can turn the pony out onto the tennis court, or some rough grass alongside the house.' So many seem to think that any old bit of grass and the occasional hay net is all that is needed for a pony's wellbeing. This is just not true. When you choose a pony, you will have to think about where you will be able to keep it, and your choice must be influenced by this. For instance, a well-bred pony, which has always been accustomed to stable life, can hardly be expected to do well if you buy it and then turn it out into a field to fend for itself. Similarly, a pony which has been used to the freedom of a field may not take kindly to being kept in a stable and given a very different diet.

Remember that a pony which is normally kept in a field is usually referred to in advertisements as 'lives out'. Before setting out to buy a pony, however, make sure that you really have enough room for him.

If the field is to provide most of the food for a year, it should not be less than one and a half acres for a pony up to 14 hands in height. If the pony is larger, then between one and a half and two acres will be needed. Ponies love company, and if you have a friend with a pony living nearby, it may be better to see whether your friend will be willing for them to graze together and then change over fields every few months so that one field can be rested while the other is being grazed.

When ponies are left out at night, they usually settle down to

a routine pattern of behaviour. They start grazing soon after dawn and then drink about a gallon of water. A constant supply of clean drinking water must, consequently, be available in each paddock, because water is essential for the pony's digestive system.

Fields vary enormously from very poor to very good. Neither extreme is good for a pony. Poor grass has a low nutritive value and often contains weeds which can be harmful. Few fields are entirely free from dangerous weeds, but fortunately poisonous plants are seldom eaten unless a pony is extremely hungry and there is almost no choice. Also, most plants are only dangerous when they are eaten in quantity. It is when eating hay that poisoning is more likely to occur, because animals often cannot tell the difference between wholesome and poisonous plants like ragwort or horsetails.

High-quality grass like that used for dairy cows is too rich for ponies and can cause fever of the feet, known as laminitis or digestive troubles like colic.

Ponies do best on medium quality grass, but a pasture which can provide most of the needs of one pony during the winter months will usually have too much grass during the spring or early summer. The field should either be grazed for a few weeks by two or three bullocks, or cut by a mowing machine when the grass is about six or eight inches in length.

Any field used for a pony must either be properly fenced or have hedges to prevent the pony from straying and possibly causing damage to itself or to other people's property. Barbed wire is temptingly easy to erect, but when an animal becomes restless or excited, rusty barbed wire can be a menace. Plain wire can be used if it is put up properly, but even so it should have a top rail made of timber. Post and rail fences, although expensive, are by far the best, and four feet is a good height.

A pony out in a field during the winter will usually need a good, well-fitting New Zealand rug to keep it warm. It will also need an open-fronted shed for shelter from the wind and rain in winter and the flies in summer. It should not have a corrugated iron roof, because in summer the sun will make the roof too hot and the shed will become unpleasant for the pony.

Remember that a pony must be kept warm if it is to keep well and strong, or it will use up precious energy trying to keep out the cold. Regular worming about every three months will also prevent loss of condition, and teeth must be checked regularly, because if a pony cannot chew properly, it will not be able to eat its food.

Feed your pony according to the work it is expected to do, but hay will always be required in the winter when the grass has little food value. If the pony is expected to do any hard work, some concentrates like pony nuts and bran will be needed. Oats can make a pony 'over fresh' and should be used very sparingly, if at all.

If you are lucky enough to have a stable for your pony, make sure it has a good, well-drained floor and is warm and dry and free from draughts. Your pony will need a clean, dry bed made of either straw, wood shavings, sawdust or peat. But make sure you obtain good quality straw, because the poorer quality is usually dusty and can make a pony cough. Wood shavings are far better than poor straw, and can be mucked out more quickly.

The stable should be large enough for your pony to be able to lie down easily without getting 'cast', and all the light fittings must be either well covered, or of the safety variety that won't get broken. The doors must be wide enough for the pony to walk through when tacked-up without damaging the saddle, and should have safety bolts which it can't open. Buckets of fresh water should be kept in a part of the stable where they can be seen easily and checked but not liable to be knocked over.

Proper exercise is very important for a stabled pony. Horses and ponies of all types must have exercise because it stimulates the digestive system, improves the circulation, and helps to expand and contract the lungs.

All ponies enjoy a good roll,

Top left: **If your pony is stabled make sure the loose box is well ventilated but free from draughts. The hay net is the correct height**
Bottom left: **Position the schooling jumps where the going is as good as possible at all times of the year**
Above: **Variety prevents boredom and this Connemara pony is obviously enjoying his schooling session.**

and if the weather is fine, turn yours out for an hour or so, but leave the head collar on, otherwise it may be rather difficult to catch.

Ponies have small stomachs in comparison to their size, so they should be fed little and often. Good quality hay is very important all the year round when a pony is stabled, but a pony will require more food nutriment than hay if it is to be kept in hard, fit, working condition.

If your pony finishes its hay and then begins to eat the straw of its bedding, it usually means that it is getting less hay or roughage than it requires. On the other hand, if it leaves good hay untouched, it is usually getting too much and the daily amount should be reduced.

Concentrates like barley, bran and nuts should be fed at least three times a day, but the amount fed will depend on the size of your pony and the work it is asked to do.

Finally remember that each pony is an individual and will vary in its requirements. They all, however, will need regular visits from the blacksmith to keep their feet in good condition. The old saying 'no foot – no horse' is very true.

Having made sure that you have the necessary facilities for keeping a pony fit and well, you will then have to set out to find the right pony, depending on the type you want.

A good pony is valued at whatever it will fetch, and there is no fixed scale of prices. The first thing is to have an absolutely clear picture in mind of just what sort of pony you will need. Is it going to be a first pony? Will you want it to hunt or to show, or perhaps show-jump or event? Do you want a gymkhana pony whose main merit will lie in being quick and agile and able to win gymkhana games? Or do you want a general utility pony which will probably excel at nothing in particular, but will serve you faithfully and well?

Height must be one of the first considerations, because apart from being comfortable to ride, if you intend doing any jumping or showing, it must also be the right height for the class you may want to compete in. Age is also important because it will affect the price you pay, and an older pony will usually have a shorter expectation of life. A pony is mature at five years of age and in its prime at six. After the age of nine it usually begins to drop in value, slightly at first, but more rapidly after the age of twelve.

Parents are wrong to insist on buying young ponies in the mistaken belief that they and their children will 'grow up together'. A young pony doesn't know enough to teach a youngster, and a young rider won't be experienced enough to teach the pony.

The shape of a pony is also important. Round, fat ponies are uncomfortable and quickly tire the legs of their riders and make them feel insecure in the saddle.

A reasonably narrow pony is more preferable, providing it is not narrow chested or flat ribbed. A pony with a thick neck is also tiring to the arms, and frequently difficult to hold. The withers are also important because they help keep the saddle in position. A long-backed pony never makes a good riding pony, and one that is narrow in the chest sometimes proves to be an unsafe ride, because the forelegs, being too close together, can interfere with one another. A pony with faulty hocks is also one to be avoided.

Good temperament is an essential qualification for a children's pony. Docility, obedience and willingness are more part of a pony's nature than the result of breaking or training. A pony with the right temperament will give confidence and pleasure to its rider, whereas one which is obstinate, nappy and disobedient can be nothing but a nuisance.

After deciding on the type of pony you want, the next problem is how to find it. This can take time, but it is better to end up with the right animal than to buy in haste and repent at leisure.

The first essential is to get the help of someone who is really knowledgeable and able to advise on the suitability of each animal. When a choice is finally made, have the pony examined by a qualified veterinary surgeon before the deal is completed.

Most horse and pony magazines and local papers carry details of ponies for sale. When answering advertisements for ponies that are some distance away, it is usually wise to ask for a photograph to be sent to you along with as much information as possible. Doing so can prevent a long and perhaps disappointing journey.

Horse sales are where the majority of ponies are sold in Britain. The ponies can usually be inspected before they are auctioned and those that have been examined and passed by a veterinary surgeon will have a certificate which you will be able to examine. Sometimes the ponies carry what are known as 'warranties', so that if, when you buy a pony, it does not match up to what its owner said in the warranty, you can return it within a given time. Ponies bought at auctions are something of a gamble unless you happen to know the pony, but bargains can be had.

Most riding schools sell ponies, and going to a riding school means you have the advantage of being able to hire the pony first. Don't forget, however, that riding-school ponies are used to being together, and when they are away from the other ponies they can be nappy in their behaviour.

The most reliable method of finding the right pony however, is to buy one from someone you know, which has probably been outgrown. Most owners with good ponies will be anxious to find a good home for them and will not object to a trial, but if you are planning to keep the pony at grass, do make sure it is easy to catch. When you are satisfied that you have found a pony that is really suitable for you and meets your requirements and the vet has given it a clean bill of health, all that remains is for the money to be paid and you can look forward to really getting to know your new friend.

Once you get your pony home, make sure that the saddle and bridle you are planning to use fit correctly, and that the bit is not only comfortable in the pony's mouth, but is also of the type best suited to its temperament and behaviour. Very often it is as well to try and purchase the saddle and bridle with the pony. If it has been outgrown, the owners may well be willing to sell the 'tack', including head-collar and rugs, at a reasonable price.

You will, however, need a suitable grooming kit. If the pony is to be stabled you will also need buckets, a broom, shovel, rake, fork and skip, as well as a haynet and a feeding bowl if the stable is not equipped with a manger. Feeding bowls, providing they do not tip up easily, are usually better because mangers are difficult to keep clean, and a bowl on the ground will mean that the pony can eat in a more natural feeding position.

(1) Grooming promotes good health. First remove the mud with a dandy brush

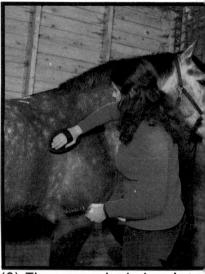

(2) Then use a body brush to remove the dust and scurf

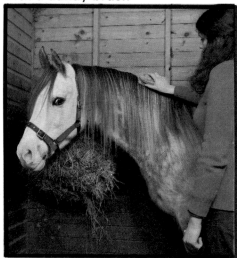

(3) The water brush can be used damp on the mane, tail and feet

(4) Clean the eyes, muzzle and dock with a sponge

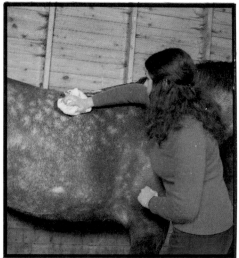

(5) The stable rubber will give a final polish to the coat

(6) A tail bandage will help keep the hairs in position

Ponies enjoy a change of scenery and so vary the rides as much as possible

You will also need dry, rat-proof bins for the pony's food. Plastic dustbins are fairly inexpensive and quite satisfactory for the purpose, and a scoop or bowl for you to measure the feed can also usually be purchased from the local hardware store.

A stabled pony will need regular grooming each day in order to keep it healthy, clean and in good condition, as well as to improve its appearance.

The main items you will need for grooming are a hoof pick for cleaning out the feet; a dandy brush for removing dirt, dry mud and dust; a body brush which should be used for removing dust and scurf from the pony's coat, mane and tail; a curry comb for cleaning the body brush; a water brush for the mane, tail and feet; a wisp for helping to promote circulation; a sponge for cleaning the eyes, muzzle and dock; a stable rubber to give the coat a final polish after grooming, and a tail bandage.

During the early autumn the pony's coat will usually appear dull and rough, and the winter coat will begin to grow. About October, if your pony is stabled, you will want to think about arranging for it to have its first clip. If the coat is very thick and grows quickly another one may be needed in January.

There are four main types of clip. The full clip, when the whole of the coat is removed; the hunter clip, when the hair is left on the legs and where the saddle goes on the pony's back; the blanket clip, when the hair is only removed from the pony's neck and tummy so that a patch of hair in the shape of a blanket is left on its back and body, and the trace-high clip when the hair is removed from beneath the neck and along the tummy as far up as the traces, and from the legs as far as half way down the forearm and thighs. The trace-high clip will be particularly useful if your pony is being kept out at grass with a New Zealand rug.

A smartly turned out pony is a pride to its owner and a joy to look at, and the time taken to make your pony look really good is always time well spent.

Saddlery and Equipment

by Robert Owen

The most popular saddle in use today is the one known as the all-purpose saddle. As the name implies, this is suitable for all disciplines of riding. We illustrate below the details of this saddle and show the names given to the various parts.

Other saddles in fairly common use are those used for dressage, the show ring and racing, as well as the Western. This last saddle is from the United States, but it is being seen quite a lot in Great Britain nowadays. Each of these is made to a different style and, as will be seen, for a different purpose.

A saddle, of whatever type, is built around a specially prepared frame called a 'tree'. The tree is made from wood and metal, or sometimes from plastic. These can be very easily broken if dropped or badly handled, and once this has happened the saddle is quite unusable until repaired.

Some ponies and horses, with their individual conformation, will require their own special saddle. But this is an expensive piece of equipment and great care must be taken with it.

As you will know, all tack and equipment must be regularly cleaned, not only to remove mud and staining, but to keep the leather supple and prevent cracking. Cleaning also gives an opportunity to examine the stitching and fastenings to make certain these are not becoming worn and unsafe. There is nothing more dangerous to both rider and pony than faulty equipment.

The way you 'turn out' is quite important. Be as smart as you can at all times, and remember your pony – let him have well-polished leathers and brightly shining buckles and bits.

It is essential that a saddle fits properly; a badly fitted saddle can be very uncomfortable for the rider as well as unkind to the pony.

When fitting, make sure that no part of the saddle touches the pony's spine. This is something you can easily see and check with your hands. But if you are not certain that all is well do talk to someone who has experience.

When fitting a saddle make sure it rests at the point of the rise of the withers, and that the weight of the saddle and rider is taken on the muscles which cover the upper part of the pony's ribs.

When 'saddling up' you should stand on the near side of the pony and place the saddle carefully on the high part of the withers. Next, gently slide the saddle back to the correct position.

Now move to the off side and check that all is well and that no hairs from the pony's back are being rubbed the wrong way. If you are using a numnah you should check that it is still flat and tidy. Returning to the near side, you then reach under the pony's tummy and pull the girth towards you. Begin to tighten this into the buckles on the saddle.

However, never tighten the girths to their maximum at this stage, just make sure the saddle will not slip when you begin to mount. Once you have mounted, reach down and tighten the girth.

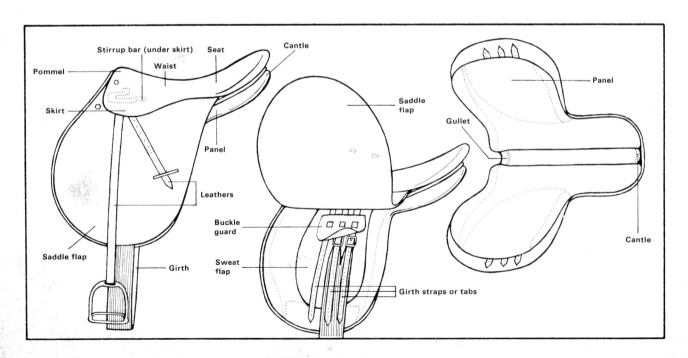

The Local Show
by John Bullock

Sheila Jenkins gave a yawn, slipped on a dressing gown, and drew back the bedroom curtains, the sound of the alarm clock still ringing in her ears.

A ray of sunlight lit the room and she gave a grateful smile. The weather had improved. Her husband Peter was still sleeping peacefully as she slipped downstairs to make a cup of tea.

It was just 6.30 in the morning and all sorts of problems were rushing through her head.

'Did I remember to ask Mary to collect the Junior Open Cup from the Robsons who were due back from holiday last night?'

'I hope Jenny remembered to call in at the bank and pick up enough change for the gatemen and the Secretary's Tent?' Everyone always seemed to pay with five-pound notes at the start of every show. 'I hope the Jumping Judge will be all right, he sounded terrible on the phone last night! I don't know what we will do if he has 'flu,' Sheila thought to herself. The kettle began to boil and she made the tea.

'Oh well,' she muttered to herself, 'it's too late to do anything about it now. Today's the day and at least the sun is shining.'

Just then the telephone rang and Sheila took time for a quick sip of tea before answering it. She knew that once the telephone started ringing on Show Day there would be little time for tea.

'That you, Sheila? Oh you're up! Good! I just thought I'd give you a ring and make sure that our Show Secretary is all right.'

It was Tom Whitemore's voice, the Chairman of the Committee.

'Looks as though the weather is going to be kind to us, after all. Just as well as we decided not to insure against it. That should save us a pound or two.'

Sheila mumbled a rather sleepy, 'Yes, I suppose you're right, Tom,' as the voice the other end said

cheerfully, 'Oh well, I mustn't keep you. I'm sure you've still plenty to do. Give my regards to Peter, I'll see you on the showground about 8.30. Goodbye.'

The phone clicked and the line went clear as Sheila's husband walked into the room.

'Who was that? Any chance of a cup of tea? I suppose today's the day, eh darling? Anything I can do?'

'Yes,' said Sheila as the telephone began to ring again. 'Answer that phone, and if anyone wants to know whether the Show is on, tell them it is, and that we are planning to start the first class on time at nine o'clock.'

An hour later when she drove her car through the gate into the showground, she was relieved to see that the marquee and tents were still standing despite the storm in the night, and that her two assistants had already arrived. One, a short blonde girl, was opening the door of the Secretary's Caravan, while the other, a middle-aged woman with glasses, was putting out a table and chairs beneath the awning.

'Morning Jenny, morning Mary,'

Bending is still one of the most popular gymkhana events

she called out as she parked her car alongside the caravan. 'Looks as though the first horse-boxes are arriving already. Have you got all the numbers ready, Betty? Good!'

'Anyone seen Peter Willett, the Jumping Judge, this morning? He sounded terrible last night. Oh thank goodness, there's his car now.'

For Sheila Jenkins this was the climax of weeks of planning and scores of telephone calls, letters, visits to the printers, finding sponsors, hiring jumps, collecting trophies from the winners of the last year's show, arranging schedules, dealing with caterers and exhibitors, contacting judges, keeping in touch with the British Horse Society and all the people whose help was essential to the smooth running of the show.

It had all started at a meeting in Tom Whitemore's house about four months previously.

Tom Whitemore was the new President of the local Rotary Club, and as soon as the Club had decided to hold another horse show in aid of local charities, he had been made Chairman of the Horse Show Committee responsible for making all the necessary arrangements, and Sheila had again been asked to be Show Secretary.

A date had been chosen so as not to clash with other shows in the area, and a suitable ground had been arranged, which was large and flat enough to allow for five large rings to be set out, and still leave enough space in neighbouring fields for car and horse-box parks and a warming-up area for the competitors' horses and ponies.

Judges had to be arranged, not only for the jumping, but also for the various show classes. Then someone had to be found to organise the gymkhana events which were always so popular among the younger riders.

The gymkhana classes always provided very keen competition, and Sheila wanted to make sure that the person she chose not only knew all the rules, but would also be able to cope with those over-

A competitor does her individual 'show'

zealous parents who were always sure that their child had been overlooked when it came to handing out the rosettes.

Peter Watson was a local riding-school proprietor, and he had detailed three of his assistants to help him. Sheila knew that he would deal with any awkward situation with firmness and tact.

She just had time to check that Jenny had collected the change, and had despatched her with a bag of it in the direction of the gatemen, when a bright-eyed little girl with long brown hair tied in a bow under a hat that looked a size too big came to collect her number.

'Can I have the numbers for Susan James and Peter James,' she piped up in a rather nervous voice. 'The ponies are Peter Piper and Muffin, and were in classes two, seven, eight and ten. Do I get gymkhana tickets here or do we pay in the collecting ring?'

Sheila handed her over to Jenny Wright, the Assistant Secretary, who had already placed the numbers in long boxes in alphabetical order, and went to deal with a rather haughty woman who was trying to alter her entry.

'I entered Deidre on Happy Man in the 13.2 jumping, but he has a bruised foot and is lame. I want to enter Just William instead. I did try to ring you but I couldn't get any reply.'

Sheila altered the entry and turned to help a young rider who was having trouble with his pony and was finding it a problem staying in the queue long enough to get his number.

As the morning wore on and the judges and their stewards had been despatched to the various rings, she managed to drink a quick cup of coffee from a flask that she had fortunately had time to fill before leaving home.

Her rest was short lived. One of the ring stewards rushed across to the caravan. 'Have you got the cup for the Working Hunter Pony, and could we have an extra rosette? The judges have given a tie for third place.'

A tall, smartly dressed boy, sporting a black jacket and pony club tie, handed in a stick and pair of string gloves which had been found behind the refreshment tent.

The voice of the announcer came clearly over the loudspeakers. 'Judging for the best rider in class three, children sixteen years and under, will commence in Ring Four in five minutes. Will all competitors please go to the collecting ring immediately?'

Sheila looked anxiously across at Ring Two where the 14.2 jumping was still in progress.

'Gosh!' she muttered, 'I thought we had allowed plenty of time for the jumping to finish before the best rider class. Most of the best riders are doing the jumping as well. I'd better warn the judges.'

Mrs Joan Talbot, who had been judging the Mountain and Moorland class in Ring Four, broke away from a group of young riders who had been tackling her about a Pony Club rally she was due to instruct at the following Monday, and came across to the caravan.

'Anything else I can do to help, Sheila? Would you like me to relieve you for a while, you look as though you could do with a break?'

'Oh would you, Joan? I'm a bit worried about the 14.2 jumping running so late. It's going to make the rest of our classes late, and we always pride ourselves on running to time. I'd like to have a quick word with the judges, then it will be time for you to go to lunch. The judges' refreshment tent is behind that ice cream van over there.'

Tom Jenkins drove alongside Sheila in his Land Rover as she was making her way across to Ring Two. 'Mark Sommers, the pop singer, has arrived early to judge the Fancy Dress. Where can I give him a drink? Someone told him the class was at twelve o'clock not two, and he hasn't had any lunch either.'

Sheila gave a sigh. 'Oh well, it can't be helped. Take him over to the judges' tent, and I will go and see Jill Drewitt, and try and get her to squeeze in another lunch. I don't think I will be very popular, because three of the judges decided to bring their families with them at the last minute, although they told me yesterday they would be coming alone.'

A shout came from the direction of the collecting ring as a riderless grey pony galloped through the crowd, and headed for the lines of horse-boxes in the adjoining field.

There was a murmur among the crowd as the calm voice of the announcer said:

'There is a loose pony on the showground, will someone shut that gate please.'

A girl with pigtails ran across the field after the pony, obviously none the worse for her tumble, except perhaps her pride which had been hurt slightly. The pony galloped round in a circle, bucking and kicking as it went, and then stood still, while a man in a check coat and cap walked slowly up to him, speaking quietly as he went, and holding out a small scoop of pony nuts. Sheila watched while

However young you are, there is always work to do

Removing the tail bandage on arrival at a show

the little girl and her pony were safely re-united and cantered gently back to the collecting ring.

She had to make her way through the long queue of people waiting at the ice cream van, and saw with relief that the 14.2 jumping had finished, and the course builder and ring stewards were already re-arranging the jumps for the Junior Open while the prizes were being presented to the winners by the wife of the local Member of Parliament.

A dark cloud brought a quick shower of rain and sent the competitors in the Fancy Dress scurrying for cover.

Youngsters dressed up as packets of flour, scarecrows, Humpty Dumpty, and a fairy queen were hurriedly covered up with raincoats by anxious parents, and Sheila saw that one of the Indians' war paint was beginning to run.

She remembered the times when

Going clear to win

her children had been younger, and she had spent hours preparing costumes and grooming ponies for them to take part in the Fancy Dress Parade.

Her children were grown up now, but she felt sorry for the parents of the little Red Indian, who by now was beginning to shiver and sob with cold.

The shower was over quickly, however, and the sun shone through the clouds to bring groups

Hours of work go into the Fancy Dress Parade

Getting the sack . . . and a rosette?

of competitors and spectators out of shelter.

Sheila gave a sigh of relief. It was time to go and relieve Mrs Talbot for lunch, and then, if she was lucky, she might be able to take a few minutes off to get some lunch herself.

The stewards' and judges' tent was a babble of voices when she finally managed to get a quick snack before the final classes took place.

Most of the talk was about young Peter Willis, who had beaten one of Britain's international riders into second place in the Open Jumping.

Peter was still only seventeen and a local schoolboy. His parents farmed near the showground and his win was tremendously popular with the locals, who had followed his show-jumping career with great interest ever since he had ridden his old pony Rusty Red to win the Junior Open at Wembley two years previously.

Now with his new horse, Merryman, he had ridden two clear rounds, and then a final one against the clock, to win the biggest competition of the day by a fifth of a second.

His parents had produced a bottle of champagne and were being congratulated by friends, who were predicting a great future for Peter and Merryman.

As Sheila left the tent a queue of horse-boxes and trailers was starting to leave the showground.

Soon there were only a handful of spectators and riders left, as the prizes for the last of the gymkhana races were being competed for with just as much enthusiasm and verve as any jockey hoping to win a Derby.

Helpers were beginning to dismantle the ropes round the collecting rings, and the jumps were being loaded on to a Land Rover and trailer.

The contractor's men would be arriving early the following morning to take down the marquees and tents, and by evening only a few bare patches of turf would be left as evidence that a show had been held.

After bidding goodbye to the army of helpers and gathering up the remains of the rosettes and numbers, Sheila thanked the policeman on the gate and drove home exhausted, but pleased that everything had run so smoothly without major problems. The Treasurer had taken the money with him, and a quick calculation had indicated a profit of £183. Not bad, thought Sheila. All that remained for her to do now was to send details of all the results to the local newspaper, and write letters of thanks to the judges and stewards.

I'd better remember to end each letter, 'and I do hope you will be free to help us again next year,' thought Sheila, as she got out her writing paper and pen.

Top: **A nicely turned-out pony and rider**
Centre: **A very competitive Working Hunter class**

Left: **Another potato goes into the bucket**
Below: **The rider's winning, but what about the pony?**

Peter And The Grey Pony

by John Bullock

The young boy looked pensively at the grey pony. 'There boy,' he said soothingly as the pony hobbled a few paces until the chain tethering him became taut, and the leather strap round his neck bit into the flesh.

The pony turned to look with big proud eyes. Then he arched his neck and gave a little whinny that brought a dark-skinned man out of the caravan nearby.

'Hey. You leave that pony alone,' said the man. 'Be off with you. I don't want the likes of you round here.'

But the boy stood his ground as the gipsy ambled over to stand between the boy and the pony.

'That pony's hurt,' said the boy, running his hands nervously through his mass of curly blonde hair.

'I know he is,' said the gipsy. 'That's why he's off to the knacker's tomorrow. Can't do anything with a leg like that. Pity 'cos he's been a bit of a jumper in his day, but he'll still make a quid or two as a dead 'un.'

As the gipsy was speaking, the boy slipped past to fondle the pony's soft grey muzzle. 'Seems a pity that nothing can be done,' he said, feeling in his pocket for the crumpled remains of a bag of peppermints. 'Surely there must be some way of saving him.'

The dark man shrugged his shoulders. 'His tendon's gone. I haven't got time to mess about with him, and travelling around the country as I do, there's only one place for him, and that's the knacker's for sure.'

'Seems such a pity,' said Peter Simons to his father as the family were having supper that evening in the kitchen of the big stone farmhouse that had been Peter's home for all of his twelve years.

'Won't you come and see him, Dad? He's only about a mile up the road, and you always take Dodger for a walk after supper.'

As though to bear out the truth of the boy's words, the shaggy great collie that had been lying on the hearthrug suddenly came to life, and beat a steady tattoo on the table leg with his tail.

Mr Simons methodically cleaned and refilled his pipe. The tobacco smoke rose slowly up to the ceiling before he spoke.

'Can't do any harm to go and look,' he said, giving a broad smile as he saw the look of relief of his son's face. 'I'd like to take a look at what the gipsy fellow is doing anyway. A lame pony is the last thing I want, but the knacker's place is some way away, and if the worst comes to the worst, we could at least run the poor thing there in our horse-box.'

The gipsy was sitting on the steps of the caravan savouring the smell of pheasant that caught the breeze and wafted across from the stew pot bubbling nearby.

He got up and walked quickly towards Peter and his father, hoping to keep them far enough away from the tell-tale aroma.

'Evening, sir,' he mumbled, giving what was meant to look like a respectful tug to his

forelock. 'Hope you don't mind my camping here. I'll be off in the morning, unless there's any jobs you'd like me to do before I go, sir.'

The gipsy looked anxiously towards the stew pot, as he saw Mr Simons' nostrils twitch.

The unmistakable smell of pheasant had reached Peter's father even before the gipsy had spoken. 'No thanks, but I hope you aren't planning to stay long, or I shan't have any pheasants left.'

The man looked sheepish and started mumbling some excuse about finding the bird in the road after being hit by a passing car, when Mr Simons cut him short. 'Where's that grey pony my son has been telling me about?'

At that moment Dodger gave a playful bark, and the grey pony trotted painfully from behind the caravan, shaking his head and sniffing at the collie bounding alongside.

'Come here, Dodger! You know better than that!'

The collie looked soulfully at Mr Simons and, as though ashamed at the rebuke, walked tail down over to the fire.

The grey pony stopped to nibble some grass, but kept the dog in view out of the corner of his eye.

'His tendon's gone, and I can't do nothing with it,' said the man, holding the pony by the head-collar as Mr Simons ran his hand slowly down each leg in turn, before taking a long careful look at the pony's feet.

Then he gently opened the pony's mouth and looked at his teeth before replying.

'Tell you what I'll do. I'll give you fifty pounds for the pony, and if he's sound by the next time you're round here, I'll give you another fifty and forget about that pheasant.'

The man opened his mouth to argue. It was second nature for him to haggle over any price, but Mr Simons cut him short.

'Come on, man. It's a good deal. For two pins I'd have you up for poaching. After all, you are about to eat one of my pheasants.'

The gipsy gave a shrug and nodded his head in agreement.

Mr Simons smiled 'You enjoy your dinner, and we'll be back later to collect the pony.'

Then, putting his arm round Peter's shoulder, they walked slowly back to the house.

Two hours later the grey pony walked contentedly into the stable at the rear of the big house, and snatched a mouthful of hay from the bulging hay net before taking stock of his surroundings.

His own box was old but clean and had a generous supply of fresh straw on the floor. A bucket of cool water stood in the corner.

Across the way two hunters and a chestnut pony looked inquisitively at the new arrival out of half-open stable doors.

Peter and his father laughed with amusement as the grey pony sniffed carefully into each corner of his new home. Then, with a grunt, he lay down on the soft straw and methodically rolled.

Getting to his feet and shaking himself so that bits of straw flew in all directions round the box, he limped back to the hay net and munched away contentedly.

'You're sure we can cure him, Dad?' Peter looked hopefully at his father.

'I don't see why not. He's young and sound apart from that leg. Rest can work wonders, but I'll get the vet over tomorrow, and we'll see what we can do. You'll have to be patient, because even if his leg responds to treatment he'll still have to be turned out for a while.'

'I don't mind, Dad, just so long as he does get better. But can he be turned out in the meadow by the house?'

Mr Simons nodded. 'Even if you won't be able to ride him yet, you can at least get to know him and earn his trust.'

Peter looked pensive for a minute, then he said, 'I'd like to call him "Stewpot" because

if it hadn't been for that pheasant stew he might not have been ours.'

As the weeks went by, the pony's lameness gradually disappeared, and every time he saw Peter he would gallop round the field kicking his legs in the air before nuzzling into the pocket of Peter's coat where he knew there was usually a bag of peppermints.

One Saturday morning after watching the pony's bronco act, Mr Simons called across to Peter.

'Go and get a head-collar. It's about time that pony started to do a bit of work.'

Peter's yelp of glee caught the pony by surprise. Legs outstretched, he looked inquisitively at the boy for a second, and then with a squeal of annoyance galloped, tail flying, to the far corner of the field.

Peter looked shamefacedly at his father. 'Sorry Dad, but you don't know how I have been waiting for you to say that.'

His father smiled. 'I think I do, son, but you'd better go and catch Stewpot, and take him into the stable. You can give him a brush down while I go and get the tack.'

Peter was brushing the last of the mud from the pony's legs when his father entered the stable carrying a rather strange-looking head-collar with a long rein looped over his arm.

'As he hasn't been ridden for some time we will have to lunge him first before you can ride him. Let's see whether this Cavesson will fit Stewpot.'

Peter's father fitted the Cavesson and, clipping the lunge rein through one of the metal rings on the padded noseband, led the pony out of the stable into the field.

Standing in the middle of the field, Peter's father made the pony walk and trot round him at the end of the lunge rein. At first the pony showed off and refused to do as he was told, but he soon realised he had met his match in Mr Simons.

'Go and get a saddle and bridle, Peter, and don't forget your hard hat.'

Peter needed no second bidding, and a few minutes later watched excitedly as Mr Simons adjusted the bridle, and gently tightened the girth round the pony's plump middle.

'There you are, Peter, I'll give you a leg up, but slide into the saddle gently, because he hasn't had anyone on his back for some time.'

Peter could hardly believe that the moment he had been longing for had really arrived. Gathering up the reins, he sprang lightly into the saddle. He felt the pony arch his back, and saw patches of sweat break out on the pony's neck.

'There now, Stewpot, there's nothing to get excited about. Just settle down.' Peter ran his hand slowly along the pony's mane as he tried to reassure him.

'Steady now boy, let's take a walk.'

Peter could feel Stewpot slowly relax as, with a gentle squeeze of his legs, they set off round the field, jogging at first, but then settling down to a steady walk.

A pheasant that had been hiding in the ditch suddenly took off across their path with a squark and a flap of wings, taking Peter and the pony by surprise.

Stewpot gave a squeal and a buck, and as all four legs left the ground, Peter left the saddle. The pony pawed the ground and looked down at Peter in surprise. But before he could gallop off, Peter gathered the reins, and swung back into the saddle.

'Phew! He can certainly buck,' said Peter, as his father came up, but you can't really blame Stewpot.'

Mr Simons spoke soothingly to the pony, who was sweating with excitement. 'No, I don't suppose you can, but now let's see you walk him round the field a few times without any more circus acts.'

Later, as he unsaddled Stewpot and rubbed him down with handfuls of fresh straw, Peter stopped to wipe the perspiration from his brow.

'He feels terrific, Dad. I could sense how keen he really is. When can I start jumping him?'

Mr Simons' face broke into a smile at the boy's enthusiasm. 'Steady now, Peter. We have a long way to go yet. While you were walking Stewpot round the field, I telephoned the blacksmith, because the first thing we've got to do now is to have him shod.

'Then you must get him really fit by giving him steady walking and trotting exercise each day. We'll have to watch his diet, and I think tomorrow you had better start bringing him into the stable each morning and just letting him out at night.

'Being in that meadow for so long has made him very fat, and we'll have to get him trimmed down before you can start galloping and jumping him.'

The next few weeks saw a change in Stewpot. Each morning Peter got up early, and before his friends were awake he walked and trotted Stewpot round the country lanes.

At first the pony returned to the stable covered in sweat from his exertions, but as the days went by his fat turned into muscle and his coat took on a new shine.

Peter groomed Stewpot each day until he glistened. His father helped him trim the pony's mane and tail, so that when they went out people made admiring remarks about 'that beautiful grey pony' that made Peter glow with pride.

One Friday evening as they were having dinner, Mr Simons said to Peter: 'It's time we started the next part of Stewpot's training.

'For a pony to be a really good show jumper he has to learn obedience and become really supple. Tomorrow we will start what's known as flatwork, and we'll see what he knows about dressage.'

Stewpot responded quickly. 'I think he must have been very well schooled at some time,' Mr Simons told Peter after a particularly good training session. 'I think the time has come when we can start to jump him.'

The little pony pricked up his ears when he saw the jump of coloured poles Mr Simons had put up in the paddock.

'Just take him gently, and don't hurry him,' Mr Simons told Peter.

Stewpot gave a little leap of pleasure as he turned into the jump, and when Peter gave him the signal to take off, he gathered up his legs, stretched out his neck, and cleared the poles with inches to spare.

To Peter it felt as though he had just jumped over the moon.

'Wow!' he said, patting Stewpot. 'Did you see that? Can we put it up a bit?'

'All in good time, let's concentrate on small fences to begin with. There's plenty of time to see how high he can jump when you have formed a real partnership.'

It was Peter's mother who let the cat out of the bag several weeks later. 'If we are going to spend next Saturday at the show, I'd better arrange a picnic.'

'What show?' asked Peter. 'Where?'

Mr Simons laughed. 'I wanted to surprise you, but I've entered you and Stewpot in the junior jumping at Albrighton on Saturday. I think it's about time we really found out what you can both do.'

It was the longest week Peter could remember. He hardly slept a wink all Friday night, and when the alarm went off he was already dressed and making his way to the stables.

Stewpot eyed him suspiciously. He was used to early morning rides, but today seemed different.

Peter filled up the water bucket and mixed Stewpot's feed. The pony tucked in with gusto. Whatever was being planned, he wasn't going to let it interfere with his breakfast.

'There, Stewpot,' said Peter, giving the little grey a pat. 'Eat up, we've got to show them all today. I'll be back soon, I'm just off to get my own breakfast.'

The smell of bacon and eggs from the kitchen told Peter that he wasn't the only one up early that morning.

'Come on,' said his mother, 'you can't ride that pony on an empty stomach, and you won't be able to do anything until Stewpot has finished his feed.'

Peter was gulping down the last piece of toast when Mr Simons poked his head round the door. 'Ready, Peter? We'll have to leave in less than an hour.'

With so much fussing around him at that time in the morning, Stewpot knew that it was no ordinary day.

His coat shone as Peter tackled the grooming with extra enthusiasm, and after he had been bandaged and was being led out to the horse-box, Mrs Simons ran out of the house with a parcel under her arm.

'Wait a minute. Take that rug off, I've got something special for him,' she called to Peter, tearing open the parcel to reveal a brand new blue travelling rug, with the initials 'P.S.' embroidered in the corner.

'Thank goodness the postman arrived before we left. I never thought my present for Stewpot would arrive in time.'

The showground was bustling with activity as Mr Simons parked the horse-box alongside a bright blue Land Rover and trailer.

'I'll go and get your number while you and father walk the course,' Mrs Simons called over her shoulder as she headed for the secretary's tent. 'We've timed it just right. The class is due to start soon, and it looks as though they are just putting the final touches to the course.'

Mr Simons had been careful not to arrive at the ground too early. There were more than sixty entries in the Junior Open Class, and he didn't want Stewpot to get too excited before it was his turn to go into the ring.

'We don't know how he will behave,' he told Peter as they led the pony down the ramp of the horsebox. 'For all we know this could be his first show.'

They need not have worried. Stewpot stood quietly while Peter and his father removed the travelling bandages. Then, raising his handsome grey head in the air, he gave an impatient snort, as though to say: 'Let's get on with it. I know what I'm here for!'

The announcer's voice came clearly across the showground. 'The judges have given permission for competitors in Class Two, the Junior Open Jumping Competition, to walk the course. The Class will begin in fifteen minutes time.'

'Come on,' said Mr Simons, 'Stewpot will be quite safe tied up to the box while we go and see the course.'

By the time they reached the ring, groups of young riders were already busily pacing out the distances between fences, and giving some of the brightly coloured poles a push to see how firmly they were held in their rather flimsy looking cups.

The black coats and white cravats worn by some of the competitors made them look very smart, and Peter's heart sank when he saw how professional many of them looked.

Mr Simons seemed to read Peter's thoughts. 'It's the horse and rider that matters. You and Stewpot won't be left out of it, you'll see. This is where all that training and hours of hard work will pay dividends. That's all that matters in the end.'

Peter didn't look convinced. He was too busy trying to memorise the course and listen to the advice his father was giving him.

The first fence looked easy, but the third was a real stinker with a big spread, followed soon afterwards by a very formidable looking wall.

'Gosh!' Peter muttered, as his father measured out the distance between the three elements of the treble.

'Come on, Peter. It's not as bad as it looks. I think the bogey fences are going to be that upright of planks and that narrow stile. They'll have to be jumped very accurately, so let's take another look at your approach.'

Peter tried hard to concentrate on what his father was saying. It all looked terribly big, and he was sure he would make a mess of things. He didn't care so much for himself. It was letting Stewpot down that worried him.

The announcer's voice boomed out. 'The first to jump in the Junior Open will be Miss Prunella Thompson riding Ragamuffin the Fourth.'

As they made their way back to the horse-box, out of the corner of his eye he saw a tall girl with pigtails riding a rather bouncy skewbald into the ring.

They cleared the first three easily enough, and made nothing of the big double, but they hit the planks hard. Peter heard the announcer say 'Ragamuffin had four faults and now we have . . .'

But the rest of the announcement was lost as the crowd clapped one of their local favourites.

Stewpot looked a picture. While they had been walking the course, Mrs Simons had been busy getting him saddled up, and was walking him slowly round.

Peter's mother called out 'Hurry up and get ready. I've got your number, you're twenty-seven.'

Peter pulled his Pony Club tie straight and smoothed down the flaps of his tweed jacket as he hurried across to mount Stewpot.

The little grey stood quietly enough, but the moment Peter was in the saddle he started to dance as though every blade of grass was too hot to tread on.

Mr Simons slid the tail bandage free and called out to Peter as Stewpot danced away: 'You've got plenty of time to ride him in. Find a quiet corner and I'll meet you by the practice jump in about twenty minutes.'

Stewpot was so obviously enjoying himself

and the time passed so quickly that it was only when he heard the announcer saying, 'With ten more to jump there are only four clear rounds,' that he realised that he was almost due in the ring.

'Just pop him over those poles. There are four to jump before you,' his father said as Peter cantered up to the practice jump.

Stewpot carelessly rattled the top pole, and Peter gave the little grey a slap with his stick, as they went round to take the jump again.

This time Stewpot made no mistake, and cleared the poles with a good six inches to spare.

'That's better,' said his father. 'Now leave it at that. You're about due in the ring.'

'The next to jump is Peter Simons riding Stewpot.'

Peter saw a sea of faces as they trotted into the ring and cantered round waiting for the bell to start.

The little grey arched his neck as the bell went, and headed for the first of the twelve fences.

Peter had never felt such power. They were over the third before he got his breath back and remembered his father's words, 'the bogey fences are going to be the planks and the stile.'

The planks loomed ahead of them and Stewpot seemed to be going far too fast. He tried to check him, but it was too late.

The little grey took off miles too soon, and Peter heard the rattle as Stewpot's hind legs hit the top plank.

He hardly dared to look. The plank swung from side to side, but somehow stayed on.

Peter gave a quick sigh of relief, but he wasn't going to let Stewpot make the same mistake again.

Measuring the double perfectly, Stewpot cleared the big parallel with ease. Peter checked him slightly going into the stile and then rode on over the wall, the white gate, and another spread fence.

One by one the fences seemed to fly by until they reached the imposing-looking treble at the end of the course.

Peter's arms were aching, and the wind made his eyes water.

Stewpot, his ears pricked, measured the first element. 'Come on, Stewpot!' Peter thought he had said the words under his breath, but to his surprise he heard his voice echoing across the ring.

The crowd roared encouragement, and Stewpot responded with three enormous leaps that made Peter feel as though he was jumping over a line of houses.

As they cantered through the finish, the announcer was saying 'A very game performance by Stewpot and Peter Simons for our

sixth clear round.'

Peter slid to the ground and loosened Stewpot's girth. It all seemed like a dream. They had got into the jump-off!

'Well done, Peter, but you haven't time to hang about. They're just drawing the order for the jump-off.'

Mr Simons gave Stewpot a mouthful of grass as he stroked the pony's nose.

'You were the last to go clear and so there are just the six of you. Because they're running late, it's been decided that you'll go straight against the clock.'

The voice of the announcer came over the loudspeaker once more. 'The jump-off will be against the clock over a shortened course. The fences have been raised and those to be jumped will be numbers one, three, four six, ten, eleven and twelve.

'The judges have drawn the order of jumping, and first to go will be number twenty-nine, followed by three, seventeen, fifty-six, twelve and twenty-seven.'

'Let's hope your luck holds, Peter, you're last to go. That'll give you a chance to watch the others and see where you can save precious seconds.'

As Peter led Stewpot across to the collecting ring, a boy on a rather nice bay pony trotted into the ring.

'Four faults for Happy Man in fifty-eight seconds,' said the announcer shortly afterwards, as the bay pony hit the last part of the treble.

The first four riders all had faults, and Peter's hopes rose.

'Two to jump and still no clear round. Next in the ring will be number twelve, Jupiter Boy ridden by Nancy Bolan.'

The announcer gave the news, and the crowd became hushed as a young girl on a big dun pony cantered into the ring.

The cheers from the crowd as Peter prepared to mount almost drowned the announcer's words a few minutes later.

'Our first clear round, and Jupiter Boy's time was a very fast one – forty-six seconds.

'And last to go will be number twenty-seven, Peter Simons on Stewpot.'

Peter pulled his cap firmly over his eyes. Leaning forward, he gave Stewpot's ears a reassuring tug and whispered, 'Come on Stewpot, I know you can do it.'

As the bell went the little grey leapt forward. Peter steered him over the first, and galloping past the second, turned quickly into the third and fourth.

Stewpot simply flew.

A rapid turn took them inside fence five, and heading for the stile and a big brush filled fence. 'Steady boy, steady.'

Stewpot slid slightly turning into the final line of fences, but his stride hardly faltered as he stood right back at the spread and made for the final treble.

The seconds ticked away on the big clock in the middle of the ring. Forty, forty-one, forty-two . . .

Peter felt Stewpot put every ounce of strength into a final leap, and as they galloped over the finish the crowd became hushed. Then a roar went up as the announcer said, 'There's our winner, ladies and gentlemen, Stewpot was clear in forty-four seconds.'

★   ★   ★

That evening as they were nearing home, Mr Simons pulled up alongside an old gipsy caravan parked by the side of the road.

The smell of stewed pheasant wafted into the cab of the horsebox when Mr Simons wound down the window, and hailed the tall dark gipsy who was kindling the fire.

'If you come up to the house I've got fifty pounds for you. But enjoy your supper first. We're rather fond of Stewpot ourselves.'

Peter looked at his parents, and their laughter echoed along the lane as they drove home.

My First Pony

Malcolm Pyrah

Malcolm Pyrah's first pony was a ten-year-old, 13-hand chestnut called Flash.

Although Flash had a wonderful temperament, and was a brilliant gymkhana pony, he absolutely refused to jump.

The result was that Malcolm spent most of his time practising trick riding and mounted games, and frequently he rode Flash without a saddle which, he feels, helped his grip and balance.

All his successes on the little chestnut were in gymkhana events at local shows around Hull during the early 1950s, and the money he won went towards keeping Flash. 'This gave me a great incentive to win,' explains Malcolm.

Eight internationally
known riders tell the
story of their first pony
and how they began
in the world of show
jumping and eventing.

Paddy McMahon

Marion Mould

Paddy McMahon started riding when he was eleven, but he didn't have a pony of his own until he was fourteen, when a schoolfriend's father bought him Bella B, an eight-year-old grey.

'Before then I used to ride any pony I could get hold of,' Paddy explains. 'I never had any real riding lessons, but I went to school with Mr Tommy Mullholland's son who used to let me ride his pony, until that day in 1949 when his father bought me Bella B to learn to jump on.'

Bella B had formerly been ridden by Mr Gerald Barnes' children, and Paddy did very well with him in local ghymkhana and jumping classes.

Marion Mould's first pony was bought for her when she was five, a pretty little chestnut called Amber-Light, who had a long flaxen mane and tail. She was seven years old and stood 12.2 hands high.

Amber-Light had once been owned by the Duchess of Abergavenny, and became very successful in showing classes. Marion's first successes with her were in leading-rein classes, and they went on to win many cups and rosettes together at local shows in Hampshire before Marion decided to devote all her time and attention to show jumping.

Peter Robeson

The first pony Peter Robeson owned was an eight-year-old brown gelding called Billy Bunter, which Peter's parents bought in 1935 from the famous air pilot, Mr O. P. Jones.

Billy Bunter was 13.2 hands high, and disliked all men except Peter, whom he adored. Peter's two young brothers tried to ride him, but kept on being bucked off until eventually it was decided that he should be ridden only by Peter. The pair scored successes at local shows in the South of England, such as Cobham, Ashtead, Langton Green and Tunbridge Wells; and went on to victories at some of the larger shows, like Blackpool, Windsor, Maidstone, and Sussex County.

Tom Brake

Tom Brake's first pony was bought from a local farmer. This animal had a habit of jumping out of his field into the corn, and the farmer was afraid that all the corn he ate might prove fatal.

He was a brown gelding called Hope, standing 14.2 hands high, and Tom broke him with the help of his father when he was a three-year-old in 1927. Hope obviously had tremendous jumping ability, and he was first given a chance to show it at the Bath and West Show at Dorchester, where they jumped in the Open Competition. Hope had a brick out of the wall that time, but very soon he and his young rider were winning at all the leading county shows including the Bath and West, the Devon County, the Royal Cornwall, the Sussex County and the Royal Counties. They also competed successfully at the Agricultural Hall at Islington, London. To reach this show Tom had to ride Hope through the streets of London from Paddington Station.

Hope also won the weight-carrying cob championship with Tom's father riding him, and proved himself to be a really remarkable pony. As Tom says, 'He was a grand pony who loved sugar, but he always became very frightened when he saw pieces of paper blowing about, and we never managed to cure him of that habit.'

Aileen Fraser

The first *jumping* pony owned by Aileen Ross (now Lady Fraser) was a 13.2-hand mare called Irish Jig. Her parents bought the mare from Mr John Bailie soon after her eleventh birthday.

Lady Fraser's first inspiration towards a career with horses was the wooden lid of a Singer sewing machine which she used to sit on and then slide up and down the corridors, much to the horror of her parents' housekeeper.

Her parents could not afford a pony for her at the time and so she had to make do with the lid of the sewing machine until, at the age of four, an aunt presented her with a 10.2-hand show pony which had been rescued from a knacker's yard.

Lady Fraser's first ride was on an 11-hands brown Icelandic mare called Dolly who belonged to her eldest brother. He used to go round in a governess cart pulled by Dolly, who was twenty-four years old at the time.

Her show successes were on a 13.2-hand pony called Highlight, which her parents bought at Kelso sales for £100. Soon afterwards she was given Irish Jig and her show-jumping career began in earnest.

Alison Oliver

Alison Oliver's first pony was a six-year-old, 13.2 hands mare called Minnie. As Alison was only seven at the time, the pony was much too big for her and, to make matters worse, her parents had bought her from the local riding school because of her looks rather than her temperament, and Alison had great difficulty in staying on board.

She didn't like to complain to her parents, however, and for the first few months Alison used to go out riding with an older friend who was a more experienced rider. This friend had a smaller and quieter pony. As soon as they were out of sight of Alison's house they used to swop over.

After a while, however, Alison realised that she had to learn to master Minnie, and they had many successes together, not only in gymkhanas but also at Pony Club shows.

Debbie Johnsey

Debbie Johnsey's first pony, Silver, was bought for her in 1960 as a seven-year-old. She was black with four white socks, a silver blaze and silver-blue eyes.

Although Silver is now twenty-one years old she is still a firm favourite. Debbie says: 'I used to ride her along the banks of the canal near my home with only a halter. I'm sure this helped me with my balance and grip.'

'When Silver was purchased she had a foal at foot, and since then she has been mother of ten beautiful foals. The father of her most recent foal is Count Cristo, who was also the father of Champ VI, the gallant little pony stallion who won so many show-jumping prizes for me and who is now jumped by my younger sister, Clare. Silver's delightful temperament seems to have been passed on to all her foals, and I'm told that her silver-blue eyes are only found in the really old strains of Welsh mountain ponies.'

When Debbie became keen on jumping she used to build practice fences from buckets and broomsticks. Silver was her very first 'show jumper'.

'When we first had her,' says Debbie, 'we had great difficulty in catching her. She would even jump over a gate to get away from being caught. But once she got to know me she became a really super and obedient pony.

Riding Holidays the World Over

by John Ruler

If you were riding in Australia, a monster lizard could well meander across your pony's path, while in Wyoming, in America's former Wild West, you might be warned to look out for a bull moose. They're unpredictable animals and could easily charge your horse!

Fortunately, riding holidays are usually less dramatic, though riding in a strange setting is always exciting even if it is only in another part of your own country.

If it is abroad then so much the better. You might go to a place where it is usually hot and sunny, like Spain, in which case you could find yourself riding through orange and fig groves aboard an Andalusian pony who will prance *piaffe* fashion along the dusty tracks. Or you could pick somewhere cold like Iceland where they have 13-hand ponies, introduced by the Norse Vikings back in the tenth century, who can take you through this strange land of primeval fire, hot springs and glimmering glaciers.

But most riders are usually holidaying somewhere nearer home – and what happy days you can have if you pick a spot which is definitely different from your daily or weekly rides.

If you live in Southern England, why not head for Scotland where the scenery is startling and there is a chance to ride a Highland pony, those sure-footed creatures who are reckoned to be the sturdiest breed in the British Isles?

But it is as well to realise that there is a vast difference between pony trekking and trail riding, where you are expected to be 'able to ride at sustained speeds for long distances over tough country'. And even if you are fit and experienced, check on the age limit for riders – usually you have to be at least twelve years old.

If you are going pony-trekking age is not so important, but even so you should select a riding centre to suit your particular tem-

perament. You might choose a farm-house, but find it boring in the evening. If so, the Aviemore centre might be more suitable because it has so many other activities. Or you could try a pony trekking Course run by the Scottish Youth Hostels Association, or improve your schooling, dressage or jumping at the Iverclyde National Recreation Centre, which is approved by the British Horse Society.

Whatever you decide, Scotland is refreshingly new. There is generally very little road work.

Instead you climb through hills, tracks and forest paths. Perhaps you will be in Rob Roy country – or even riding round Loch Ness if the weather is fine.

If you go trail riding, it is possible to concentrate on 400 square miles of border country in the Cheviot Hills, mainly on drove roads and open hill country, but for a full list of centres approved by the Scottish Sports Council, it is as well to contact the Scottish Tourist Board.

All you need after that is good weather – but, to be on the safe

side, warm clothes, sensible shoes with heels and, please, a hard hat. You should always be prepared to groom and tack up your pony because, after all, half the fun of a holiday is to feel responsible for your own mount even if it is only yours for a week or so.

Trekking is also all the rage in Wales. But, once again, it is important to check on the facilities available by obtaining the pony trekking and riding booklet from the Welsh Tourist Board.

Certainly the Welsh mountains seem made for pony-trekking – and are rarely more than 3000 feet high. And the scenery is really magnificent! The bracken and gorse on the lower slopes are speckled with pine and oak, while further up you can see red kites flying round the sheep, and perhaps hear the cry of a curlew.

For those tough and experienced enough, the Llanigon trail ride in Brecon is worth tackling. Riders with their guide cover between 100 and 130 miles, and accommodation for seven nights usually takes in everything from farm-houses to a converted work-house!

Sizes of the Welsh centres vary from those with less than fifteen ponies to those with over twenty-five – such as the one at Tregaron which has its own trekking association. Some feature just a few hours hacking along with show jumping, dressage and use of a manège.

It is sometimes easy to overlook other riding possibilities in the British Isles. In the West Country, around Hexworthy, in Devon, for instance, there is virtually unlimited riding country among the high rugged tors and along boulder-strewn streams and rivers.

If you like the more wild and rugged splendour of Cornwall, several centres are situated on the edge of Bodmin. The Bodmin Moor Riding Centre Association is always pleased to give further information.

Many riders take their own pony with them on holiday. But do be careful. There is a true story of two girls who went with their ponies to Wales, asked the way to a certain village, and landed up in a bog. It took a helicopter to winch

out the ponies! So always heed the advice given by people like the tourist authorities – it is much better to be safe than sorry.

Don't be too ambitious to begin with. Riding every day for perhaps twenty miles is very different from a few hours hacking each week.

Another challenging county is Yorkshire, which has excellent trekking at Pately Bridge (Nidderdale), Clapham Greenfield at the head of Wharfedale and at Stalling Beck near Senerwater. And do not forget Northumbria, especially round Bamburgh Castle, a huge pink place set amid sands along which you canter.

If you want somewhere more gentle, the New Forest with its woods, graceful hills and moorland, along with the wild ponies and deer, provides an ideal holiday setting. Stables abound, and many hotels have their own. One group not only includes lessons for beginners, but also the hire of a pony and trap.

Now for selecting those holiday stables or centres. You can do no better than consult the various publications prepared by the

British Horse Society, Ponies of Britain or the Association of British Riding Schools.

Southern Ireland has one thing in common with Wales – horse-drawn caravan holidays. In the case of Wales, you hire them and spend a week exploring the rich valley and mountain scenery of the Ystwyth and Rheidol rivers. In Eire, the choice is wider still, with centres near to Dublin, Cork, Galway and Limerick.

Remember, however, that Eire's roads, though virtually free outside the towns, change considerably in character. So, indeed, does the scenery – and your ten to fifteen miles a day could vary a lot from region to region. There is a vast difference between the prim little hills topped with powder puffs of mist in Wicklow and Wexford, and the craggy splendour of Connemara with its tumbledown stone walls and donkeys laden with panniers of peat.

Northern Ireland is always eager to attract holiday riders, with pony-trekking at places such as Rostrevor in the lovely Mountains of Mourne in County Down. Here you can enjoy forest, sea and mountain views.

England's off-shore islands should not be overlooked. The Isle of Man, for instance, has pony-trekking centres at Douglas and Port Erin.

If you are a little fearful of foreign parts, but fancy a slight Continental flavour, try the Channel Islands. There is excellent riding round St Ouen's Bay in Jersey where you can gallop along a four-mile stretch of sands.

France, of course, is not only one of our nearest neighbours, but is also a country which provides an abundance of interest for the holiday rider. It is possible to cross the English Channel for a week-end's riding in the Orne district of Normandy.

If you wish to stay longer, there are week-long treks there, and you can perhaps include a call at the famous Les Pins du Haras stud. A similar short stay is possible at Le Touquet, a large, fashionable resort with superb sands.

The Dordogne region is also delightful for a holiday further south, where the horse fits in as naturally as the fairy-tale châteaux or the great, green strips of tobacco leaves yellowing in the hot sun.

There are stables at Lalinde, not far from Bergerac, and at other centres such as St Cere, a market town of medieval origins, and at Sarlat, an historic hotch-potch of Gothic, Romanesque and Rennaissance buildings.

Riding holidays can be had at the equestrian centres in Valencay in South Loire, while the Etampes Riding Society, south-west of Paris, has Portuguese and Lipizzaner horses for learning the 'secrets of academic riding as taught by La Guérinière!'

Special holidays for young people are held at the Roursaudes Estate in the French Ardennes, where you can combine riding with learning to climb, and at the Gunkel Stables, Granjalna, in Alsace – a land of vineyards, storks, pine forests and pastures.

A pony trekking party in Wales
A group of riders at Rostrevor, County Down, known as Ulster's Riviera, where the winters are especially mild

If you really want to be casual, and see some sun, head for the Camargue which is famed for its white horses. The main centre is at Mejanes, but you can find places along the road to Les Saintes Maries-de-la-Mer.

Another relaxed holiday is that offered by the horse-drawn caravans, similar to those in Wales or Ireland, though more rectangular in shape. The main centre is at Assier in the Lot Valley, regarded as part of the Dordogne region, where you can also ride around in a stage coach. In Brittany you can try a tilbury, a light hooded carriage with two seats, or take an ordinary caravan trip round the countryside behind Le Touquet.

Little Luxembourg is a happy mixture of farmland, hills, woods and a grape valley along the Moselle. It is just right for riders, with a special week-long ride in the summer organised by the Luxembourg Federation of Equestrian Sports.

Pleasant riding facilities are available at Stegen, with two- or three-day tours with riders staying overnight in cabins and being given the opportunity of visiting famous castles.

In Belgium, although you can ride in the pines behind the coastal resort of Knokke-le-Zoute, it is best to go inland, especially around the Ardennes.

Of the Alpine countries, Austria has the advantage of being the home of the Hafflinger, the perfect holiday horse. With their long blond manes, they provide attractive mounts and are superbly cut out for taking you round this land of chalets, lakes and flower-strewn meadows.

But you will of course have to pay for your pleasures. Both Austria and Switzerland are expensive, so make full use of their respective holiday tickets which allow generous concessions on trains, boats and postal coaches. You can also find private rooms at a cheaper rate, while camping facilities, certainly in Switzerland, are good. So, too, are the youth hostels.

Austria offers ideal riding country, and includes the well-known

Above: **Hafflingers are the perfect holiday horses in Austria**

Markhof centre, near Marchegg, in Carinthia. There is both instruction and trekking alongside the river Danube.

In Upper Austria there is the horsemen's 'village' of Ampflwang, and in Vienna the superb Spanish Riding School. Special tours are arranged there by a number of companies to coincide with the dressage demonstrations.

Of the Swiss holiday centres, Davos offers weekly excursions and moonlight rides; while at St Moritz, again in The Grisons, there is an indoor riding school offering dressage, jumping and livery stables for those with their own pony. The area around Lausanne is also attractive with good riding, and ponies are also available at Montreux, Vevay and Leysin.

In complete contrast are the Swiss Jura, rugged and severe mountain ridges where horses and walking are the accepted means of transport.

Riding is featured in many of the villages and towns of West Germany, among them Munich, Bayreuth, Berchtesgaden, Mittenwald and Nuremburg. Hesse is another German region which particularly caters for riders and has both schools and dude ranches. And the woods and meadows around Bad Harzburg in the Harz Mountains, are reputed to be the original home of white horses.

It is easy to imagine that all of Scandinavia looks the same. But each country has something unique for the horse lover. Norway is nearest to England, and one of its loveliest cities is Oslo, which has a rural charm, and marvellous countryside around the western reaches of the Oslofjord.

Week-long tours are held in the Hallingdal Mountains during the summer, and one is available through the Norwegian Youth Hostels Association. There is also riding at Geilo, one of Norway's foremost winter sports resorts, and at Lillehammer, which is surrounded by farmland and forests.

Denmark is a land of fields, farm-houses, forests and small hamlets. There is a considerable amount of casual riding, with the

Young holidaymakers enjoy the sunshine in the hills overlooking Oslo

emphasis on farm-house holidays. These are generally centred on the East Jutland countryside or on the 'garden isle' of Funen.

It is in Jutland you will find the Vejle Riding Institute, which has an offshoot, a Wild West Camp for children, near Billund of Legoland fame. The Institute itself runs eight- to fifteen-day courses in the summer for both beginners and advanced riders. Children are also welcome at Højmarken, a Danish thatched-roof farm at Rabjerg, seven miles from Skagen, the furthest point north on the Jutland peninsula.

Sweden has about ninety riding camps, with the most attractive riding country along the West Coast, which rather resembles Cornwall. There are two schools at Varberg and one at Falkenberg.

One of the most publicised trekking ponies must be the Icelandic, although the country itself consists largely of rocks, stones, deserts or sandy wastes. The most popular centre is at Lake Laugarvatn. Alternatively, try Gullfloss, Geysir and Thingvellir.

Finland is a fun country of forests and lakes and charming people. Much of the riding, and there is plenty of it, is concentrated in the central area with carpets of pines, thousands of them like black notes from a Sibelius symphony. You can also ride in Finnish Lapland and there is a centre at Rovaniemi, the administrative capital.

Of course it is not only Western Europe that provides riding holidays. For instance, there are wonderful holidays available in Hungary, with tours for the more expert at Hortobagy, Lake Balaton, the Danube Bend, and in Trans-Danubia.

There is the Tata Riding Centre, which was formerly the Court stable of the Eszterhazy counts and, in the fourteenth century, the Hungarian King and Emperor of the Holy Roman Empire had a stud of 5000 horses there.

Stud farms, incidentally, flourish in Poland, where top breeding horses are kept in State-owned farms at which it is possible to stay.

There is magnificent mountain scenery for riders in Germany

And don't overlook Yugoslavia. Lipice, after all, is the original cradle of the Lipizzaners, and there has been a stud farm there for nearly 400 years.

You can also find good horses at Porec, a modern Yugoslav resort close to the old medieval town. This type of place can give us the best of both worlds.

It is in the more popular 'places in the sun' that holiday riding can provide rather a problem. Spain and Italy are no exceptions. So often riding is listed alongside other holiday sports, with little regard, in some cases, to the standard set. So you sometimes take potluck on whether you land up with a half-starved looking pony, or something very much the type you would ride at home.

Of course, there are notable exceptions. In Spain there are many well-run riding schools in the major cities and resorts. But it is when you go inland that you often find the best riding.

The Alondra riding parties are run by a Spanish count, from Alora in Malaga. In Andalusia,

The rolling hills of the Swiss Jura are ideal riding country

an exciting region of folklore, fiesta and flamenco, you can ride over good country before relaxing in two old houses dating back to the early part of the seventeenth century.

Also recommended, for the more rugged type of horseman, are the fifteen-day riding expeditions which take one from the orange and olive groves around the tiny town of Orgiva right over the snowline in the Sierra Nevada range of mountains.

In Italy, in the Rome area, riding is available at Le Palazzo Country Club, Spoleti, where it is possible to ride out to visit the castles built in the Tofa Mountains. There is also a permanent horse-lovers holiday centre at Soleschiamo di Manzano, a town in the Udine in the Po Valley. And should you want beach riding why not try Rimini, Cattolica, Lido di Jesolo and Lido di Salvio. As we have said, good ponies are available in

many parts of Italy – and there is some very good riding country as well.

The Algarve area of Portugal has all the advantages for the holiday rider. It is still less commercialised than neighbouring Spain, and has sands sweeping up to orange groves in which you can trot and canter at will. In the capital city of Lisbon there are several very good riding centres, as there are in most resorts along the coast.

No review of riding holidays can be complete without reference to the United States of America. The trail rides in the Yellowstone National Park in Wyoming are justly famous. This is a land of green sage, swaying grasses, and woods of spruce and aspen. The place is known for its many boulders over which your trail pony picks his way. There are holidays, too, in Kentucky's famous Bluegrass region, and in Florida

with its sunshine and golden beaches.

In fact, throughout the United States riding can be enjoyed both in the towns and countryside. And all the main seaside towns have their centres, with excellent stretches of beach.

Canada and Australia also offer excellent riding facilities and excitement. Australia, particularly, is a land of the horse! A vast number of younger riders belong to the various branches of the Pony Club, and enjoy expert tuition from the many schools and riding centres spread far and wide across this continent.

Riding must always have an element of fun – and riding holidays can provide fun in practically every country of the world.

Left: **A Saturday outing at Canberra, Australia.** *Below:* **Trail riders in Waterton Lakes National Park, Canada, zigzag up the mountain sides**

The great Dutch painter of the 17th century, Rembrandt, painted a number of works which included horses. This detail is one of the finest

Day with a Farrier

In the picturesque Surrey village of Abinger Hammer the blacksmith's forge is still the centre of interest, in much the same way as it has been for hundreds of years.

There are two main differences. The old fashioned hand pumped bellows have been replaced with a modern electrically driven fan, and each morning Howard Cooper or his assistant set off in a beautifully equipped Mobile Forge to visit outlying districts, because some of their customers live in the neighbouring county of Sussex.

Howard Cooper bears little resemblance to the village blacksmith of the famous poem. A Freeman of the City of London and a Liveryman of the Worshipful Company of Farriers, he is one of Britain's best known farriers and his work is featured frequently on television. As a lecturer, consultant, examiner and judge he is also well known in Canada where he ran training courses for young farriers.

When he left school Howard Cooper became apprenticed to a Master Farrier at Abingdon, and after a five year apprenticeship he passed the examination of the Worshipful Company of Farriers to become a Registered Shoeing Smith, able to set up in business on his own.

With further experience he became an Associate of the Farriers Company of London, and then a Fellow of the Worshipful Company of Farriers, which is the highest qualification a farrier can have.

Howard Cooper passed all of the necessary examinations with honours, and was soon in demand as a lecturer not only for Pony Clubs and Riding Clubs, but also for various educational organisations. Even at weekends much of his time is spent with horses and ponies. His wife Christine is a riding instructor with the Surrey Union Branch of the Pony Club, and their four young children are all keen and successful riders.

After helping to prepare their seven ponies for the various showing classes, he drives the family horsebox to the Shows, and hopes that none of his customers will choose that time to bring him horses or ponies with loose shoes.

'They often do', he says rather ruefully, 'and I usually carry a leather apron and a bag of nails around with me in the box. I'd hate to see their enjoyment spoilt, but they can be a nuisance at times, particularly when they arrive as we are all spruced up ready to go into the ring.'

At his well-known forge at Abinger Hammer, Howard Cooper spoke of the wide variety of horses and ponies that they have to shoe each week. Show ponies, hunters, event horses, show jumpers, driving horses, cart horses, race horses, and family pets all visit the forge or, when it is more convenient, the mobile forge visits them.

The watercress beds at Abinger Hammer are famous throughout the south of England, 'But,' says Howard Cooper, 'even they owe their existence to the forge and the local iron industry because the watercress is now grown in the old hammer ponds, which date from the time when Abinger was famous for its iron smelting.'

When Monarch, a big 17-hand hunter arrived at the forge for a new set of shoes, Howard Cooper explained the process of shoeing.

Monarch proved the perfect model for this series on shoeing because at no time was he disturbed by the photographer's use of the flash lamp for close-up photographs. Indeed he seemed to enjoy the experience, but Monarch has already appeared in other books about horses.

First he knocks up or cuts off the clenches of the old shoe, using the hammer and the chisel sharpened end of the buffer. The clenches must then be either chopped off or straightened to enable the shoe to be pulled off without damaging the hoof.

The shoe is then levered off the foot using the pinchers, starting at the heels and levering downwards towards the toe on alternate sides of the shoe, so that it can be removed gradually with a straight pull. It must not be twisted sideways, as this would break the wall of the foot.

Then, with the cutting edge of his searcher or drawing knife, the excess sole which has grown since the last shoeing is scraped away. In this way he can reveal the depth, or length of foot which has grown since the horse was last shod and which needs to be trimmed back before a new shoe can be nailed on to the hoof.

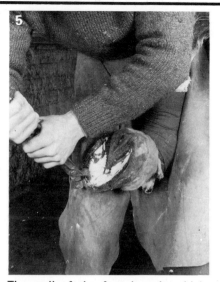

The wall of the foot is quite thick, varying between a quarter of an inch on a small pony or thoroughbred to three quarters of an inch on a cart-horse. Unless great care is taken the tendency is to cut too much off the outside of the wall, making the sole surface higher than the outside of the hoof. This would mean that too much pressure would be placed on the sole of the foot and lameness could result.

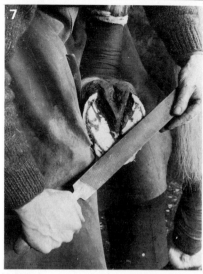

Using the rasp, which is really a coarse toothed file, the foot is rasped absolutely level, and Howard Cooper makes sure that both sides of the foot are of equal height. The toe and the heels must also be level and in correct alignment to the rest of the foot. A perfectly level hoof is essential before the shoe if fitted to allow for an equal bearing on all parts of the foot when the horse stands on it.

Once the old shoe has been removed the dirt and bits are scraped out of the foot with the blunt side of the farrier's drawing knife or searcher. Howard Cooper pays careful attention to the sides of the frog, making sure they are clean, and there are no pieces of grit or stones buried deep in the foot.

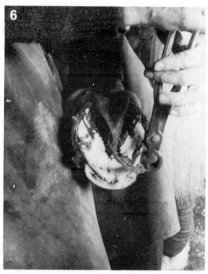

Using the hoof parers, or cutters, the excess of the wall is cut off with a pinching action. Care must be taken to ensure that the cut is made at the correct angle to the foot or too much wall may be taken away.

When the shoe has been made it is taken from the fire at a dull red heat, and carried by means of a pritchel, which has been lightly hammered into one of the nail holes. The shoe is then placed on the foot to scorch the hoof slightly. The shoe is then removed and the correct place for the clips of the shoe are cut in the wall. The shoe is then bedded on to the hoof with a steady pressure. If it does not fit correctly it is taken back to the anvil, altered, and tried on again until a perfect fit can be obtained. The wall of the hoof is not at all sensitive to heat or cold, and so the horse does not feel any discomfort when the outer surface of the hoof is scorched.

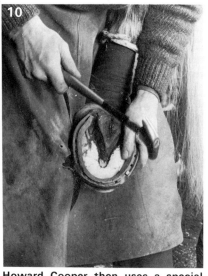

Howard Cooper then uses a special driving hammer for nailing on the shoe. He starts with a nail at the toe so that he can hold the shoe on to the foot and guide the nail into the correct part of the wall of the foot at the same time. He gets the nail to come out of the wall about one and a quarter inches above the shoe. Having got the first nail in, he then balances the shoe by putting a nail on the other side and checks that the shoe is in the correct position before nailing the other inside nails. He continues round the foot hammering in the outside nails finishing with the outside heel nail.

The shoe is then cooled, and the nail holes are checked to make sure they are all clean and clear. The shoe is tried on the foot once more to make sure that there has not been any distortion since it was fitted hot. A perfectly fitting shoe has a correct length at the heels which is neither too long nor too short, giving clearance between the heels of the shoe and the frog, which enables the frog to work correctly without any stones becoming ledged there.

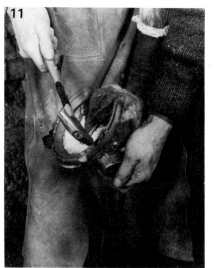

After all the nails have been driven into the shoe, they must be tightened up by putting the pinchers under the 'clenches', or 'wrung off' nail ends and hammering each nail tight.

The foot is then taken forward for 'finishing-off'. First of all the clenches are rasped until they are the same height. The corner or edge of the rasp is then passed underneath the clenches making a small groove in the wall of the foot. Then with the pinchers held under each nail head, the clench is tapped down into the wall. When all the clenches have been dealt with in this way, the rasp is passed over them to make sure they are all perfectly smooth and there are no sharp edges to cut into the horse.

Using the anvil the red hot metal is then bent in the middle almost at right angles. The heel is then hammered into shape.

The blacksmith's forge fire has changed little over the centuries. It is still basically a coal or coke fire which has a draught of cold air blown through a small hole into the bottom to induce an intense heat in the middle of the fire. Originally a hand pumped bellows was used but now an electric motor and fan does the work. After the metal for the shoe has been cut to the correct length it is held by a pair of tongs and placed in the fire until it is hot.

The shoe is then turned over and any 'bumps' are flattened out. The other half is then placed in the fire and the same process is repeated, except that only three nail holes are placed in the inside half of the shoe.

The shoe is returned to the fire to get the toe hot. It is then placed on the edge of the anvil and a small portion of the shoe is drawn down and hammered into a triangular shape. There is one central toe clip on the front shoe and two clips on the hind shoes.

The shoe is then curved on the bick iron. Either a cross pien or a cat's head hammer is used. The shoe is placed on the anvil, and the nail holes are made with a 'stamp', a tool that has a sharpened end the same size as the heads of the nails which will be used to nail on the shoe.
The shoe is then placed over the anvil hole and the pritchel, a sharp pointed hand tool, is driven right through the metal.

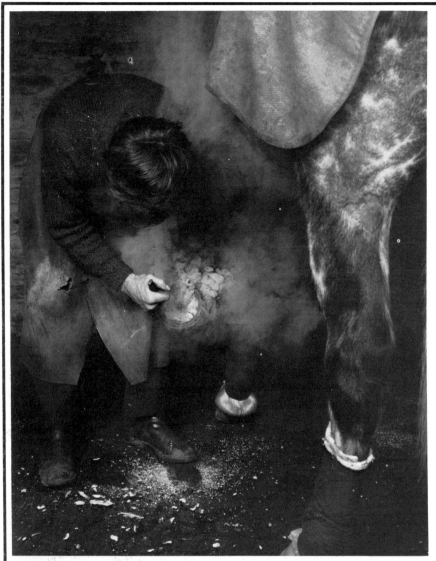

Howard Cooper holds the shoe with the pritchel and places it on the hoof to scorch it slightly. He can then see how the shoe fits and also know where to shape the hoof to take the clips which help to hold the shoe in place.

The tools needed for shoeing the horse are from left to right:
a) The driving hammer for nailing on the shoes.
b) A buffer for cutting clenches on old shoes.
c) A pair of pinchers for removing old shoes.
d) The curved wooden handled or sometimes horn handled drawing knife, or 'searcher' for cleaning out the foot and cutting away the excess hoof.
e) The hoof pairers or cutters for cutting off, or trimming the excess wall of the foot.
f) Above the pairers is the toe knife which is used in conjunction with the hammer to chip away the excess wall.
g) The rasp is used for levelling the foot and smoothing the horn of the hoof rather like a large nail file.
h) The tools are all laid out in the farrier's apron which has a split up the middle to enable the horses leg to be placed between the legs of the farrier. It is made of strong leather to protect his legs if the horse starts pulling about.

Two Great Shows In Two Great Places
by Raymond Brooks Ward

1 The International Show Jumping at Hickstead, Sussex

Every year, in the first week of May, a vast fleet of horse boxes and caravans set out for the start of another year's show season. People like David Broome, Harvey Smith and Marion Mould will be away from home, often seven days a week, competing at shows up and down the country. In the course of the season they and their grooms will travel thousands of miles in Great Britain alone, to say nothing of the trips to International Shows on the Continent. One night the show jumping 'circus' could be at the great Yorkshire Show and the next day 300 miles away at Hickstead in Sussex.

Obviously the itinerary has to be planned down to the smallest detail. Is it possible to get from A to B in time for the first class at 11 o'clock? Have we got plenty of hay and oats on the lorry? Will the farrier at the Bath and West be able to put a set of shoes on in time to jump at lunchtime? What time do declarations close? What stables have we been allocated? A thousand and one things to think about as the horse boxes are loaded ready for another long journey between shows.

It is not surprising that with such a tough schedule to maintain the riders nearly all have caravans so that wherever they are they have an instant base to work from. Take a typical overnight move from North Wales down to Hickstead for an International Show Jumping Meeting. At 6 o'clock at night the last class is still in progress. The caravans will be packed for the

Tony Newberry on Warwick II jumping at Hickstead

journey and, as soon as the rosettes have been presented, the horses will be bandaged and rugged and loaded straight into the lorries. The caravan will be hitched up behind and within fifteen minutes the whole 'circus' will be on the move.

The drivers will have ahead of them a journey of five to six hours, with only a quick stop for supper at a café en route. Somehow it always seems to be raining as the lorries pull into Hickstead in the small hours of the morning. Sleepy horses are unloaded by even

Well clear in front of the Member's Stand at Hickstead

sleepier grooms searching frantic-ally in the dark for the correct stables. Half an hour later the horses are bedded down, fed and watered, and the caravan is pushed to a good site, and there is time for a quick cup of tea before bed. Next morning it's another early start: the novice horses have to be got ready for the first class of the day. Jumping in the four outside rings begins at 9 o'clock. By 8.00 a.m. the loudspeakers in the horse lines are plaintively asking for 'Willie Snooks' to please declare his horses, while down in the secretary's office there is a flurry of last minute activity as owners rush in to make their declarations.

In the caravans, riders snatch a hasty breakfast before going to walk the course. Ten minutes to go and Gerald Barnes, Senior Judge of the outside rings, has made sure that everybody is on duty. Have all the judges turned up? No — one judge missing in ring two, so will Gerald have to do the first hour himself? Meanwhile

Tom Stammas, who apart from judging in the international arena is responsible for all the electric timing, has made sure that the sets are working in all the rings. In the secretary's office Anita Arnett and her staff have slowly made order out of the apparent chaos and by 9 o'clock the judges have their duplicate orders of jumping, the collecting ring stewards have been hard at work calling up the first few horses, and with a bit of luck in comes the first competitor.

The knowledgeable are already assembled around the ringside anxious to weigh up the chances of their own and other people's horses, whilst in the ring the equally anxious course builder watches the first round to get some idea of how the course will ride. Have I made it too easy? 20 clear rounds will put the whole day's schedule out! Is the distance in the double all right? Did I make that last parallel big enough? The unfortunate course builder knows he will never make everybody

happy, except of course the winner.

'Not a bad course,' says David Broome, as he leaves the ring on the first of his novices. He has jumped a clear round. 'Bad dis-tance' is Harvey Smith's comment. His horse had eight faults. The first thing a course builder learns is to be philosophical. The Show Director, Bob Warren, who has just retired, used to be up and about by 6 o'clock, checking that all the flags were flying correctly. The Show Director also has to make sure that an ambulance party is on duty, gate men are ready to take the money, rosettes are sent out to the rings, and a veterinary surgeon is in attendance. He even has the mundane task of checking that everything required is in the loos.

By 10.00 a.m. all the rings will be happily ticking along, with riders and grooms and horses rushing from the stables to the arena with hardly time for a cup of tea or a chat. Meanwhile in the vast expanse of the international

Marion Mould brings Stroller down the Derby Bank

arena, Mrs Pamela Carruthers, one of the world's top course builders will be putting the finishing touches to the fences her arena party had put up the night before. The first day of the meeting is always an anxious one for her, just as it is for the other course builders. Mrs Carruthers has the added responsibility of television. Too many clear rounds and bang go plans to finish the transmission at 4 o'clock. At the same time she is always anxious to get the horses jumping well and accustomed to the big arena — a complete change from the average agricultural show ring. An added problem on the first

day is that she will not know how the horses are going or how strong the international opposition is.

At 11 o'clock, Douglas Bunn, 'Master of Hickstead', Fred Viner, the senior BBC Producer, the Show Director, and Mrs Carruthers meet in Mr Bunn's private room overlooking the arena to plan the day's television. 'We go on the air at 2 o'clock,' Fred Viner tells the meeting, 'and we have to be off by 4 o'clock.' 'Can we finish the Wills Embassy Stakes by 3.55 p.m.?' 'Forty starters,' says Douglas Bunn. 'How long is the course Pam?' 'About 600 yards finishing near the collecting ring, which

should help, and I'm aiming for ten clear rounds.' 'Right, that means we must start the big class at 1.45 p.m.,' says Bunn. Fred Viner then decides to record the jump off for the first class in case the major class under runs. 'Right,' says Bunn, 'we had better start that class at 12 o'clock.' So the pattern for the day is established. The riders, judges, timekeepers, collecting ring stewards and arena party are all warned that jumping will start at midday.

Fred Viner goes back to brief his team. At Hickstead he usually has four to five cameras at his disposal and it is his job to make sure that they are sited so that every fence can be covered — ideally by two cameras, just in case one goes wrong. This is a more complicated task at Hickstead than for example the Horse of the Year Show because of the huge size of the arena. A typical plan is to have one camera on a hydraulic lorry hoist, the same sort of hoist that you see men cleaning High Street lamps from. This will be sited at the far end of the arena, looking down from twenty feet up to the water ditches and the Derby Bank. At a lower level there is probably one on the Club House verandah; there is a third one with a roving commission in the ring itself; while the fourth is up on the Judges' Box balcony (this will also be used by David Vine to introduce the programme and, if necessary, for interviews). The fifth is the highly mobile Mini Camera which is carried by the cameraman at the entrance to the collecting ring.

Up in the commentary box Dorian Williams puts on his earphones and tests his microphone and television monitors — most important at Hickstead since you cannot see the fences at the other end of the arena. Noel Philips-Brown, the commentator for the arena, settles in his seat; the judges check the timing and the starting bell and check their own television monitor.

With two minutes to go, Noel welcomes everybody to the international arena. Fred Viner, tucked away behind the grandstand in the BBC scanner says: 'We are ready to record.' In comes the first horse. Behind the commentator the caption is put into the special machine and up on the screen comes Caroline Bradley on Middle Road. One hour later the class is over, the ten minute jump-off edited and held ready on the machine. At 2 o'clock, David Vine sets the scene and the big class starts. Down below in the tunnel the riders all rush forward to see how the course will ride. Nobody wants to be first but it is a drawn order which changes in each class, horses slowly moving down the list. This time it is Ted Edgar, and he cannot resist a few choice remarks as he goes past the entrance, much to the delight of the crowd. Everest M'Lord hits the last fence, not a bad round for four faults. 'Looks all right,' says Lionel Dunning to Graham Fletcher. 'Watch the double David, it is riding a bit short,' grunts Ted as he comes out. Out in the ring Pam Carruthers turns to her assistant John Dovey, 'I think we are going to be all right. Keep pushing, however, is the order from the Show Director. We can always slow up if we get too many clear rounds.'

Out the back the grooms are busy walking the horses around, listening for their turn. 'Harvey Smith, please get ready,' booms the collecting ring loud speakers. Harvey has a final jump over the practice fence and adjusts his girths. 'How many clear, Hazel?' he asks his groom. 'Five so far.' 'Right, let's get in.' As soon as Volvo is in the ring Hazel rushes to the front of the tunnel. This is the big moment for her just as much as for Harvey. 'Half way round and still clear! 'Steady, that was nearly a bad one. Here comes the last — he's done it.'

3.40 p.m. now, and nine horses to jump off against the clock. Just about right for television. Fifteen minutes later and it's all over. Graham Fletcher, narrowly beating David Broome, by $\frac{2}{5}$ second. There is a final interview with Graham, and David Vine wishes everybody 'goodbye' from Hickstead.

But it is not goodbye for the

The winner of a major Junior Competition with her sash of honour at Hickstead, Sussex

riders and grooms. Two hours later and the final round in the last competition has been jumped. As the crowds stream on to the Brighton Road the horses are led back to the stable, fed, watered and tucked up for the night. Then it is time for supper and the portable 'telly', or to get together over coffee in someone's caravan. What do they talk about? You've guessed — show jumping.

2 The Dunhill International Show at Olympia in London

To be successful every show has to have a character of its own. There are particularly good examples of this. One is the Royal International Horse Show which has that great tradition stretching back over the years with magic names, like the King George V Gold Cup, the Queen Elizabeth Cup and the Prince of Wales Cup — all for jumping.

The other is the Horse of the Year Show, which is a complete contrast.

It could almost be called the kaleidoscope of the horse — with fun, variety and excitement and something of an end-of-term atmosphere about it. To stage a new show was therefore a tremendous challenge to us and we were fortunate when Dunhill's asked us to produce an entirely new concept at Olympia. We had always thought that circus and show jumping could go together and when it was decided to stage the first event at Olympia in 1972 this seemed to make sense, since Olympia was for so long the home of the Bertram Mills Circus. So a new idea was born — of having top-class show jumping, circus and, because it was essentially a family show, a pantomime.

In the first year we asked the Enfield Chace Pony Club to produce Snow White and the Seven Dwarfs.

Mary Chipperfield located the original Schumann Liberty Horses in France and brought these to London. Dunhill guaranteed probably the strongest foreign opposition seen in this country, by bringing the winners of the trophy events held during the year all over Europe.

But Olympia has its own nightmare problems unlike Wembley where the seating is already in existence. We take over the vast echoing empty spaces of Olympia five days before the show and have to build it from scratch. That means bringing in portable grandstands to hold 7,000 people, putting in hundreds of tons of earth for the arena and the collecting ring, building 150 temporary stables, to say nothing of providing 50 shops of various shapes and sizes for the trade stand exhibitors.

As you can imagine this requires very careful planning, for if the seating contractors get behind,

The ring at Olympia in London has been cleared for awards to be made to the winners

this delays Alan Spearman, who is responsible for putting down the earth. If he gets delayed then Woodhouses have difficulty in putting up the stables. It all boils down to a last minute dash to get everything finished and approved by the Licensing Authorities as the first horse boxes come rolling through the doors.

We have another headache at Olympia, since the Brussels International Horse Show finishes the night before the Dunhill starts, and as we cannot take chances with storms in the channel, an air lift of 32 horses starts from Brussels at 8.00 a.m. on the opening morning! If all goes well these horses are in their stables at Olympia by 2.00 p.m., to join the horses from competitors who have come from all over Great Britain.

Then comes the frantic rush to rehearse the displays by 5.30 p.m. Despair sets in. Everything has gone wrong. All the items are over-running. The band are not quite sure what the High School

horses are going to do. And the only thing we can do is pray at opening time – 7.00 p.m.

However, there is a very true adage. A bad dress rehearsal can mean a successful opening night and at 7.00 p.m. the arena comes to life, with the stirring Christmas fanfare from the Band of The Royal Corps of Transport. In comes the first horse and the show is on its way.

Throughout the week, the jumping classes all have Christmas names: The Christmas Pudding Stakes, The Cracker Stakes; The Turkey Championship. The riders enter into the spirit of the festive season and hand round the mince pies at the end of each class. On Saturday night we have the Pair Fancy dress, and who can forget one particularly outrageous Christmas fairy in the large person of Ted Edgar, with his ample measurements suitably adorned in the right places, and accompanied by brother-in-law, David Broome, as Father Christmas. The riders go to

tremendous trouble in great secrecy to produce their costumes. In 1974 Paul and Monica Weier from Switzerland appeared beautifully dressed in Alpine costume – they had even borrowed a St Bernard dog and a donkey for the occasion, but the class was stolen by the two Frenchmen, Monsieur Marc Pelissier and Hubert Parot, who appeared as Paris tramps.

At the end of the first class the entertainment starts. Mary Chipperfield – a member of the famous Chipperfield Circus family – has her High School horses, Domino and Amber, on the long rein and, as a complete contrast, brings in her show jumping monkeys on Thelwell ponies.

Then it is time for the Pony Club. Throughout the year the Enfield Chace branch have been busy rehearsing a cast of forty children, while behind the scenes, Mrs Hacker, assisted by various Pony Club mums has been busy stitching away at the costumes. A considerable task when you think

that in 1974 we had 'Tales from Nursery Rhymes' with a whole variety of characters from Humpty Dumpty to the King and Queen of Hearts. This, of course, is one of the highlights for all the children in the afternoon performances, but it is also tremendously popular with the adults! In the evening there is the pantomime and than a quick change of emphasis as the lights come back on to show the Cossack riders in the circus arena.

Out they go and then it is time for tent pegging, with representatives from the army and the police taking part.

There is a tradition at Olympia that the Chelsea Pensioners come to one of the evening performances. Several of these gallant veterans ride into the arena on the tent peggers' horses, and there is a fair amount of expert criticism by the old cavalry soldiers, many of whom competed at the old Royal Tournament at Olympia in the 1930s.

After this there is a twenty minute interval, during which Alan Ball and his team of course builders

have to erect the fences for the Dunhill Puissance and show jumping is under way once more. But the jumping event does not close the programme, as it does at most other shows. Dorian Williams, the Chairman of the Show, was always determined that the Dunhill should be entirely different to the other famous indoor events and so we always finish with a Christmas Finale.

In previous years we have had 'Mr Pickwick at Dingley Dell', 'A Meet of Mr Jorrocks' Hounds on Christmas Eve' and Dickens' 'London On Christmas Eve'. Most of our riders are delighted to play characters in this Christmas finale and things do tend to get a little out of hand at the final performance on Saturday, with water pistols and packs of flour appearing at unexpected moments!

Traditionally a stage coach comes galloping into the ring and we finish with Father Christmas on his sleigh and as the snow falls in the centre of the arena the whole audience sings 'Good King Wenceslas'.

Raymond Brooks-Ward, dressed as James Pigg, the huntsman of Mr Jorrocks' hounds

Harvey Smith on Summertime shows how it is done

Pony Club members as they appear in their now traditional mounted pantomime

Fences and Courses
by Robert Owen

The objects of a jumping course are to be attractive to look at and good fun to ride over, while providing an interesting event for those who watch. Also, of course, the course must give the variety so necessary to today's demanding standards, and provide the type of competition best suited to those who are taking part. Obviously a course for ponies will have very different heights and spreads of fences to a course set for horses of 16 hands or so.

The British Show Jumping Association, the official body controlling the sport in Britain, has for many years realised that the building and planning of courses is a job for experts. Each area of the BSJA has a panel of Course Builders, men and women who have the skills and experience to undertake this important work.

There are only four main types of fences: the upright or vertical; the parallel; the staircase or triple-bar; and the pyramid or hog's back. Then, of course, there is the water jump, which is in a class of its own. These are illustrated on the right.

But, of course, there are many variations of these basic fence shapes. For example, a parallel can be built which is not absolutely 'true' (meaning that the heights of the top poles are exactly the same), but may, from certain parts of the ring, look as if it *is* 'true'. This kind of near-parallel is called an oxer, and is usually built with brush placed between the front part and the back part.

Now for a short description of the types of fences mentioned.

An upright might be a gate, or a vertical made from poles or perhaps planks. A wall can also be classed as an upright fence. These are easier to jump when a ground line has been included, because a horse judges the height of a fence by first setting his sight on a ground line. When there is no ground line it is up to the rider to bring his horse to the correct point of take-off before asking him to jump.

A parallel is the most difficult jump of all. The spread between the front upright part of the fence and the single back pole can be set to any standard depending on the competition. But the back pole is sometimes not seen by the horse or pony as he comes to the point of take-off. Unless the rider 'pushes' hard, it is possible that the animal will imagine he is jumping an upright. Then he will not allow for the spread, and will invariably knock the back pole down.

A staircase is possibly the easiest jump of all. Because the horse can see the whole jump it is natural that he will jump it long, and the trajectory (another word meaning the arc of jumping) will enable him to clear the obstacle with ease. But if there is no ground line it is not quite so easy. Be careful to look for this when walking the course before the competition begins.

A hog's back is tricky, rather than difficult, since it is a confusing jump to look at when the approach is made. A pony must be asked to jump big so that his back legs will clear the back pole.

A water jump is one quite on its own! It should be jumped as if a triple bar were being taken, though the approach, balance and ability of both rider and horse or pony is very important. This is a jump that must be practised as often as possible, since more and more shows are including a water jump in competitions for younger riders.

No fence is ever easy – they are not designed to be so! The course builder sets out to pose certain problems and hopes the riders will solve them. If each obstacle were to be approached properly, at the right speed and with the correct balance, and if the pony

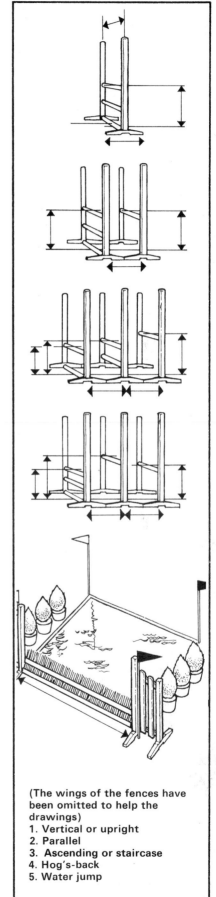

(The wings of the fences have been omitted to help the drawings)
1. **Vertical or upright**
2. **Parallel**
3. **Ascending or staircase**
4. **Hog's-back**
5. **Water jump**

Buttevant Boy with Graham Fletcher clearing a well-built obstacle

took off each time at exactly the right point, there would be a clear round for everybody. But neither riders nor their mounts are the same all the time, and both can make mistakes. This is what makes it so exciting for the spectators and frequently frustrating for the riders.

Courses are designed over selected distances. The overall distance is carefully measured by the course builders, and this is known as the track to be taken. When the speed of riding the course is known, the time for the course can then be set. For example, if a course was 450 metres in 'track' and it was being jumped by ponies at 225 metres per minute, the time allowed would be exactly 2 minutes.

Courses are also designed, as we have said, to set problems or questions. And one of the biggest questions is asked at a combina-

tion obstacle, whether a double or a treble. The distances between each element are very, very carefully measured – as the distances set between each fence on the course should be.

Course builders know the actual stride a horse or pony *should* take – either a jumping or a non-jumping stride. A horse jumping a one-stride double, say from an upright to another upright, would be asked to accept a distance of

8 metres (26 ft) between each element. A pony being asked to jump a similar obstacle would be set a distance of 6.86 metres (22 ft 6 ins). But if the two elements were, say, an upright to a parallel, the measurements would be: for a horse 7.6 metres (25 ft); for a pony, 6.55 metres (21 ft 6 ins).

These measurements might be slightly varied when the course is on an uphill or a downhill track.

Listed below are some of the so-called 'true' distances for a combination obstacle:
Upright to upright:
    Horses: 8 m (26 ft)
    Ponies: 6.85 m (22 ft 6 ins)
Upright to parallel:
    Horses: 7.60 m (25 ft)
    Ponies: 6.55 m (21 ft 6 ins)
Upright to ascending oxer:
    Horses: 7.50 m (24 ft 6 ins)
    Ponies: 6.40 m (21 ft)
Ascending oxer to upright:
    Horses: 8 m (26 ft)
    Ponies: 6.85 m (22 ft 6 ins)
Parallel to upright:
    Horses: 7.85 m (25 ft 6 ins)
    Ponies: 6.70 m (22 ft)

The course builders have a tremendous responsibility to see that the competition is a good one, and fair both to the rider and his mount. And he is set with a number of different problems, particularly in the case of an indoor show, where the related distances are very much closer. Under BSJA rules the judge appointed for the competition finally decides whether the course as set should be jumped without any final slight alteration. In other words, the judge is responsible for what he is judging.

Course builders and judges do everything they possibly can to ensure that the skill of the riders and the ability of their horses or ponies are tested by the right standards. They are also much concerned for the safety of all who take part in the sport of show jumping. Sometimes, because of the state of the ground or the weather, which can change during a show, both course builders and judges will make adjustments to the fences and courses to make sure that no one gets hurt.

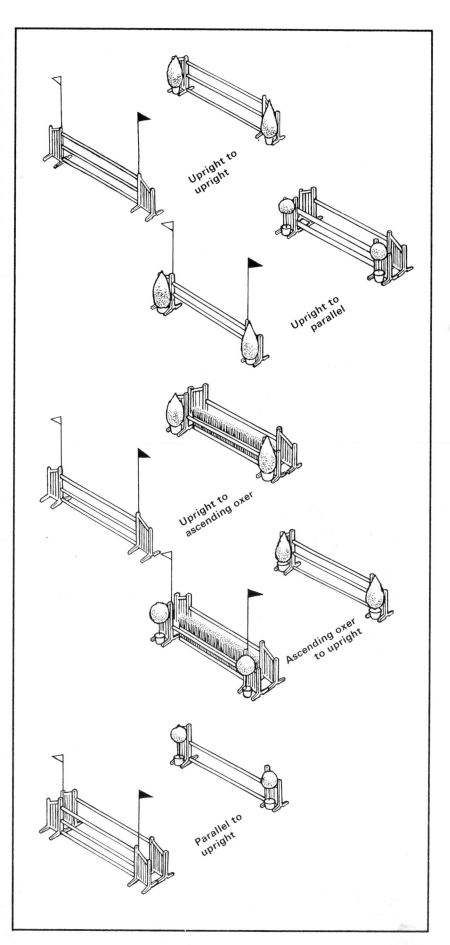

Upright to upright

Upright to parallel

Upright to ascending oxer

Ascending oxer to upright

Parallel to upright

Copra- A Shetland Pony

by Stella Ranns

'Look at that!' Joanna pointed to a new notice tied to a tree. SHETLAND FOALS ON VIEW, it said.

'On view,' repeated Wendy. 'Do you think we can just go in, then?'

'Of course,' said Joanna, already halfway up the steep drive, bordered with gay tulips and aubretia.

They turned a corner and there, across a wide lawn, was a small herd of Shetland ponies sunning themselves in front of a large shed. There were grey and chestnut ones, golden dun and black ones, and all less than 38 inches (one metre) high. The foals were just about half their size.

'Come to see the ponies?' called a cheery voice from a window before the girls had really had time to take in the scene. 'The liver chestnut with the white mane and tail is the stallion. Be respectful of him, best stay this side of the fence till I come.' But the stallion, Gabriel, was having a siesta and didn't even bother to inspect the visitors. The foals, though, were very curious.

'Aren't they gorgeous?' exclaimed Wendy, rubbing and patting their soft coats. 'I expect the black one came out of that shiny black mare.'

'No, it didn't,' said a teasing voice behind them, and a kindly man, ready to spend all afternoon showing his ponies, introduced himself. 'Climb through the fence,' he said, 'and have a look.'

The coal-black filly was obviously used to being inspected. 'See all those white hairs around the eyes? She'll be a grey, and a pale grey at that.' On being released, the black foal bent to suckle a chestnut mare.

'Well I never,' exclaimed Wendy.

'The colour of their "spectacles" is the clue to their final colour. Actually, when their foal coats start coming out in midsummer I feel like taking my notice down for a few weeks because they really look like spotted leopards for a bit.'

Wendy suddenly squealed with delight. 'This foal's undone my shoe.'

'I'm afraid pulling at laces is her special trick.' But when a chestnut filly took hold of a button on his jacket and nearly pulled it off she received a sharp tap on the nose. 'She's tame enough now to learn some manners,' he explained. 'Come on, let's make up and shake a hoof,' he went on, lifting each foot in turn. 'The blacksmith won't have any trouble with you when he comes to trim your hooves,' he added, stroking the blond mane with pride. 'We're very proud of this filly; she's called Gold Dust.'

'What about this one?' asked Joanna quietly. It was the first time she had spoken and she pointed to the smallest foal standing at the end of the line. He was the colour of steel wool, with a brown eel-stripe down his back. He had the prettiest head of them all, with tiny ears full of fawn fluff and a nose like velvet.

'This is our only colt. He's out of the grey mare by our own stallion. He'll be mouse black eventually, and how he managed to turn out so drab I wouldn't know, but he's a lovely little animal – that small head and ears and chunky little body. He's called Copra. Come on, Copra, show these young ladies your teeth. See, a perfect bite, absolutely together.'

Suddenly the fillies decided to take a run in the field and tore round at an incredible speed. The mares trundled after them to graze, but Copra stayed with Joanna.

* * *

One evening about a week later Joanna's father came home tired after his long journey from London to find his wife looking perplexed.

'I don't know what's got into Joanna,' she said. 'Can you guess what she wants? A Shetland pony of all things!'

'Whatever for?' asked Mr Moffat, taken aback.

'You'd better ask her, she won't say much to me. But I must say she really has a gift with animals, the way she tamed that wild stray cat and never misses going to groom Doug's Shadow. If it isn't this animal she wants it will be something else, no doubt.'

Now it must be explained that Mr Moffat had a friend called Doug, and but for him this story would end here. He was an enterprising fellow, owned poultry, pigs and property, but most important, he owned fields almost opposite Joanna's house where his pony, Shadow, used to graze with a donkey and a couple of bullocks. So, with some friendly arrangement, it would in fact be possible for Joanna to keep a Shetland.

'But here she is, almost twelve,' thought Mr Moffat, 'and wanting a pony she can never ride. It just doesn't make sense.' So he tackled his daughter right away.

'He's beautiful, Daddy, and the smallest, and he's lonely.'

'How can he be lonely with his mother?' interrupted Mr Moffat.

'But he is,' persisted Joanna, 'because all the frisky fillies play together and leave him out, and he's so gentle and such a baby. I *do* want him, Daddy, really I do.'

There was something about his daughter's earnestness that made Mr Moffat realise this was no passing whim. 'But it's like falling for a day-old chick, Jo. He won't stay a baby for ever.'

'I know he won't, but I can go every week-end to see him. In any case I can't have him until October when he's weaned. He's pure-bred Shetland,' she continued, 'Section A. That means his pedigree can be traced through two generations, and I've seen his papers and he goes way back, much farther than that, to the first Shetlands ever registered.'

'Oh dear,' sighed Mr Moffat. 'That will make him expensive.'

'He's less than half the price of a filly, though, that can be bred from,' persuaded Joanna. 'And the true Shetland breed is important because of their gentle temperaments, and the fantastic coats they grow, two in fact – a woolly undercoat and long hair as well. He can live out all the year . . .'

'All right, all right,' Mr Moffat interrupted the flow, 'we'll go and see him at the weekend.'

Joanna threw her arms round her father. At that moment she knew that Copra was hers. 'They've only got to see him,' she thought.

*　　*　　*

When Joanna went to collect her Copra in October he was gelded, weaned and could eat hay and pony cubes. Because of her owner's skill and patience he was halter-broken and Joanna actually led him all the way home with the help of his breeder. Occasionally she had to push him from behind when he was sus-picious of a mend in the road or a flapping cover on a haystack. She loved the sensation of burying her fingers in his thick coat. He was the colour of bitter chocolate now and like a little bear.

'That's not Copra,' shouted her father as they passed the gate.

'It *is*,' came the prompt reply, 'we've never had a foal who could lead like Joanna's.'

When the tired little pony first saw Shadow he must have thought, 'That's my grey mother,' for he tried to suckle. Shadow sniffed him, approved, and from that moment on they became inseparable. Anything Shadow did Copra would do too, and when, later on, Joanna tried to teach Shadow to jump Copra followed, clearing the obstacles like a champion.

On very wet, cold nights he had other company. Joanna had arranged with Doug that Copra could share the big shed for this first winter with two cows, two bullocks and a sow. Not only did he take charge of the farmyard menagerie at night, but he taught them how to tear open bags of potatoes, much to Doug's annoyance.

'How could you, Copra?' scolded Joanna, 'when I give you pony cubes every night. And you'll only get those while you are a baby. After that it's grass and hay and no more, or you'll get like a barrel,' she threatened.

One day, early the following spring, Copra was feeling very hot in his winter woollies, which were starting to mat in lumps under his tummy.

'Look at that pathetic little pony,' said one prim lady to another passing the gate.

Joanna overheard and laughed to herself. 'You'd be pathetic, Copra, if you lived in a backyard with no company, wouldn't you? But I must admit you do look a sight.' And from that day, until his plump little body emerged with a new silk coat, Joanna brushed him for half an hour twice a day.

*　　*　　*

All the village thought Joanna had a new pony when she took him out. 'I'd give anything to have him for my grandchildren,' said one lady, admiring his tameness and love of small children.

'Mary had a little lamb...' teased an elderly gentleman, making Joanna annoyed.

'He's not a lamb, or a large dog, he's a proper small horse,' she protested.

If anyone doubted her word they should have taken a look in Doug's field a few weeks later.

Copra always took kindly to animals and humans alike and he welcomed the new mare, Lady, who came to share his field. But he realised that there were now too many bigger than he was and he decided he must stick up for himself. His heels could flash out like lightning, and he gave such impressive displays of bucking and kicking that the two other ponies and the donkey eyed him with a new respect and had to admit that Copra was indeed 'the Boss'. It was therefore Copra who had the first taste of a new salt-lick and chose the best bit of shade. Joanna laughed to see her gentle pet so mightily in charge.

On the day that Copra earned for himself the title of 'the bravest Shetland ever' he unhappily disgraced himself. How many Shetlands are challenged to a duel by a huge horse and stand their ground? Especially when the charger is disguised in flapping gold and black trappings and mounted by a knight in glittering armour!

It all happened when some dashing horsemen staged a real-life medieval jousting tournament at the Village Carnival. The Black Knight was the bragging villain, and was looking for a last chance to entertain the departing crowd. Suddenly he saw Copra. With lance couched he bore down on the little pony, who stood unflinching.

'Fair damsel,' shouted the Black Knight, towering above Joanna, 'mount thy trusty steed and I'll challenge thee to a duel.'

There were roars of laughter all round, and clapping, and more laughter at the incongruous pair. Joanna blushed and giggled helplessly, but inside Copra there grew a new, strange feeling – RAGE! He was being laughed at, laughed at because he was small, and his tail began to swish menacingly. Having had his sport the Black Knight turned his charger and galloped off.

Copra seethed inside, his tail swished violently, and he started to trot at a brisker pace than was comfortable for Joanna among

the crowd. The bit of his new bridle, that he had accepted so willingly, hurt him as Joanna tried to restrain him. Out on the road there were cars and more cars, all trying to get away before the crush.

'Cars!' thought Copra. 'They're just like chargers, always taking liberties and coming too close.' Before Joanna could stop him he lashed out at a passing car, and was ready to tackle the next, and the next. The drivers swerved and looked alarmed and one shook his fist. Luckily Joanna had the presence of mind to take Copra down a side lane and there waited until the crowds had gone and the little pony had recovered from his slight.

'I'm sorry, Copra,' said Joanna, smoothing his nose and scratching his neck affectionately. 'It was all my fault. I shouldn't have taken you. Perhaps it will stop people wanting to buy you for a bit,' she added, cheering up. 'How could I part with you when you've still everything to learn? I'll tell you a secret,' she whispered. 'When you're three you can learn to pull a little cart and we'll go to the shows together!'

Almost as though he understood Copra pricked his ears, Joanna clicked her tongue, gave him a long rein, and together they trotted home straight and true.

Three Girls At The Top

by Brian Giles

A few years ago anyone who mentioned that women should ride against men in flat races were considered slightly odd and not to be taken seriously. Now, however, things have changed and it is a common sight to see young ladies riding a finish against their male rivals on a racecourse.

Perhaps some racing fans still consider mixed amateur races a joke, but for those who take part, the business is deadly serious. It has to be to progress. Too much money and effort have gone into the buying, keeping and training of the horses for the owners to treat it as a game.

One young lady who has made a big impact on the racing world is Brooke Sanders, a brown-eyed beauty from Epsom, the daughter of a court shorthand writer. She is a very talented jockette, and in 1974 finished the season as leading lady rider after having six wins on five different horses. She usually weighs in at 8 st 2 lb.

Like most people who love horses, Brooke started riding at an early age. In fact, she was only four when she sat on her first pony. Six years later she was given a horse called Sweet William, a giant which stood over 18 hands and dwarfed the then ten-year-old Brooke.

Sweet William, however, had a liking for roses, and when turned out in the back garden of the Sanders' house, would take to eating those growing in the next-door neighbour's plot. It was a situation that could not be toler-ated and Mr and Mrs Sanders decided he must go. Brooke adored the horse and found the decision difficult to accept. She even ran away for a night to sleep in Sweet William's stable, but she became lonely and decided to return to the warmth of the family home the next morning. Shortly afterwards, her parents bought her a pony.

Having attended a convent school, at sixteen Brooke had made up her mind to work with horses, so she joined Ian Benstead, a local trainer, as a stable girl. She knew and liked Benstead because during the school holidays he had allowed her to visit his yard and help out with the race horses. She loved the life, but after a spell with Benstead and Staff Ingham, another local trainer, she moved on to work and ride for Brian Swift, who must have been very proud to have such a dedicated young woman in his employ.

But although Brooke ended the 1974 season as the champion jockette she still has to work alongside the other stable boys and girls. Each morning while most of us are still sound asleep, Brooke is busily mucking out three horses. When we wake, she is exercising horses on Epsom Downs no matter what the weather is doing, because come rain or shine they must be given the correct amount of work to keep them in super-fit condition. Brooke

Brooke Sanders ready for action

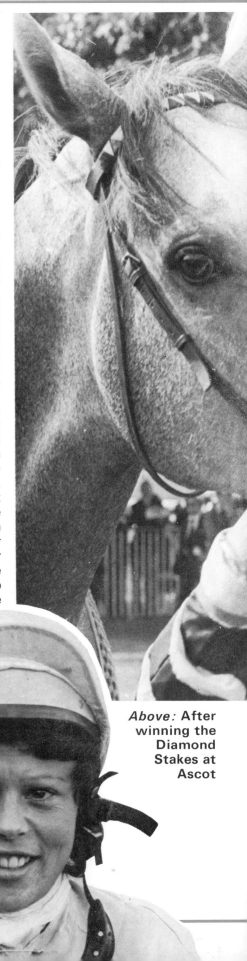

Above: **After winning the Diamond Stakes at Ascot**

opportunity because it makes a change.'

Brooke maintains that she would much rather race ride against men than girls. 'They seem to know what they are doing!' she says. 'I once raced in Jersey against girls and got pushed all over the place, because most of my rivals were galloping their mounts flat out with their eyes firmly shut.

'It was all the more hair-raising because if you were not lucky enough to get the inside during the race the chances were you would end up going over a cliff!

'But it was good fun and I would not swop jobs with anyone. My ambition was to win the Lady Jockey's Championship and I did. Now I think I would like to win it again!'

Brooke has very firm ideas about other young girls wanting to carve out a career in racing as a jockette. 'The only way to do it really', she said, 'is to start as a stable girl. People do not realise how fit you have to be to compete in races, and the only way is to ride regularly and that can be achieved if you work in stables. There are other ways, but I think my idea is best!'

Even if some other lady riders take out professional jockey licences, Brooke would not turn pro. 'I need a lot more experience', she said. 'And I have not got the right connections to make a good living. My parents are not in racing and if I turned professional I would not get good horses to ride. As an amateur, I am offered some of the best rides and because of that I have been able to win a championship!'

During her years with horses, Brooke has had many accidents. Her injuries to date include two broken arms, an ankle, a collar bone and a twisted pelvis. Many people would shy away from such physical damage even for an undying love of horses. But those who stand head and shoulders above everyone else have to make sacrifices even if it means suffering pain in the climb to the top.

And anyone who wants to embark on the long trail that leads to success in the saddle must be

is also a very good instructress and on many occasions can be seen teaching apprentice jockeys how to ride. At the start of the 1975 flat racing season Brooke moved to work at Arthur Pitts yard.

When the racehorses return from the gallops they are groomed and their straw beds straightened. At midday, Brooke and the other stable staff have time off to rest before evening 'stables' start. Then the horses are groomed again and their beds skipped out before they

are fed their last meal for the day.

When Brooke finds the time she likes to ride to hounds and she also takes an interest in show jumping. She competes whenever she can on a horse called Arctic Gladiator, and has won several Foxhunter classes with him, but she doesn't think she will ever be a top-flight show-jumping rider.

'I am no Harvey Smith', she explained. 'And I am not as knowledgable as most in the sport. I like to take part when I get the prepared to buy some alarm clocks. Those who doubt these pearls of wisdom should take a look in Brooke's bedroom. She has several that shriek together at the unearthly hour of 5.30 a.m. every day.

Debbie Johnsey

Like eventing, show jumping has a habit of occasionally throwing up stars – people who have that special ingredient that enables them to stand out from the pack. One such person who has emerged as a future champion is Debbie Johnsey from Devauden in Wales.

Debbie, who is still in her 'teens, was first selected to ride for Britain at the age of eleven, and it was intended that she should take part in the Junior European Championship at Linards in France. She was delighted; for her, it was a dream come true. Her joy was short-lived, however, because other nations in the championship pointed out that the minimum age for a junior under the rules of the Federation Equestrian Internationale was fourteen.

Although many people hated the idea of telling Debbie, it had to be because the rules had been made, and of course, had to be respected. But in 1973, those early years of frustration were forgotten when young Debbie, justifying the faith put in her, took the European title on Speculator at Ekeren.

It was a just reward for her efforts and a particularly good win because she beat Stany van Paesschen of Belgium by five seconds in a jump-off.

Debbie's first season in adult show jumping was in 1972, and again she was in superb form, finishing second in the Leading Show Jumper of the Year competition at Wembley, and equal runner-up for the national title. A year later, Debbie took second place behind Ann Backhouse in the Ladies National Championship at Windsor.

But it was at the 1973 Bath and West Show that she gave the public a glimpse of something new and exciting when taking the Babycham Gold Cup on Speculator.

Only five of the twenty-five starters managed clear rounds and Debbie won the contest after having four faults in 57.7 seconds. It was a truly brilliant performance for such a young girl against seasoned campaigners.

In 1974, Debbie and her father produced a new horse called Assam, then a seven-year-old, who was an ex-American racehorse related to British Derby winner Mahmoud. At Hickstead in the Wills Embassy Stakes, those watching witnessed the devastating speed of the gelding when he shot round the course in deep mud to win as he liked in 59.8 seconds.

Reporters clustered round young Debbie and asked how she came to ride Assam. It transpired that her neighbour David Broome had seen the horse on one of his trips to America and had phoned Mr Johnsey from New York suggesting that Assam looked suitable for his daughter.

Shortly afterwards, Debbie flew to America to ride Assam, liked the way he performed, and a deal was struck.

If anyone deserves to succeed in the world of show jumping, Debbie does. Since she was three years old she has had a liking for horses and a desire to ride.

At eight years of age she made her mark in show jumping when winning the Junior 12.2-hands Championship of Wales. A remarkable achievement when you consider that Debbie never had a paid-for riding lesson. Honours must go to her father, Terence, because it was he who put in all the hard work and taught his daughter the way to sit, gallop and jump.

Debbie's mother also plays a big part in the young future champion's career. She bought Debbie the pony which was to take her to the top of the juniors and keep her there for several years. The pony's name was Champ VI, and he is now ridden by Debbie's sister Claire, who also is galloping rapidly in the right direction.

When Debbie reached the age of fourteen, her father bought

Debbie Johnsey in winning form with the brilliant horse, Speculator

Speculator, a big, rangy horse with a lot of potential. This was made clear by the way he strode away with the Junior European Championship in Belgium.

But life for Debbie is not all glamour, because in her quest for perfection and her many, many victories, she travels more than 3000 miles a season to get to shows all over Britain.

She also considers that stable work and training must play a major role in her life, and spends most days exercising her horses in order to get them fit and keep them in peak condition. Debbie also believes that working her mounts on the flat and schooling them in figures of eight helps to keep them supple and agile enough to cope with the various courses they have to face in the international show jumping arena.

And if she feels they are becoming bored with the scenery, she changes their routine and exercises them in a nearby wood. She is always thinking about them and keeping *their* welfare uppermost in her mind.

Ask Debbie what her ambition in life is and the reply comes quickly. 'I would like to ride in the Olympics, because I would love to win a gold medal, and feel I have the horses to help me do so.'

To get a true picture of the situation it is always best to consult those who spend their life watching horses and riders both in this country and abroad; Ronnie Massarella has the key to Debbie's success. 'She is a wonderful rider,' he explained, 'and a natural!'

Although Debbie has had a few good wins, she has, in fact, suffered hard times. In 1968 she broke a collarbone after a riding accident, but amazed everyone by bouncing back into the saddle in next to no time.

The countries she has ridden in include Belgium, Holland, Switzerland, Austria and South Africa.

In future years, Debbie Johnsey will be either a world champion, an Olympic gold medallist, or both. These are not idle prophecies: she has the will, the ability and the horses to win.

Janet Hodgson

Although flat racing can be exciting there is nothing quite like eventing. It has everything; glamour, pace and colour, and one of the finest riders in the sport is Janet Hodgson, still in her twenties and as tough as they come.

In September 1973, Janet was chosen to ride for Britain in the European Championship at Kiev, in Russia, on Larkspur. Little did she know that by the time the second stage of the event was over, her name and picture would be in every national newspaper in the country. Janet made the headlines not because she won, but because she gave a personal sacrifice and contributed more than anyone had the right to ask.

The drama had started at the second fence, an upright of solid poles set over a ditch. Larkspur took off, hit the top, crumpled on landing and buried poor Janet. The ground that day was fairly firm, and when Janet remounted her face was badly battered and she had lost a tooth. Then at the twenty-first fence, Larkspur came down again, but instead of giving up, Janet got back on and finished the course.

She knew that at least three of the four team members had to get round, and as one had already

been eliminated, Janet's efforts helped Britain to gain a bronze medal behind the German and Russian teams. So impressed were the Russians that they presented her with a gold watch for courage. Later that year, she was honoured again by members of the British Equestrian Writers Association who voted her Equestrian Personality of the year. Most journalists, when writing about her escapades in the Ukraine had called her 'the heroine of Kiev'. Janet, who is very modest, said 'I just wanted to be treated like everyone else and I also want to thank all those people who were so kind!'

It was in 1971 that Janet, who lives at Sutton Coldfield in Warwickshire, really caught the eye of those who follow eventing. Riding the 17.1-hands Larkspur, she galloped the opposition into the ground to win the Advanced Class at Chatsworth. The same season she made the trip to Holland with Larkspur and took honours in the major three-day event at Boekelo. It was another example of the Warwickshire girl's courage, because at Badminton in the April of 1971, Janet had taken a fall and been badly injured.

She returned to show such good form that the British selectors put her on the short-list for the

Left: Janet Hodgson win the Burghley Horse Trials

Above: Negotiating the Trout Hatchery on Larkspur in the World Three-Day Championships

By the time the cross-country section had been completed, her total score was only 89.47 penalty points. A clear round show jumping pushed her into fourth place behind eventual winner, Bruce Davidson on Irish Cap.

It was a superb effort, because when the results are studied carefully, the nearest any British team member got was seventh place, a position filled by triple Olympic gold medallist Richard Meade on Wayfarer II.

Three years earlier, Janet had proved that she was a highly talented event rider when winning the Burghley trials on Larkspur, and even though she was afterwards to suffer pain and injury, her love for the sport did not diminish.

Training plays a very special part in Janet's life and she believes that hunting is one of the best ways to teach a horse the job of eventing. During the winter all of her young mounts, including the very promising Gretna Green, are ridden to hounds.

'I take them hunting,' she said, 'because it teaches them to cope with the unexpected. It also keeps them fit and gives them an added interest in life!'

Although no other horse will take the place of Janet's Larkspur, the Warwickshire girl does have a lot of feeling for Gretna Green and thinks he might one day make up into an Olympic hope. She rode him at Boekelo in October 1974 and although they finished in fourteenth place, Janet was delighted with the performance.

'The ground conditions out there were dreadful,' she explained, 'and it tipped down with rain most of the time. But Gretna Green jumped very well and I was very pleased with him.'

The trip back from Holland proved a headache for Janet and the other British riders with her. They were delayed at the coast for three days before returning to their homes!

'The weather was bad', she said, 'and we couldn't get on the transport provided. In the end, the journey seemed like something out of one of the 'Carry-On' films.'

1972 Munich Olympic Games, but for some reason did not pick her for the team who went to West Germany and eventually won a gold medal.

Eventing, unlike show jumping, is more a vocation than a business. There is very little prize money involved, and those who take part in the sport usually start in the hunting field. Janet began her long haul to success as a member of the South Staffordshire Pony Club. And it wasn't long before she could be seen galloping across the field in hot pursuit of those who follow hounds.

Ask Janet what her ambition in life is and she will say: 'All I want to do is ride horses well!' It is not much to ask and as far as most people are concerned, she does that already.

In September of 1974 she was by-passed by the selectors who chose the British team for the Rayleigh World three-day event championship held at Burghley in Lincolnshire.

Janet, however, still competed and rode with such inspiration that it soon became obvious that she was very much a force to be reckoned with. In the dressage phase she and Larkspur finished with a total of 54.67 penalty points.

Training for Police Work

by Denis Colton

Of all the partnerships in this world, perhaps the strangest is the one that exists between a rider and his horse. Here you have a creature of some intelligence and great physical strength (the horse) completely giving itself over to the service of another creature (man) who, though far more intelligent, is physically the weaker. He will then demand that the horse should perform actions completely against its normal way of life and basic instincts.

In the wild, a horse is a lazy, rather indolent creature. Look at a group of horses in a field. If they wish to move from one part of the field to another, they will do so at a slow walk. Only if pressed will they break into a slow canter or trot and then, as soon as possible, will revert to their original pace. Yet this basically rather lazy creature will, when trained, run itself to almost complete physical exhaustion to try and beat other horses in a race like the Epsom Derby. And this at the urging of a very small human being called a jockey.

Horses in nature do not jump obstacles from choice. A herd of horses in a field containing show jumps will, when moving from one part of the field to another, invariably go around the jumps, even when those fences lie directly in their path. Occasionally a horse will jump a natural obstacle, but then only because he has no other choice! Yet this same animal will, when trained, jump a series of different obstacles of all shapes and sizes, even bravely attempting heights far beyond his own physical strength in response to the command of his show-jumping rider.

Horses are not, by nature, either very intelligent or very brave. Strange objects frighten them, and they are not clever enough to understand why they are frightened. If startled, their defence is in flight; they use their strength and speed to carry themselves

An immaculately turned-out horse and rider

away from the thing that frightened them. And their fear is catching. If one horse among a herd in a field is startled and runs away, the others will also run without pausing to see why, or what was the cause of the panic. Yet this same timid creature will, after training, stand motionless amid the noise and tumult of a near riot and will use his great strength to gently move, or restrain, large numbers of human beings at the command of his rider, the mounted policeman.

In the training of a horse for police work, two things are of primary importance. First, the horse must be strong enough to do the work required of him and second, he must have the temperament to carry out the job without panic or fuss. The whole art of training lies in the skill of knowing what

and how much you can demand or expect of your young horse, both physically and mentally. If in training a horse, you are thoughtless or stupid enough to demand obedience beyond his ability, it can only lead to the horse refusing to obey. If you were to persist in your demands it would lead to a trial of strength, a fight which you, as the weaker half of the partnership, would lose. All you would have taught the horse is that he is stronger than you and that if he does not want to do what you wish he has only to use his physical strength to beat you and get his own way.

The whole object of training the police horse is to achieve complete obedience, and you certainly cannot train a frightened horse by fear or punishment. You do not cure a fear by replacing it with another, you only make the first fear the greater.

As students must have confidence in their teacher's ability to impart knowledge in a proper manner, so must the trainer of a young horse gain that horse's confidence before attempting to teach him his lessons. The thought that must always be foremost in a trainer's mind is: 'Does the horse understand what I want him to do and is he physically strong enough to carry out my wishes?' If ever it came to a disagreement, the trainer must ask himself: 'Is the horse saying "I can't" or "I won't"?' There is a world of difference between the two, and in any case, it is nearly always the former.

The end product of this training should be a quiet, well-mannered horse. He must be strong and well-balanced to carry out the demanding work required of him; completely obedient to the command of his rider at all paces and under all circumstances; calm and responsive in all situations and in all kinds of traffic. He must also become accustomed to strange sights and sounds and, most

A schooling session indoors at Imber Court

Getting used to the feel of harness before being ridden

important, since horses are creatures of the herd and love one another's company, he must be able to work completely on his own without fretting.

The whole system of training is based on the principle of reward – if the horse is obedient and does what is asked of him, then he is rewarded. The reward might be something to eat, such as oats, bread or sugar, or a pat with the rider's hand, even a soft-spoken word. But whatever it is, it is the 'Well Done' for obedience. If the horse misbehaves, or does not do what the trainer wishes, then he is not rewarded, it is as simple as that. He is not punished physically, just not rewarded, until in the horse's simple but very logical mind, there is built up an unbroken association between the pleasure of receiving the reward in response to the obedience to his trainer's wishes.

The majority of police horses working in London are purchased in Yorkshire. In the main they are a three-quarter-bred type of horse, the sort you see in the middle or heavy-weight Show Hunter classes at horse shows. Good bone structure is essential to ensure the horses' ability to carry weight, since the average policeman 'rides' at around fourteen stone when all the saddlery and equipment of the horse is added. Good feet are also important, since all the horses' work will be done on hard metalled roads, and the concussion and continued beat of hoof meeting road surface would play havoc with any weakness. Lastly, the horses must have quiet temperaments which will enable them to accept the demands of their training for the job they have to do.

Ideally, they should should be bought between the ages of four and five, when their development and strength are sufficiently advanced for them to start training for work under the saddle. The majority are completely unbroken, apart from being handled and led round on a halter. Certainly they have never had a rider on their backs. The normal period of training lasts about nine months and is divided into three separate stages as follows:

Stage 1:
Handling and Lungeing
                    six weeks
Stage 2:
Mounted Training
                    ten weeks
Stage 3:
Advanced Mounted Training
        about five months

The length of time a horse spends in any one of these stages depends entirely on how quickly and well he learns his lessons and on his physical development.

Nothing must be hurried, nor must there be any short-cuts to success in these early stages. No demand must be made on the horse that is too much for him, and he must never attempt something beyond his ability, or he will lose confidence in his trainer. Patience and understanding are the orders of the day throughout this whole period of work. Patience is needed for the trainer to be able to spell out the lesson time and time again until he is certain the horse knows what is required of him; and complete understanding of that particular animal's mental and physical ability is a must, since all horses are different. Such an understanding ensures that the horse is able to perform the

task required of him. In other words, the clever trainer makes it easier for the horse to say 'Yes' instead of 'No'.

The young horses, or remounts as they are now called, arrive at Imber Court, the Mounted Police Training School, near London, after a long journey in a horse-box from Yorkshire. They are settled down in roomy, well-bedded loose-boxes in the 'Remount Stable' and given a feed and water. They are usually left for a day to get used to their new home and each officer who is entrusted with a particular horse's training will spend this time quietly getting to know the animal by petting him and talking to him. The horse also gets to know the man. This is the person who brings him his food, who carries oats in the pocket of his jacket which are good to eat, who has a soft cherishing voice and hand. A person to have confidence in, someone from whom good things can be expected.

By the second day, the horse is accepting the feel of a brush on the matted hair of his coat over most of the non-sensitive parts of his body, as part of the stroking of the trainer's hand.

Once confidence in handling is established, the trainer leads the horse round the whole of the

training school on a strong halter called a cavesson. They visit every part of the place where the horse is likely to go in his time in the school, and everywhere they visit he is given a small handful of oats from his trainer's hand. They stand by the forge, where he will eventually be shod, and with his head in the doorway, he waits with his trainer, absorbing the sight and smell of this strange place. Usually, another horse is in the forge being shod, and the sight of his fellow creature standing there quietly serves to give the younger animal confidence. All the time, his trainer is talking, patting him and giving him little tit-bits until the remount accepts the 'feel' of the place. So it goes on until the horse follows the trainer everywhere with confidence.

Work on the lunge consists of making the horse obedient to the command of the trainer's voice, and building up the horse's balance and muscle. The lunge school, called a manège, is an area some twenty-five yards square, with a good sand flooring, completely enclosed so that there are no distractions from outside.

Wearing only a cavesson, with protective bandages on his lower legs, the horse moves round in a wide circle around the trainer, controlled only by a lunge line, of soft webbing attached to the cavesson, and a long whip. The trainer stands in the centre and, at first, an assistant leads the horse around the outside track. When the trainer says 'Walk-March', the assistant moves forward with the horse following. As soon as the horse moves in obedience he is patted and rewarded.

This goes on time and time again until the horse learns the meaning of the words 'Walk' and 'Halt' or 'Whoa', and once this occurs the assistant is dispensed with. So it goes on until the horse learns the meaning of the words 'Walk', 'Trot', 'Canter' as well as 'Halt' and 'Whoa'. Gradually the intensity of the work increases as the horse becomes fitter and more equipment is added. A surcingle or body roller is put on his back

A Police horse must get used to banners and noise . . .

. . . and being jostled by a crowd

where he will eventually carry a saddle, he learns to wear a bridle and he progresses to taking small fences while being lunged, starting from poles laid on the ground.

Eventually he accepts the weight of the saddle proper, and he is ready and obedient enough to carry the weight of a rider. He will, of course, by now have become used to working anywhere in the training school, in the open manèges or in the riding school in company with other horses, and it is in here he will first feel the weight of a rider on his back.

Of all times in his training, this is the crucial one, when there must be no snags or unpleasant incidents. Usually it is best done towards the end of the week when the horse has been well worked. He is taken into the riding school and goes through all his routine on the lunge wearing a saddle and bridle. All doors to the school are shut and the trainer has at least one, possibly two, experienced helpers. At the end of the work period the young horse is led forward by one of the helpers who has a bowl of oats in one hand. While this person holds the remount still and lets him feed on the corn, the second helper quietly and very steadily 'legs-ups' the trainer until he is lying across the

saddle.

As soon as the horse accepts this weight, a great fuss is made of him, and the trainer quietly and gently lowers himself back to the ground. This is repeated time and time again until the horse stands quite steady. Then, with the trainer still lying across the saddle, the horse is led forward in a straight line for a few strides. Again, he is made a fuss of and told what a great chap he is, then the trainer is lifted up again, and with much care, carries one leg over the back of the horse and slowly lowers his weight until he is actually sitting in the saddle, without putting his feet in the stirrups. All this time the assistants are making sure that there are no distractions and keeping the horse's attention occupied with the contents of the feed bowl.

With the trainer sitting in the riding position the horse is again led forward at a walk for a few strides and then, if all is well, the trainer lowers himself from the horse's back with the same care as he used in mounting. The most important lesson in the horse's training is over. This lesson is gone through daily until both assistants are dispensed with and the remount accepts the movement of his trainer mounting in the normal

manner, and moves forward in response to the same spoken word of command that he learned while on the lunge.

Nothing in this stage of training must be rushed or done haphazardly, nothing must be left to chance. If the horse becomes unsteady or resentful of the rider's weight, then the rider must slip off and wait a few minutes for the horse to become settled before trying again. If the horse does not move forward willingly in response to the word of command or the assistant's leading, he should be induced to walk forward towards the bowl of corn held away from his nose. Nothing must be forced on him or done while he is upset or fretful, because this is the foundation of confidence on which all future training and development must be built.

Now that the horse accepts the weight of the rider and will move forward with that weight on his back, his training goes on apace, but always that pace is set by his physical and mental development. At first all turns and changes of direction, increases and decreases of pace are very gradual, but as the horse becomes fitter and more advanced in his education, so do the demands made upon him.

He works with other remounts in the school as a 'ride' at least once a week and during these sessions music is played through a loud-speaker system, very softly at first and then, as the remounts become accustomed to it, gradually louder and louder. 'Nuisances' are also introduced, such as sudden movements, people with flags and rattles, anything the horse is likely to meet in his varied duties as a police horse. At first the flags are merely held, with no movement at all, the helper holding them folded in one hand with a bowl of oats in the other. The remount is induced to move forward to the oats and, while he is enjoying them, the flag is slowly opened and held still. Very, very slowly so as not to startle or upset the remount, the assistant moves the flag and, if the horse accepts the movement, the lesson is over.

The movement and nearness of the flag is gradually increased until, after some time, the horse can be induced to push his head through or under the flag to get the corn. If anything happens to frighten or upset the horse then the trainer is prepared to go right back to the beginning and start all over again.

So the training goes on, adding to the noise, the number of people and variety of strange objects until, some weeks later, there is almost a full-scale demonstration going on in the riding school! But at all times the amount of the activity is governed by what the horses themselves will accept.

It is during this latter part of his training that the remount starts his preparation for road work proper. At first, after his lessons in the riding school, he is ridden up to the front gate of the building and stands there for a while just watching the traffic go by.

Then one day, usually at the end of the week when he has been well worked, he is ridden out in the streets, always in the company of an older, well-trained horse, and at first, always round the quieter streets in the neighbourhood. The youngster gains confidence from the behaviour of the older animal and gradually, day by day, a little bit more each time, the two horses and riders can venture farther afield and into more heavily used roads until the remount accepts the rush and movement of London's traffic.

The two trainers are very careful not to try the horse too much. If they know there are road works in one street, they avoid that place on the way out and only go down the street on the way home, using the horse's natural homing instinct to draw him past something that might have frightened him under normal circumstances. If a large lorry or dustcart is being loaded, they wait until all movement has stopped and then, with the older horse between him and the lorry, allow the younger animal to find his way past.

Once they are sure the remount has confidence in his surroundings, the experienced horse is ridden a little way behind. He stays rather close at first, so that he can be on hand to help if the pupil gets into trouble, then farther and farther behind until the remount is going on his own in traffic, quiet and unafraid.

During the last few weeks of his training the horse is introduced to the officer who will ride him on duty in London. Usually the policeman is very experienced and has been serving for some time. He comes down to the training establishment for about two or three weeks and takes over complete responsibility for his new mount. He cleans its stable, grooms and feeds it, in fact does everything to make it comfortable and gain its confidence.

He rides it in the riding school at first until he is sure that he knows how the remount reacts to the new rider. Once he is sure the horse has confidence in him, then the road work begins again. As before, with an older and well-trained horse as a 'schoolmaster' escorting them round the streets, they repeat the sequence of training, with nothing forced and nothing rushed, letting the young horse find its own way through confidence, patience and understanding.

When everyone is satisfied that the new partnership of man and horse is going to work, then the remount and its rider leave the training school, and go to duty on divisions. Here the programme of acclimatisation is repeated. The remount will always be ridden out in company and he will be sent on the quieter patrols to start off with. His rider will always have the Sunday off duty so that he is able to keep the remount well worked through the week and not run the risk of the animal becoming 'fresh' through lack of work when he has a day off during the week.

Everything possible is done to make the remount's passage an easy one. His first duty at a football match is usually at one where only a small crowd is expected, and he is able to stand aside and get used to seeing what is for him large numbers of people. Again,

he is ridden up to watch the Changing of the Guard, not as one of the police horses on duty, required to control the crowds, but more as a spectator. He is allowed to wait some way away and listen to the bands, the commands and all the noise and bustle that goes with the colourful ceremony. When it is all over and the old Guard are marching back to barracks, if he has been calm and well-behaved he will be ridden at the rear of the Guard, alongside the older police horse whose rider is acting as rear escort and controlling the flow of traffic. He will probably do this quite a number of times, gradually working his way towards the larger crowds and greater noise until his rider is sure the horse is accepting everything.

Time does not matter, the pace is the horse's own and it is foolish to think it can be rushed.

In some cases two years would not be considered too long a period in which to change a rather gangling, nervous remount into a strong, well-balanced, trained police horse. It would be true to say, especially in the first few years of its duty, that the police horse never stops learning, but if its early teaching has been done correctly, if obedience has been achieved by patience and complete understanding of the horse's mental and physical capabilities, then confidence and complete acceptance of the rider's wishes come naturally in any circumstances.

Remember, the horse that carries Her Majesty the Queen at the Trooping the Colour ceremony, the horse that stands like a rock during the inferno of demonstration, and the horse you see controlling crowds going into football matches, have all been trained by the same methods, and you must agree, it seems to work very well indeed.

Top left: **On patrol in one of London's open spaces**
Above: **When the Guards are on parade**
Left: **Keeping a quiet eye on the crowds outside Buckingham Palace**

Working Horses

by Vivien Batchelor

When the motor car first appeared it replaced the working horse as the main means of transport. For centuries the horse had been the only way of getting around the country. Apart from pulling the coaches of the aristocracy, he had also drawn the carts of the farmers and peasants in the country, and the buses and hansom cabs in the towns. The blood horse had supplied the needs of the people who would today own sports cars, while the solid cob carried the parsons, doctors and professional men, who now have to rely on the less exciting family saloon.

The invention of the car changed all that. Now everyone could move around at the press of a starter button – the journey from Bath to London, for example, took only hours instead of days. Stables and mews which once were fragrant with the smell of horses, hay and carriage oil today reek of fumes from the cars of people who live in the mews, and a horse-drawn vehicle seen in a city turns more heads than the first horseless carriages did at the turn of the century.

The army, which at one time used more horses than any other organisation, almost gave them up altogether, and even the farmers began to use machinery instead of the well-loved and picturesque 'working horses'.

All this makes it all the more surprising that there are more horses at work today than there were in about 1914.

It could, of course, be said that all the many thousands of horses in the British Isles and other countries are working in a way. After all, horses kept for pleasure and for show jumping are work horses in a sense of the word. Show jumpers are still called upon to travel the country, and sometimes the world, jumping several strenuous rounds each day (although the British Show Jumping Association has recently introduced a rule forbidding a competitor to ride the same horse in more than two competitions at a show on the same day). From the horses' point of view this must seem like 'work'.

But the types we usually think of as 'working horses' are police horses, who are so much in the public eye, the heavy horses which pull brewers' drays in some British cities, and those which still play a big part in farming or forestry work.

Every major police force has its mounted section which undertakes such duties as helping in crowd control, as well as quite a lot of ordinary patrol work.

The Metropolitan Police Force in London has about 200 horses, and all of them have completed a long and thorough training to make sure that they never panic at any sudden bangs, rattles and explosions, and are never upset, even when hundreds of people are waving flags all around them. (This training is described in detail in another chapter.)

For the last few years the Metropolitan police have been justly proud of their record, and they are particularly pleased that one of their horses, Sandown, won the Supreme Horse Championship at the South of England Show two years running against competition from 2000 horses of all types, including Arabs, hunters, hacks, cobs, working hunters, hackneys and many others. Sandown, like every other police horse, is used for routine duties; the police force do not keep 'show' horses.

When the Queen rides at the head of her troops each year for the Trooping the Colour, one of the most colourful ceremonies in London, which marks the Sovereign's official birthday, she usually rides a police horse. For although she has a magnificent

Top: Her Majesty the Queen at the Horse Guards Parade in London
Above: Police horses are famous for their obedience

Right: The Household Cavalry ride on parade
Below: Horses are still used for ploughing in parts of Britain

Above: Dray horses at work in the old Billingsgate market in London
Below: The last horse drawn tram being used in London in 1905

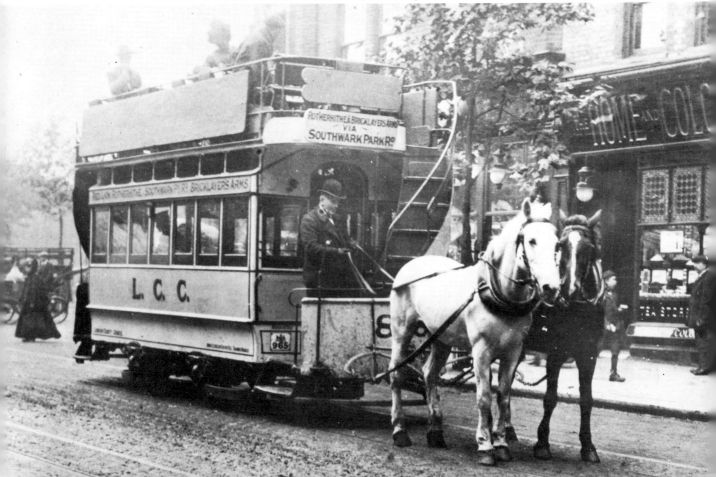

Above: A farm horse on his way home from work
Below: Two fine and well matched fellows deliver the beer

selection of horses of her own, none are trained to cope with the flag waving, cheering crowds which come to watch. Several different horses have been trained for special duty, and two of them, Imperial and Winston, are well known and loved by the crowds.

A less well-known kind of mounted 'police' work is carried out by the Rangers, who patrol many of the open heaths and parks surrounding central London. They keep a watch for fire and other dangers, and help to deal with bad behaviour from the public, lost children, straying animals and other day-to-day problems.

There is one place where horses are still used for public transport in the British Isles. This is the Isle of Man. In Douglas, the corporation owns seventy horses which are used to draw the Island's trams, and the Isle of Man is believed to be the only place in the world where horse-drawn trams are still used.

London's streets are still brightened up from time to time by other types of working horses pulling various vehicles. For instance there are still some costers left in London, though no one is sure how many. Probably there are about fifty. Certainly there are between thirty-five and forty entries each year in the costers' light and heavy trade turn-out classes at the Greater London Horse Show on Clapham Common.

In recent years this Show has included a Shetland pony called Peanuts and a beautiful and powerful Welsh cob called Regency Cream Boy. They take their place in London's streets alongside the famous pair of horses, Pell and Mell, who regularly pull a hundred-year-old coach in the West End, delivering cigarettes to palaces, embassies, consulates and clubs.

But the bravest sights in the streets of London for many people are the magnificent Shires who pull the brewer's drays. The famous Whitbread greys – chestnuts are used occasionally – make daily deliveries of beer, and each year pull the Lord Mayor's Coach on

The Lord Mayor's Coach outside the Law Courts in London

its journey from Guildhall to Temple Bar on Lord Mayor's Day. The horses stand 18 hands high and, with their ceremonial trappings and bewigged drivers and coachmen, always provide the high spot of the Show.

Young and Company are another famous London brewery known for their horses. They specialise in huge black Shires with great white feathered feet.

Their biggest is a young horse, called Henry Cooper, who is already more than 18 hands high and weighs nearly one and a half tons.

Young's is the only brewery company which shows a harness team of eight horses. The team, however, is most often shown with four horses, or as two pairs and, together with the Whitbread horses, they regularly perform in

the now famous Musical Drive of the Heavy Horses at the Royal International Horse Show at Wembley. Young's brewery horses each do three journeys a day delivering something like 10,000 tons of beer a year!

Watney Mann, another London brewery, also regularly uses Shire horses which take part in various shows, including the Musical Drive.

But it is not only in London that horses are still regularly used for delivering beer. Every day, in the streets of Blackburn in Lancashire, a team of black, 17.1-hand Shire geldings, Major and Star, deliver for Daniel Thwaites and Company. And a team of Suffolks belonging to Truman Ltd is a regular sight in Colchester, Essex. The Suffolk, which is always chestnut in colour, is often known as the Suffolk Punch. Unlike the Shire he has no 'feathers' on his legs, which are short and powerful, supporting a very deep body. One old dictionary rather unkindly describes him as 'a short fat fellow'.

The Percheron has recently been gaining popularity among heavy horse enthusiasts in Britain. Already this strong, solid animal, grey in colour but otherwise rather like the Suffolk, is the most popular breed for heavy work in France.

The breed was first brought into Britain during the First World War, but new blood was introduced in the early 1970s by a Surrey vet, Mr C. Boyde, who imported two magnificent mares, Tulippe and Cavile, from France.

Although most farms in Britain use tractors, combine harvesters and other machinery, there are still a few where horses are used, sometimes for old times' sake, but often for sound and practical reasons. For instance, often there is steep ground to plough or seed, which would be dangerous for a tractor, and, of course, fuel is very expensive, while farm machinery needs repairing quite often. Horses are, in many cases, cheaper and more reliable, and more and more farmers are turning back to them.

It is also a sign of the times that the art of horse ploughing is becoming popular again, even with farmers who would not want to plough their own fields with horses. Much of this enthusiasm is due to the efforts of heavy horse societies like the Shire Horse Society, the Clydesdale Society, the Suffolk Horse Society, the Percheron Society and the Society of Ploughmen. Every year there are competitions for national and international Ploughing

Championships, which helps to keep up people's interest.

We must certainly call a circus horse a 'working horse', though they are not to be seen in the course of our ordinary lives. In many countries there are still touring circuses with great equestrian acts, and many still have 'liberty' horses, those beautiful, highly trained and valuable animals which give such colourful, brilliant displays to an eager public.

Top: **The famous Watney Mann team of Suffolk Punches**
Above: **Horses are used for logging in parts of Britain**

At last men are beginning to realise that a horse is not only a friend and ally in peace and war, uncomplaining and obedient, and willing to work until he drops, but that he must be given something in return – dignity.

The Indoor Show
by Dorian Williams

It is often forgotten that the first really big horse show, perhaps even the most important in the world, was an indoor show. This was the International Horse Show that opened at Olympia in London in 1907. After a lapse during the First World War it was revived at Olympia in 1921 and continued until the outbreak of the Second World War in 1939.

During all this time it was not only a splendid show, it was one of the great highlights of London, on a standing with Wimbledon, Ascot, the Eton and Harrow cricket match at Lords and polo at Hurlingham.

The show was staged in a very lavish style with magnificent chandeliers suspended from the ceiling, gilt chairs, private boxes, and all sorts of other embellishments. And it lost a lot of money.

After the Second World War it was obviously quite impossible to put on such a show under the conditions existing, and so the International was re-founded and held at the White City, in London.

In view of the fact that it was in 1939 that the Olympia show had finally closed down it seems extraordinary that the Horse of the Year Show, when it was opened in Harringay in 1949, only ten years later, was considered such a novelty.

An indoor show! People spoke as though nothing similar had ever happened before.

The Horse of the Year Show at Harringay was, of course, totally different from the old International Horse Show at Olympia. The latter was all elegance, style, society. The former was a spectacle for the people.

Shortly after the War an indoor show had been put on in Paris, called *Le Jumping*. There was something of the circus about this show. Certainly it attracted all Paris, who went wild over the

A drawing by Max Cowper on one of the earliest International Horse Shows held at Olympia in London

dashing Chevalier d'Orgeix, the exquisite little Michèle Cancre, and the brilliantly talented d'Oriola.

News of this show reached England after Colonel Harry Llewellyn had taken his famous horse, Foxhunter, to Paris to compete at the show. The result was that a little party of show-jumping enthusiasts flew to Paris to see the show for themselves. The three were Colonel, now Sir Michael Ansell, my late father, Colonel V. D. S. Williams, and Captain Tony Collings, the outstanding horseman who founded Porlock Vale Riding School and who, in 1950, was to win the Badminton Three Day Event.

The almost fanatical involvement of the crowd impressed them deeply. They were convinced that a similar show, with an audience participation never known before in England, could succeed in London.

Finally, such a show was presented at Harringay, in September 1949. It was a near disaster because no one involved had any experience of advertising and pub-

licity, and there was little over £60 in the box office till when the show opened!

However, word went round that the show provided good entertainment, and by the last performance the crowds were flocking in.

A great many valuable facts about the running of an indoor show were learnt from that first big indoor show in England. It was appreciated that presentation was all important if an audience was to be kept interested.

On the first day at Harringay there had been a slow hand clap as a team of amateurs built the courses. An organ sounded completely out of place in a big indoor arena for a horse show. A loudspeaker system resulting in an almost unheard commentary did not help!

Much was learnt from these lessons, and very quickly over the next year or two an organisation was built up under Sir Michael Ansell which has now proved itself in the running of an indoor show. Everything now works per-

Wembley, the present home of the Royal International Horse Show and Horse of the Year Show

fectly: there is constant variety, and not for a moment is the audience allowed to become bored. Their attention is gripped from the very second that the fanfare by the trumpeters of the Band announces the start of the show.

What, then, is this high-powered organisation that is required if a big indoor show is to be a success? success?

The planning for next year's show starts almost as soon as this year's show ends. At the heart of it all is the time-table. Roughly the pattern of a show such as the Horse of the Year Show is to have a main jumping event at the start of the programme, probably a speed event, or one that is unlikely to involve a jump-off so that it is possible to time accurately the length of the competition.

At the other end of the programme is the major event, which *should* start about $1\frac{1}{4}$ hours before the end of the performance. It is generally agreed nowadays that a single jumping class should never last more than 75 minutes. Even

the greatest enthusiasts tend to become bored by a longer competition.

Between the two jumping events there are displays, parades, perhaps show classes, anything that will entertain the public with its novelty or variety. Each of these items has to be timed exactly so that the whole show can be planned accurately and have a more or less definite finishing time, such as somewhere between 10.30 p.m. and 11.00 p.m.

Nowadays it is particularly important that this timing and planning is precise, as frequently the show is televised, and understandably, the producer of the television programme wants to know exactly how long a jumping event is likely to last and when it will end.

Once the televising of an event has been agreed, then it is up to the producer to decide how many cameras he wants and where to position them, so that he can get the most out of them. The commentator, too, must know where the cameras are placed, as obviously his commentary is going to be affected by the pictures the cameras produce.

In fact, the commentator works entirely to a monitor set so that he can be sure that he is talking about what the viewers can see. Nothing annoys viewers more than a commentator to be talking about something that they cannot see!

Care must also be taken in choosing the commentary position. It must be remembered that as well as commentating on the event he is also trying to put across the 'atmosphere' of the occasion to the huge, unseen viewing audience. He is communicating the excitement, interest and tension of the audience actually present.

Dorian Williams, well-known Commentator

The majority of the ten million or so who watch show jumping on television have little idea of how much more there is to the show than the single jumping event that they see on their screens.

The first class can start as early as 8 o'clock in the morning. Much of the preliminary judging takes place in an outside arena, leaving the indoor arena for a preliminary jumping event, a qualifier, perhaps, for the major event later in the day.

At mid-day a conference is held at which the whole programme is carefully gone through, and a post-mortem held on the events of the previous day.

In this way it is possible to co-ordinate all the different departments, each of which has a vital part to play. These include the stables, the horse-box and caravan park, the box office, the band, the collecting ring, the Members' enclosure, the restaurants and cater-

Four pictures showing some of the happenings at a major horse show at Wembley

The Pony Club competitions play an important part at the Royal International Horse Show each year

ing, the judges, the various teams of stewards, the doctors and veterinary surgeons, the trade stands, the royal box and VIPs, the arena party, to name only a few.

Each department has to be briefed, or make its report. A daily conference can easily last an hour. It may even be necessary to call a second conference between the afternoon and the evening performances.

Many people do not know that there is a matinée every day as well as an evening performance. Indeed, quite often the number of entries is so great that the arena is continuously in use from 8.00 a.m. until 5.30 p.m. Then, after only a short break, either because of the number of entries, or perhaps because of an unexpected number of clear rounds in an earlier qualifier, it is necessary to start the evening performance early.

This is avoided if at all possible: partly because people who come to the show like to spend a little time wandering round the trade stands in the perimeter alley; and partly because the opening of the show, with the arena party smartly marching in, and the fanfare of the trumpeters, the show's signature tune, is highly effective, and it is a shame for people to miss it.

Atmosphere is very much a part of an indoor show. The audience,

being so close to the performers, is always involved with the show. They feel that they are part of it, and are not just detached spectators.

That this *rapport* affects horses and riders cannot be denied, but not, I would have thought, badly. Rather it seems to me that both horse and rider is inspired and excited by the tension in the audience.

Often one is asked if the horses are affected by the bright lights. I do not think so, unless, of course, there is a sudden flash, as from a photographer's bulb, which might make a horse lose its concentration for a moment.

What no one knows for certain is the effect on horses of coming to a small indoor arena from the wide open spaces. For instance, horses coming from Hickstead, where no course is much less than half-a-mile, must find it hard to adjust to Wembley where a course takes less than a minute to jump, where the fences are tightly packed with never more than few strides between them, with sharp turns – and the atmosphere! The 'Cup Final' roar is considerably more effective inside than outside.

Yet I do not believe horses are affected too much. It may take a day or two for them to adjust, and for this reason the course builder always builds easier courses during

the first day or two. On the other hand, it is a bigger strain for a horse jumping big fences out of doors than the necessarily smaller fences indoors. The shorter courses are obviously less testing in some ways – the 'going' is always perfect, which is by no means the case out of doors!

It should be mentioned here that not all indoor arenas are small. Some – New York's Madison Square and a number on the Continent – are vast. Most, however, particularly in Britain, are about 70 m × 35 m.

One must never underestimate the adaptibility of the horse. This is perhaps his most endearing quality; the quality, incidentally, which all connected with horses, including those running shows, should make every effort not to abuse. An example of this adaptability of a horse – both fit and courageous admittedly – was the great Penwood Forgemill in 1972. In three weeks in July this horse, owned by Fred Hartill and ridden by Paddy MacMahon, won the European Championship at Hickstead, the King George V Gold Cup at Wembley and a major event at Dublin. Both Hickstead and Dublin are vast open-air arenas, though very different in character; Wembley, of course, is by comparison a very small indoor arena.

The indoor show today is, first and foremost, well-run, popular and spectacular. It is a night out, or an afternoon out, for the family, for ordinary people, for those who enjoy any activity connected with horses. It is no longer just an occasion to be enjoyed by the knowledgeable.

Not surprisingly, such a show demands sure and experienced presentation. At present big indoor shows are fortunate in that they are still able to depend on dedicated amateurs who for no more than their basic expenses – if that – are prepared to work long hours acting as judges, stewards and overseers, supporting a small permanent staff.

Obviously such shows are dependent upon organisers who have exceptional drive and enthusiasm. It may well be that such a situation can last for many more years. But it could equally well be that within the next decade most of these shows will have properly paid professional directors.

It is interesting that in the last few years there has grown up a show that can hold its own with the best of the indoor shows. Indeed, in a remarkably short time the Dunhill Christmas show has established itself as a leading indoor show with an international reputation. The interest lies in the fact that this show is held at Olympia! The indoor show has come full circle, back to its first home.

A study of concentration by both horse and rider

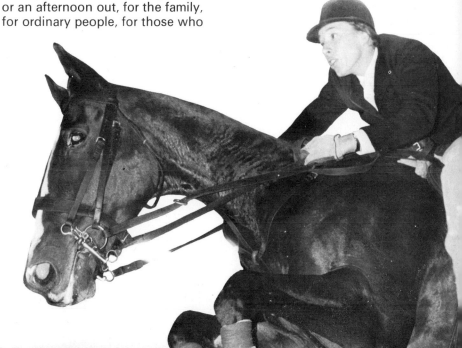

Visitors to Britain

by Brian Giles

Nelson Pessoa

Nelson was born in Rio de Janeiro on 16th December, 1935, and started riding when he was eight years old.

He was one of the first riders to become openly professional, when he was offered the sponsorship of the famous French drink company Pernod. He signed his contract in April, 1974, and rode exclusively under their name.

Already well known in this country, he decided to settle permanently in Europe in 1961. He arrived with only twenty-five dollars in his pocket, settled in Geneva, and rode horses which included Rival, Careta and Carnaval for Madame Givaudan.

Nelson has established himself as something of a Jumping Derby expert, winning the famous Hamburg Derby four times, and the Hickstead Jumping Derby twice, although not becoming one of the illustrious few to achieve a clear round. At this time he was riding the fabulous little Gran Geste, who found it so easy to flash round the very biggest of courses, and in fact won for Nelson the European Championship in Lucerne in 1966.

In 1968 he decided to move to Chantilly, just outside Paris, where he has now made his base. He has some horses in training, which he supervises himself, with the help of his head lad. It is here that his three horses, Pernod (formerly Ali Baba) aged eight, Monsieur Pernod, aged nine, and the eight-year-old Borde Loire, an attractive grey, are in training.

To date Nelson has won well over a hundred Grand Prix events. However, although he entered for the World Championships in 1974, owing to a mix up his horses did not arrive at Hickstead until 3 a.m. on the morning of the competition. Thus they were very tired, and Nelson did not manage to make the final four. This is very characteristic of this man – he always puts the welfare of his horses first and will never attempt to ask of a horse anything that he feels will upset it.

Nelson is greatly admired for his sportsmanship in Britain, and it is hoped that Pernod and Nelson will be competing with great results for a long time to come.

Henrick Snoek

One of the young 'heart-throbs' of West Germany is Henrick Snoek.

A graduate in Economics from Munster University, he manages successfully to combine show jumping with the management of his father's supermarket chain in Munster.

He started show jumping seriously at the age of twelve, and came very near to selection for the Munich Olympic Games. He learned a lot from his mother, but as he says: 'I have had no special trainer, but I try to learn from others. One rider I have great admiration for is the American, Bill Steinkraus.'

This philosophy seems to have paid off, because it was in 1972 that, riding Shirokko, he gave West Germany its first ever win at the Hickstead Jumping Derby, beating Paddy McMahon and Pennwood Forge Mill by just $\frac{1}{4}$ time fault. In 1974 he tried to follow his success, and came close to winning the Derby itself.

He is not at all daunted by the reputations of others – he has regularly beaten most of the stars in Europe, and has established himself as a regular member of the West German Team.

Henrick breeds most of his horses himself, and enjoys working with them from the beginning. 'My parents have become very involved,' he explained, 'and we have from ten to fifteen mares and one stallion.'

His sister Marion is also making a name for herself – she was the Junior European Champion in 1971, but like Henrick she is having to divide her time between study and her love of show jumping.

Henrick is a very easy-going boy, with a fluent command of English, and an infectious enthusiasm when he talks of his chosen sport. He has worked very hard to improve his natural ability, and West Germany must be extremely proud of their popular ambassador in this country.

Janou Tissot

Janou has been acclaimed the best woman show jumper of all time, and she proved that theory by winning two World Championships on her horse Rocket.

She was born in Saigon, left at the age of two to go to France, and started riding when she was ten. Her parents bought her a seven-year-old thoroughbred horse, and she began showing at the age of eleven.

She took her first title in Copenhagen, Denmark, in 1970, when she beat Britain's Marion Mould. Marion was then Champion,

having been successful at Hickstead on Stroller in 1965.

Four years' later at La Baule, in France, Janou became the first lady in history to win the World Championship twice, when she again scored on Rocket. This was a tremendous effort for both Janou and her highly talented horse, because only a year before Rocket had been plagued with injury. Before her second world title win, Janou had taken Rocket to Lucerne in Switzerland where they competed with success, but it was there that she revealed how unwell

her horse had been.

However, she hoped everything would be fine in La Baule. 'We have only just got Rocket back to his best again,' she said, 'and it would be wonderful to win the title again.'

Her wish was to come true. Shortly after she made the long journey to America and took several major events there.

Janou lives in Paris and keeps her horses at Chantilly. When she is not competing, she likes listening to classical music, especially Beethoven.

Rodney Jenkins

Rodney started riding at the age of ten, and eight years later turned professional, eventually becoming one of the best show-jumping riders in the world.

His father was a huntsman in Orange, Virginia, and was always on hand to give him valuable advice. 'My Dad always told me to ride how I feel and that is just what I do,' says Rodney.

British show-jumping fans first caught a glimpse of Rodney Jenkins when he arrived in this country for the first time to take part in the Men's World Championship at Hickstead in 1974.

He didn't win, but made up for the defeat by taking the John Player Trophy on Number One Spy at Wembley and a major class at Cardiff on Idle Dice.

In September of 1974 he returned to America to take part in a 100,000-dollar Grand Prix held at San Diego in California.

He won it on Idle Dice, beating ex-world champion David Broome in the process. David rode Sportsman.

Rodney is 5 ft 10 ins, weighs 10 st 5 lbs, and has bright red hair. Apart from show jumping, he has ridden in races, and has won ten events.

He is known to his thousands of fans as 'the Virginian'. It is easy to see why so many people rave about him; he is a marvellous rider, with his own unique style in the saddle, and his impressive record includes two 30,000-dollar American Gold Cups. Rodney has the special ability to ride any horse well, and is a first-class judge of pace.

Britain's Fred Hartill, who has seen Rodney in action, said 'the man is brilliant'. And that just about sums him up.

At one show in America, he rode more than twenty horses, and came away from the meeting having won thirteen awards.

When he travelled to Britain last year the first show he rode at was the Kent County held at Detling.

'That was great fun', he said, 'and a wonderful experience. In fact, after the show, hounds were let loose in the arena and everyone was blowing hunting horns. We all had a fine time.'

Hartwig Steenken

Hartwig Steenken's big chance to represent his country did not come until 1971 in the European Championship at Aachen in West Germany. Riding his superb horse Simona, he took on the cream of European riders, despite appalling weather, and took the title convincingly.

A very modest man, he gives all credit for this success to his horses. Hartwig is a farmer, living near Hannover in West Germany. He has been a regular member of the West German team since 1965, but because there is such a wealth of talent in West Germany, although he was selected to represent his country in the Mexico Olympics, he was in fact a reserve rider.

1974 was his greatest year, when he took the World Title from David Broome. In a thrilling championship at Hickstead in July, he again rode the great mare Simona, now seventeen years old, giving very little away in the competitions leading up to the final day. Then, as the enormous crowd held its breath, he forced a jump-off with Ireland's popular Eddie Macken. An incredible performance from a man whose leg was severely broken in a bad fall in 1973, putting him out of action for most of the season.

Hartwig has a very good string of horses to choose from, including his hope for the 1976 Olympics, Kosmos, who won the 1974 Hamburg Jumping Derby – giving Hartwig first and second placings, as Simona finished in runner-up position.

Young Erle, a pretty grey, Dodo and Winnitou have all been making names for themselves on the Continent, Dodo and Winnitou both finishing in the money in recent shows in November and December. Many of Hartwig's horses are home-bred from his first great mare, Fairness, and these are looked after on his second farm some twenty kilometres from his home. He seems to have a particularly good relationship with mares, as another of his great puissance horses, Porta Westfalica, did so well for him at the start of his career.

With the European and World Titles safely behind him, Hartwig's next objective is a gold medal at the next Olympics, and this looks quite possible.

Graziano Mancinelli

Graziano was a member of the Italian Junior Show Jumping Team for four years, and graduated to the Senior Team in 1957.

He has a superb record in show jumping, winning the European Championship in Rome in 1963 riding Rockette, the sister of Pierro D'Inzeo's horse, The Rock. He was a member of the Italian Bronze Medal team in the 1964 Olympic Games in Tokyo, and finished second behind David Broome in the World Championship in La Baule in 1970, riding the very difficult horse, Fidux.

Married to Italian show jumper Nelli Pesotti, Graziano's life revolves around horses. His greatest success came in 1972, when in a three-horse jump-off, he took the Gold Medal in the Munich Olympic Games. Riding the Irish-bred horse Ambassador, he took on Great Britain's Ann Moore on Psalm, and the American Neil Shapiro on Sloopy. Neil went first, setting a very fast time of 46.0 seconds, but paying the penalty with eight faults. Graziano then walked the strong grey into the arena, giving no indication of the speed that he was about to produce. He made an incredible round, pulling out all the stops to give Graziano not only a clear round but a time of 45.0 seconds. Ann Moore, with her customary grit, took up the challenge, but came too sharply into the second fence. Psalm had no chance, and so she finished in the Silver Medal position.

When asked about his ambitions and hopes for the future, he is very reticent. 'I just keep looking for good horses, and I hope to represent my country for many more years.' Would he like to compete in the 1976 Olympic Games? 'I don't know, we must just wait and see.'

For a few years, Graziano worked with an Italian dealer, and so has gained valuable experience in choosing horses. He is a frequent visitor to Ireland, looking for possible additions to his stable. He probably will be in Montreal, and will present many problems for the world's greatest riders.

Raimondo D'Inzeo

Strangely, riding took second place in the early life of Raimondo. Unlike his famous elder brother Piero, he went to university before eventually devoting his life to horsemanship, when he joined the famous Carabinieri.

Fortunately for the British public, he is a regular visitor to British shores. His most recent appearance was when he represented Italy in her attempt to wrest the world Championship title from Great Britain's David Broome in July 1974.

Raimondo is no stranger to the World Title, having won it twice outright, first in 1956 at Aachen in West Germany on his famous horse Merano, and then in 1960 in Venice on Gowran Girl, when he successfully retained it.

The D'Inzeo brothers became household names very soon after their arrival on the show-jumping scene, and only too often hard-pressed reporters would find themselves completely confused by these two poker-faced men, who so quickly broke into smiles and broken English.

The pair took second and third placings in the 1956 Olympic Games at Stockholm, Raimondo taking the Silver Medal on Merano, and Piero the Bronze on Uraguay.

Then in 1960 in their home country, Raimondo on Posillipe won the Gold Medal in the Olympic Games held in Rome, beating Piero on The Rock who took the Silver. The brothers then finished third in the team event to complete an Olympic Games record.

Belleview is one of Raimondo's best horses. He was thought by many to be a great hope for the last Olympic Games.

One of Raimondo's great successes in 1974 came in Dublin, where so many of the Italian riders are now buying their horses. Riding Belleview, Raimondo took on Ireland's Larry Kiely on Inis Cara in the puissance event, bringing back nostalgic memories to many of the crowd. It was in the third jump-off with the wall standing at 7 ft 1 in (1 in below the Dublin record which Belleview had set three years previously) that the two competitors met. It was characteristic of the two men that they sportingly decided to divide the prize. During the week Belleview and Raimondo went well, keeping the Italian flag flying, despite being the only representatives. They won the Players Wills International Stakes, took second place in the Thibenzole Stakes, and then he won the Guinness Gold Tankard as Leading Rider.

Raimondo sets an example to all young riders – he is always the first to congratulate and the first to commiserate, offering advice and encouragement to others.

Alwin Schockemoehle

Alwin, one of the most popular members of the West German team, started his competitive riding career after training at the West German Centre at Warendorf, where he was a pupil of Hans Gunter Winkler. At the age of nineteen he was in the reserve team for both the three-day-event team and the show-jumping team at the 1956 Stockholm Olympic Games.

From then on his success was assured. In 1960 he was in the Gold Medal team in the Rome Olympics, and in 1968 he was in the Bronze Medal team in Mexico City, riding his great horse Donald Rex.

Sadly, a World Title has eluded him. In 1974, The Robber put Alwin out of the competition, but he has finished second in three European Championships, and earned third placing in one.

Very popular with riders the world over, and plagued with serious back trouble, which put him out of the 1971 season, Alwin is very philosophical about the ups and downs of the game. 'You need a great deal of luck,' he says, 'also a good horse.' Alwin has been fortunate in the fact that he has had some very good horses during his career, Ferdl, The Robber, Rex the Robber, Weiler, and now he has just added another horse to his string – Warwick – not to be confused with Warwick III, Tony Newbury's exuberant little horse. Alwin's Warwick has had a very chequered career. He came to his stable just three weeks before the Horse of the Year Show at Wembley in 1974, but the pair settled immediately, putting Alwin in the money throughout the week, and during the following Courvoisier Trophy competitions. Alwin laughingly says: 'He has been around so much on the Continent that I could not find enough space to sign my name when I purchased him.' However, I feel sure that the next season is going to be a very successful one, and that Alwin can truly be called 'A man of all seasons'.

Frank Chapot

Not many competitors have ridden in five Olympic Games, but one man who has is the American rider, Frank Chapot. Munich, Tokyo, Mexico, Stockholm, Rome – Frank has visited them all. He has also won two Olympic team Silver Medals.

He was born in New Jersey in 1931 and in 1974 was chosen to represent America in the Men's World Show Jumping Championship at Hickstead, riding Main-spring. The pair performed with great credit, and eventually finished third behind Hartwig Steenken and Eddie Macken. Apart from Mainspring, Chapot has been associated with several other horses, including Good Twist, White Lighting and San Lucas.

Frank has been highly successful in his own country, as well as doing very well in Europe. In Chicago sixteen years ago he was a member of the team which won a Gold Medal in the Pan-American Games, and in the early 1960s he made the trip to Brazil and again won a team Gold at São Paulo.

Two years after that, Frank married Mary Mairs, a lady who had already made a big name for herself in show jumping.

When he is not competing as the first-class show jumper he is, he likes flying, and he has also taken part in national hunt racing.

Eddie Macken

It was at Hickstead in 1974 that the Irishman Eddie Macken almost won the Men's World Show Jumping Championship. So well did he do that he forced the German ace Hartwig Steenken to a jump-off, and in the end just had to be content with second place.

But it was a battle royal, and Eddie's horse Pele performed with credit against the much more experienced German horse, Simona. Eddie's superb effort in the World Title, however, was only part of the story; it is not generally known that the Irishman had only started riding show jumping five years earlier.

'I began riding at the age of nine,' he says, 'but only messing about on the ponies that we had on our farm in County Longford. It wasn't until I was nineteen that I decided to take up show jumping and went to Iris Kellett.

'I thought I would only be there a short while, but instead of returning I stayed and rode her horses.

'I have always had two ambitions in life – one is to ride in a Nations Cup for Ireland at Dublin, and the other is to compete in a puissance and jump a wall which is standing at 7 ft 2 ins.

'Luckily, I have already achieved my first aim, but am still looking forward to the other.

'The thing is you need special horses for special events, and at the moment I have not got a horse for the puissance.'

Ask the twenty-five-year-old Eddie what he thinks of his world championship mount and the answer is automatic. 'He is a wonderful horse,' he replies, 'and is full of courage.'

He has, of course, been associated with many horses including Oatfield Hills and Easter Parade.

In 1974 he returned to Britain, after the show-jumping season had ended, in order to be presented with a Martini Award.

It was an honour he justly deserved for his services to the sport he loves. Ironically, the runner-up was the man who had defeated him at Hickstead – Hartwig Steenken.

Eddie Macken has now lost his chance of winning a Gold Medal in any Olympics – unless the rules change. In 1974 he was asked to turn professional by the powers that be: the Olympics are for amateurs only.

The Artist's View

by Frederick Dawe

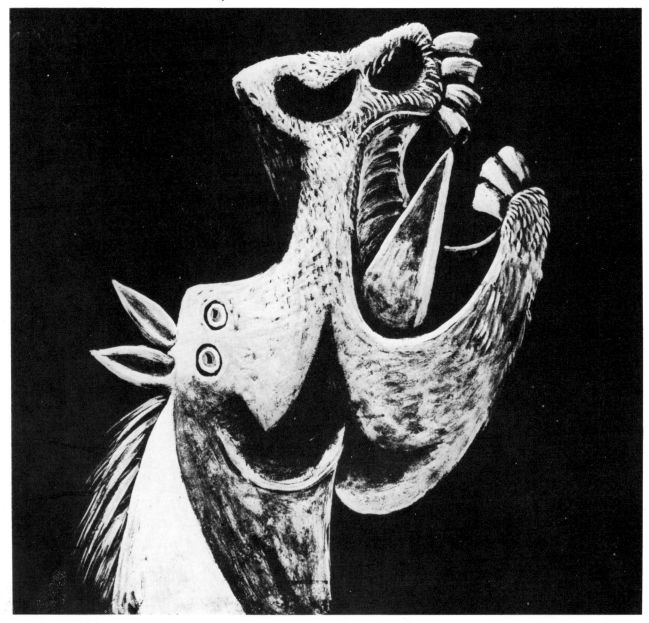

From the early cave paintings made by pre-civilisation tribes, some 20,000 years ago with simple brushes or with their fingers, until the present day, all peoples have produced representations of horses in action, in terror, in excitement, in dramatic situations and as expressions of a highly civilised and cultured way of life.

Man has always loved and painted the horse. There are literally thousands of paintings, drawings and sculptures through the centuries which show the affection and respect that man has had for this most beautiful and useful animal.

Here we can look at some ways in which the painter or the sculptor has shown his feelings for horses. What emerges is the strong feeling that artists as different as the modern Picasso, George Stubbs about 200 years ago in England, or Leonardo da Vinci about 400 years ago in Italy, felt about the anguish that this sensitive creature so easily feels. They have not expressed this feeling in the same way, which shows how differently artists can interpret feelings, and how little the actual representation of the appearance of the animal is necessary. Picasso's 'horse' looks very little like one, but it is extremely like the feelings of the Stubbs horse terri-fied by the lurking lion.

In Leonardo's drawing, the way that the mouth is pulled back to reveal the tension is very similar to that in Picasso's painting — and, incidentally, Leonardo's drawing is not exactly a straightforward representation of the animal either.

The blind obedience of excited animals controlled by man which is seen so often in Westerns is caught suddenly and effectively in Remington's painting of a group of cowboys pursued by a band of hostile Indians.

Of course the sense of wild excitement or uncomprehending terror that the paintings on these two pages express is not all that is

Left: **Frederic Remington (1861–1909)** *A dash for timber* **1899 Oil on canvas**

Below: **George Stubbs (1724–1806)** *Wild horse frightened by a lion* **1770 Oil on canvas**

Above: **Leonardo da Vinci (1452–1519)** *Study of horses' heads* **c. 1500 Ink drawing**

Left: **Pablo Picasso (1881–1973)** *Head of a horse* **1937 Oil on canvas**

Above: Benjamin Marshall (1767–1835)
Emelius c. 1823 Oil on canvas
Left: Rembrandt (1606–1669) *The Good
Samaritan* 1632/3 Oil on panel

Below: Edgar Degas (1834–1917) *Jockeys
in the rain* c. 1881 Pastel on paper

found in paintings, drawings and sculptures of the horse.

The paintings on these two pages, and the pastel by Degas, show the horse represented in a number of moods and styles. Let us now look at them separately before making any comparison. The Rembrandt, painted when he was a young man of 26, shows how he had already gained an extraordinary sympathy for the gentle nature of the horse, and in it uses it to support the idea of the pity which the good Samaritan feels for the poor unfortunate traveller. This contrasts very strongly with the formal and carefully observed painting of the particular horse *Emelius* in Benjamin Marshall's painting. This presents the social importance of the horse and expresses the fine tension of the thoroughbred animal. It also suggests the care and attention that it receives and the value that is attached to it — so very different from Rembrandt's poor workhorse.

Another and much freer treatment of the thoroughbred, in which the excited and keyed-up anticipation of the start is beautifully expressed, is Degas' pastel. The sense of movement can be related to the two paintings by David and Boccioni. David's Napoleon on his favourite horse shows him — as Napoleon himself asked to be shown — serene on a wild steed. This is the heroic treatment. Napoleon and his mount are shown as the heroes in some great event, full of splendour and eagerness. Boccioni, on the other hand, concentrates on expressing the sense of movement and internal muscular tension that is found in the horse. As a modern artist, he takes more freedom and is less concerned with the actual appearance of the horse than all the other painters, but in interlocking the strong forms in a wiry tension, and using colour to express not

Top: Jacques-Louis David (1748–1825) *Bonaparte crossing the St. Bernard Pass* 1800 Oil on canvas
Left: Umberto Boccioni (1882–1915) *Elasticity* 1912 Oil on canvas

1

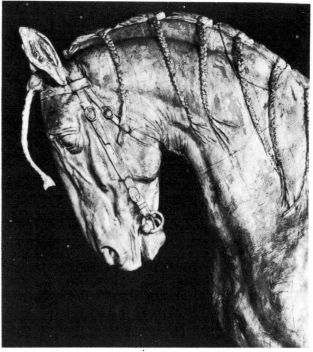

2

3

geometrically simplified forms which he believes express its power and character. The surging lines of this sculpture are strangely similar to the lines on the very accurately representational horse modelled by the Czech sculptor Myslbek (2) at the end of the 19th century. In fact, the two sculptors are separated in time by only fifteen years, and each represents the extraordinary revolution that took place in art during the first years of the 20th century. Another comparison of interest is to be made between the early Greek horse (3) carved in stone before the Parthenon was built and before the Roman Empire was formed, and the modelled figure cast in bronze by Donatello (5), the first great Italian renaissance sculptor. The styles of these two works are different but the dignity and grandeur of the horse and the pose of ·the rider are very similar. The difference lies in the great delicacy and fineness of the Greek horse which contrasts with the weight and power of the Donatello charger.

Yet one more comparison might be made between the Assyrian low-relief sculpture, in which the appearance is more of a painting than a normal sculpture (the

appearance, but emotion, he creates a sense of the movement of the horse in a fresh and exciting way.

Another modern work is shown on these two pages, which are devoted to sculptured horses. The Duchamps-Villon .(1) is a cubist work. This means that the artist has attempted to express the horse through putting together

Top left: Raymond
Duchamps-Villon (1876–1918)
The horse **1914 Bronze**
Top right: **J. V.Myslbek**
(1848–1922) *Head of a horse*
1899 Plaster
Above: A Greek warrior
c. 550 BC Bronze

4

5

6

form rises less than an inch above the surface) and the great, solid, rough-hewn form of the Watts' sculpture of Physical Energy (6) to be seen in London's Kensington Gardens. The sense of the horse's power is to be seen in the straddled forms of both horses and in the Watts the rough surface texture of the bronze seems to add to the sense of strength.

All of these sculptures, and the paintings and the drawings on the preceding pages, are only a tiny percentage of the works in art devoted to representations of the horse. Perhaps this short introduction may interest you sufficiently to get you to go to some of the art galleries, and to look at the equestrian statues that are dotted around so many cities and towns.

Top: Assyrian low relief sculpture from the Palace of Ashurbanipal, Nineveh 7th century BC
Above left: Donatello (1386–1466) *Gattamelata monument,* Padua 1443–53 Bronze
Above right: G. F. Watts (1817–1904) *Physical energy* 1904 Kensington Gardens, London Bronze

The Story of Muybridge

by Frederick Dawe

If you have ever looked at early paintings of horses running — such as the one above — you may have thought that there was something wrong about the way the artist had drawn them. They certainly do not seem to be running properly. Although horses always appear to be stretching for the next step, two legs forward and two legs back looks wrong — and it *is* wrong. Of course, it does give a feeling of the race and of swift movement, but in fact a horse is never in the position shown. It actually moves as is shown in the series of photographs illustrated below.

These were taken by Eadweard Muybridge, who was born in Kingston-on-Thames in 1830. It was Muybridge's work as a photographer, supported by an American, Dr J. D. B. Stillman and assisted by Leland Stanford, that for the first time established exactly how a horse ran.

Some of the earliest cave paintings of horses are more accurate than those done in the last two hundred years. When racing became a popular sport it was thought necessary or desirable not only to paint the portraits of horses but to depict the actual races themselves. There was also a tradition of hunting which inspired paintings of horses in action. It was at this time, some time in the 18th century, that the convention of painting running horses with their legs straddled began, and this became so firmly the view

of what happened that even such careful observers as Edouard Manet in France in the middle of the 19th century painted horses in this way.

Muybridge was an interesting and romantic figure. He was an enthusiastic photographer in the early days of photography, went to America in the 1850s where he travelled through the middle west taking a large number of historic photographs of Indians and early settlements. He went also to Alaska, was tried for the murder of his wife's lover and, eventually, in the 1870s began the series of photographs examining the way animals and humans move, which resulted in a series of books and revolutionised the study of motion both for anatomists and for artists.

His problem in producing photographs that recorded the stages of movement was to arrange a row of cameras which would take the

sequence of shots at the right instants. His solution was to set up a series of trip wires, each one of which released a camera shutter, as shown in the illustration, which is taken from the book on the subject called *The Horse in Motion*, which was published in 1882.

Using these photographs, he produced a machine which he called a 'zoogyroscope', and succeeded in projecting a number of still photographs very rapidly on a screen which gave the effect of a horse galloping. This was a direct forerunner of the motion picture. He spent the latter part of his life lecturing around America and Europe on this development, and artists such as Degas were directly influenced by him.

British Breeds

The Highland Pony

The Highland pony originates from Scotland and is the largest and strongest of the mountain and moorland breed of ponies. The larger pony is known as the Mainland, and the smaller type, bred in the Hebrides, is known as the Western Islands pony.

Highland ponies are magnificently built with short powerful limbs and short backs with well-rounded thighs. They have intelligent eyes and attractive heads set on sturdy necks.

They vary in size from 12.2 to 14.2 hands and are usually grey or dun in colour. However, there are browns and blacks, and on the Western Isles there are occasionally chestnuts with silver manes and tails. Some of the greys have a dorsal stripe running from the wither to the dock and zebra markings on their legs.

Although Highland ponies do not accept strangers quickly, they have very kind temperaments.

For many years they were used by crofters for all types of work.

They are still used for carrying deer down from the forests during the stalking season. They need to be strong, because some of the deer weigh up to twenty stone. Occasionally hunters shoot game from their backs, and the Forestry Commission in Scotland can be seen using these tough and willing ponies for hauling timber from the higher slopes down to the roadside.

On the islands the ponies are still being driven and ridden, and used for carrying peat or seaweed in panniers slung either side of their backs. The usual method of moving ponies across a stretch of water is to tow them in twos and threes behind boats, but some perform feats of swimming from one island to another.

Nowadays Highland ponies are in great demand for trekking, which is a splendid way of enjoying the beautiful Scottish scenery.

Fell Ponies

Fell and Dale ponies used to be the same breed and type, differing only by the places in which they were bred, principally the Lake District of Cumberland and Moorland, the North Riding of Yorkshire, and Durham and Northumberland. A hundred years ago, Fell ponies were mainly used as pack-ponies and carried lead from the mines and quarries to the docks on Tyneside to be loaded into sailing ships. The ponies carried up to sixteen stone of lead in panniers on either side of their backs and followed each other bridleless along the narrow paths of Westmorland to the sea.

Groups of about twenty pack-

ponies, usually in the sole charge of one mounted man, used to go on weekly trips from Kendall to Whitehaven over the passes of Hardknott and Wrynose. There are stories of these ponies travelling up to 250 miles in a week, and there are still a few pack-horse bridges and paths to show the routes they used to take.

Fell ponies were also used at the pit faces and to sledge peat down into the valleys. They are still used for shepherding and all types of light harness work, and they also make very useful all-round children's ponies. They are hardy, with strong constitutions, and are able to live out all the year round and withstand the coldest of winters.

They are real ponies standing from 13 to 14 hands in height with a pony-like head, a fairly long neck, good shoulders and muscular quarters with strong legs and clean joints. The hoofs are hard and have characteristic blue horn.

In winter the legs are covered with silky feather and the ponies have abundant manes and tails. Black, brown, bay and greys are fairly common, but duns are very rare. The brown and bay ponies usually have a mealy nose and light colour round the eyes.

Dales Ponies

The Pennine range separates the Fell ponies from the Dales breed, and because the North Riding of Yorkshire can be bleak and cold in winter, the Dales pony is a rather stronger type than the Fell from whom he is descended. The breed has lost much of its pony-like character, and by crossing with heavier breeds, mainly Clydesdale, they have become more like small horses, up to a considerable weight, stockily built and standing about 14.2 hands high.

Like the Fell pony, the Dales pony was once used for carrying lead to the coast from the mines of Northumberland and Durham. The larger ponies are sometimes used for farmwork, and are very good dual-purpose animals, being able to carry their owners riding or hunting if required. The Dales ponies are rarely allowed to run

out on the moors. They have neat heads, small ears and short necks and their bodies are very strong for their size. Usually they are black or brown in colour, but some are grey and bay. There are no chestnuts, piebalds or skewbalds.

They are ideal for farmers who want a reliable pony, which can be turned out on rough grazing and is easy to keep in winter.

Exmoor Ponies

The Exmoor is probably the oldest of the British pony breeds and it's likely that the native pony of pre-Roman times was very like the Exmoor as we know it today.

Like the Welsh, these ponies were fortunate to be living in the more isolated parts of Britain when Henry VIII ordered that all horses under 15 hands high were to be destroyed. During the First World War, however, they were not so fortunate, because during the farm depression when few people wanted to keep them, they were sold for food.

Luckily some breeders managed to keep their best mares and stallions and the breed is again

flourishing. They make ideal children's ponies, being keen jumpers, and very easy to keep, because they are very happy living out all year round. They also possess considerable strength and endurance and usually live to a great age.

Exmoor ponies have their own distinctive colouring, which is usually brown, bay or dun. Their large eyes are set in a broad forehead and their short thick ears are mealy colour inside. Their heads are rather long with 'mealy' nostrils and a deep-set jaw. They have deep, wide chests, good shoulders, and clean short legs with small hard feet. The mares usually stand about 12.2 hands high and the stallions are slightly larger.

The texture of their coats is different from any other native breed, being stringy and harsh in winter and hard and shiny in summer. The underside of their tummies is also very often mealy in colour, especially in winter.

Exmoor ponies have produced first-rate hunters and cobs, and the old Devon pack-horse was developed from them.

The Welsh Pony

The Welsh pony should not be confused with the Welsh Mountain pony or the Welsh Cob. It is a real ride and drive pony, and its breeding is a combination of the Welsh Mountain Pony and the Welsh Cob. As its breeding indicates, it is an animal of quality, having good bone and general substance and a hardy constitution.

The Welsh pony may be up to 13.2 hands in height. To get this extra size and strength some Thoroughbred Arab and Hackney blood was introduced some years ago, but to retain the hardiness of character, Welsh blood still had to predominate.

Before the height limit for polo ponies was abolished, Welsh pony mares formed the basis of some of the best polo ponies in the country.

For generations they were the main means of transport for hill farmers, who used them for shepherding, herding cattle and rounding up the wild mountain ponies. They were also used for hunting over the roughest and often the steepest ground, and many took part in pony racing at local shows and sports. They had to be quick, agile and able to gallop up and down hills without going lame.

Today there is a tremendous demand for the Welsh Pony for children. Just as the Welsh Mountain Pony is looked upon as being a child's ideal first pony, so the Welsh Pony provides the next step when the first one is outgrown.

At its best it is a miniature hunter with the strength, tough-

ness and hard bone of the native pony combined with the usual good temperament which is such an outstanding characteristic of all the Welsh breeds.

Like the Welsh Cob, the Welsh Pony may be of any colour except piebald and skewbald. The Welsh Pony and Cob Society still places great emphasis on ponies and cobs working instead of being bred for showing.

New Forest Ponies

The New Forest consists of nearly 50,000 acres of open land over which ponies and cattle are allowed to roam, and it is there that one of the most interesting of the British pony breeds may be found. Although New Forest ponies may be any colour except piebald and skewbald, the best ponies are usually bright bay, brown or black

and stand about 14.2 hands high. They have a very well-bred look, are sure-footed and have a good action. They quickly become used to traffic and are docile and make excellent family ponies. They can also sometimes be seen in harness.

The New Forest Pony Races, held on Boxing Day, are becoming very popular. The races are run over about three miles of open moorland which can provide very tricky going, and a clever, nimble-footed pony with a handy turn of speed is needed to complete the course successfully. Because of

their docile and friendly natures, the New Forest ponies are quick to make friends and like the company of people. Unfortunately, many of them are still killed on the roads every year by motorists who are driving too fast to avoid animals walking on the road.

The New Forest pony has a completely different blood-line from the other native ponies because of its very mixed background. For this reason and the fact that it is becoming one of Britain's best-known breeds, it is also one of the most interesting.

Connemara Ponies

Connemara ponies have existed for centuries in the area of Connaught to the west of Loughs Corrib and Mask. Their origins are probably similar to the ponies of the Western Island of Scotland.

The Irish have always been looked upon as being fine horsemen and clever breeders of horses and ponies, and their skill has been passed down through the centuries.

Centuries ago the ruler of a country would regard his finest horses as being the most suitable gifts to give the ruler of another country if he wanted to curry favour. For many years Ireland had a very close connection with Spain, and it is probably because of this that an interchange of horses developed and crossbreeding took place. The Spanish horse undoubtedly had quite an influence on the Connemara pony as we know it today.

The ponies, living out on the rough hillsides, had little protection from the Atlantic storms, and there was a shortage of food during the winter months so that only the cleverest and toughest survived. They also had to be very sure-footed to negotiate the rocks and boulders on the mountain slopes, and they needed all their native cunning to avoid the hazards of quagmires and bogs. The result was that the Connemara pony became famous for its sure-footedness, ruggedness, reliability, and adaptability.

The English Connemara Pony Society was founded in 1946 with the object of encouraging the breeding and use of these ponies throughout the British Isles. The height of the Connemara varies from 13 hands to 14.2 hands. They have good confirmation with plenty of bone which sometimes measures as much as eight inches below the knee.

They make excellent family ponies, being able to take part successfully in many different types of competitions.

Dartmoor Ponies

Although the Dartmoor has now developed into an entirely recognisable type and breed and is looked upon as a model show pony, they are the result of cross-breeding with a number of other breeds, including the Arab.

A true Dartmoor pony is usually black, bay, brown or grey. They have small, neat heads with small alert ears. Their backs are strong and well muscled and they have good, tough legs and evenly shaped feet. The tail is set high and is frequently full and wavy. They have the low and free action and elegant confirmation of an ideal riding pony. Although there is no minimum height, they should not exceed 12.2 hands high. Because pony trekking has become so popular, the Dartmoor is frequently used to carry riders across the tracks of the moors, enabling them to enjoy in a leisurely fashion the beautiful scenery of Dartmoor during the summer months.

The moor is rather like the fell country, with miles of unbroken and completely uncultivated grassland and scrub, interspersed with bracken. The rocks and crags offer very little shelter to the ponies during the snows, however, and despite their thick coats Dartmoors frequently suffer from the cold and lack of suitable food during really bad winters.

They are not forgotten, however, and many local farmers distribute hay and other fodder. If the weather is really bad, and the roads become impassable, this has to be done by helicopter.

It is said that even the old Irish Draught horse, which has been responsible for breeding some of the best hunters and jumpers in Europe, has Connemara pony blood in its veins.

The Shetland Pony

The Shetland pony, which some experts believe is the true descendant of the little Plains horses of Central America, is the smallest of all pony breeds.

Undoubtedly the rough climate and difficult conditions under which the ponies lived in the Shetland Islands all the year round, together with the sparseness of their diet, helped to keep them small. In late spring before the grass had grown there was nothing but seaweed for them to eat, but they became the strongest of all the equine species for their size, capable of carrying a full-grown man.

The Shetland has a small head and muzzle, neat short ears and large kindly eyes. Its compact little body with long, thick mane and tail is supported by short, sturdy legs.

They are generally used in the Shetland Isles as a saddle or pack pony, and for many generations they have been the chief method of transport on the islands. Not only can they carry their owners up to forty miles a day, but they can also carry everything else like peat, foodstuffs, or seaweed needed to fertilise the soil.

Shetlands are docile and lovable, and make exceptionally good first ponies for small children. Because they are so small, their height is usually measured in inches, instead of hands, and they vary from 39 inches to the 42 inches which is the limit permitted by the Shetland Pony Stud Book.

The Welsh Mountain Pony

The Welsh mountain pony is one of the most popular and perhaps the prettiest of the nine breeds forming the Mountain and Moorland group. They are believed to be descended from the Celtic pony, and have certainly lived in the mountains of Wales for more than a thousand years.

For centuries they endured great hardships and even, at times, persecution, with the result that they developed a hardness of constitution and an intelligence which has made them one of the finest foundations for horse and pony breeding in the world.

When Henry VIII, hoping to improve the breeds of horses, ordered the destruction of all stallions under 15 hands in height and all mares less than 13 hands, the ponies of Wales, living in their inaccessible mountain haunts, escaped the slaughter.

Today, apart from its beauty, the Welsh Mountain Pony is acknowledged to be hardy and surefooted, with the wonderful temperament needed for the ideal children's pony.

A Welsh Mountain pony should be about 12 hands high and have a small head, clean cut, well set on the neck and tapering to the muzzle, which should be soft to the touch. It should have bold eyes set well apart and small pointed ears. The neck should be of a good length with the shoulders long and sloping. The back should be strong and short, with the tail set high and carried gaily. Its action should be quick, free and straight.

Although they were exported to Australia and the United States of America many years ago, it is only fairly recently that their popularity has become world-wide. Many hundreds of Welsh Mountain ponies go abroad each year, and they are now equally at home in the heat of Texas and Africa or the snows of Canada or Sweden.

The Welsh Cob

The Welsh Cob, which must be more than 13.2 hands in height, should be strong, hardy and active with as much substance as possible. Its head should be full of quality and have pony characteristics with bold prominent eyes and neat well-set ears. The limbs should have well-developed knees and hocks with what is known as a 'lot of bone' below the knee, making them good, sturdy weight carriers.

Their action should be 'free and true', and rather 'forceful' in character. The knee should be bent and the whole of the foreleg should be extended straight from the shoulder, and as far forward as possible at the trot.

The exact origin of the Welsh Cob is unknown, but it was well established as a breed as far back as the 15th century.

Tudur Aled, a famous Welsh poet of the early sixteenth century, gave a description very similar to that laid down by the Society today when he wrote of the Cob's ability to 'carry weight, gallop, jump and swim'.

There were two major Cob-breeding areas. Cardiganshire and Pembrokeshire produced the larger Cob which, besides being a major means of transport, also did most of the work on the farm. In Breckonshire and Radnorshire, which is more mountainous country, less farmwork was needed and a smaller Cob with more pony characteristics was bred.

Between the 1920s and the later 1940s the Cob, crossed with the Thoroughbred, became the foundation of many good hunters. Today the Welsh Cob is an ideal family horse, being strong enough to carry a man, but quiet enough to carry a child.

Courage, activity, intelligence and the natural ability to jump combined with an equable temperament make them ideal hunters for rough or hilly country. They also take readily to harness and are supreme as ride and drive horses.

Some Horses and Ponies of the World
by Vivien Batchelor

Although the English Thoroughbred has probably had more influence on horses all over the world than any other breed, many other countries are just as proud of their own particular breeds which they have produced for a special purpose.

Many people think the word 'thoroughbred' means any pure-bred horse, but this is not true. It is really the running race horse of England, and it is the oldest of the breeds to be used all over the world for helping to improve other types of stock.

Most English Thoroughbreds can trace their ancestry right back to the time of King Charles II, for he was passionately interested in horse-racing, and did so much to encourage the sport that he is still known as the 'Father of the British Turf'.

United States of America

The history of the Thoroughbred goes back nearly as far in America. The leader of the British forces who invaded New Amsterdam in 1664, renaming it New York, was a Colonel Richard Nicolls, who lost no time in setting up a race-course on Long Island. That particular race-course was used for nearly a century, and during this time the racing craze spread to Maryland, Virginia and the Carolinas. The American racer was established.

Between 1730 and 1775, 113 English Thoroughbred stallions and 73 mares were sent from Britain to America to found the American Thoroughbred.

The Standard bred horse, or farmers' race horse, came from the Eastern States of America. The breed was given this name because while it was being developed, each horse had to pace a mile at the trot in a given standard of time. The Standard was produced by crossing the

Thoroughbred with other breeds and types. The horses are usually longer in the body than the Thoroughbreds and have heavier bones.

The American Quarter horse is another of the older American breeds which was started from horses brought over from Britain. It was named for its speed in running quarter-mile races – a favourite distance with the early settlers. Most Quarter horses are descended from one stallion called Janus which was sent from England in the middle of the eighteenth century. This breed is also known as the 'cuttinghorse' because today it is used mainly by cowboys for 'cutting' individual cattle from herds.

It is a thick, short, muscular animal, not usually more than 15.2 hands high, and it is descended from the Spanish breeds

which found their way into the United States. In 1940 a Breed Association was formed in America, and people once again began to take an interest in the true American Quarter Horse.

Another American breed is the useful, stylish little Morgan, standing not more than 15 hands high. This was once the most numerous and famous of all American horses, and when it seemed to be in danger of dying out, the American government took steps to make sure that it should not. Thanks to them it is now increasing in numbers. The original Morgan was a little smaller than today's version, only up to 14 hands high. He was given his name by the founder of the breed, Justin Morgan, who was not too shy to call the original sire after himself.

This sire was a remarkable animal who was believed to have

The Quarter Horse is one of America's oldest breeds

been born about 1789 and died in 1821, making him thirty-two years old. His individual strength of character can still be seen in examples of the breed today, and it is thought that his pedigree included both Thoroughbred and Arab.

The American Saddle-horse, with its short strong back and slender arched neck, is the breed mostly used today for pleasure riding, hunting and more recently, for jumping. The breed was evolved from most of the other breeds in America, and animals were selected for their easy gait and style. Saddle-horses have either three or five gaits. The walk, trot and canter are the main ones, with the rack and a slow gait, which may be a stepping pace or a running walk, added for the five-gait type. The rack is a gait in which the two feet on each side are lifted almost at the same time, so that all four feet can be off the ground at the same time. The two different types are mainly dis-

Above: Useful and stylish the Morgan was founded by Justin Morgan
Left: Carol Dawley riding Thunder's Manitcowoe in the National Appaloosa Show at Las Vegas

Johnny Johnston ©

tinguished by their manes and tails. The three-gait horse is shown with them clipped, while the five-gait horses have full manes and tails.

One of the most striking of all the American horses is the Appaloosa, or spotted horse. He is usually white with black or brown spots, but some are found with white spots on a dark colour. They are popular as circus and show horses, but they are also useful all-round animals with fine temperaments and great qualities of endurance.

They are becoming much more popular in Britain nowadays, and many have been brought in from the States by enthusiasts. They get their name from the Palouse river of Idaho, where they were once much prized by the Nez Perce Indians. In recent years some have been crossed with Arabs to improve the stock.

The Hackney is one of the most popular breeds at horse shows in America, as it is in Britain and other countries. Like so many breeds, the original horses were brought into America from Britain, and there are flourishing studs in many parts of the States today.

Poland

In Poland, horse breeding is a major industry and horses play an important part in the country's economy. Thousands are sold each year for riding, breeding and harness work. They are bred on private farms, and at Government studs. There is a system of stallion stations run by the Polish Ministry of Agriculture, and all the stallions on the stations have been bred in one of the thirty Government studs, which specialise in only one or two breeds.

All pedigree horses in Poland have to be registered in a stud book. There is one stud book for each area, and each region breeds its own particular kind of horse. The scheme was started to prevent the haphazard crossing of different types and breeds.

The two most important breeds in Poland are the Wielkpoplski, and the Malopolski. The Wielk-poplski is mainly used for riding and driving and has competed for Poland in international driving classes. The Malopolski is often called the 'original' Polish horse, and is in many ways rather like the Arab.

Arabs have been bred in Poland for more than three centuries, and Polish Arabs are highly prized all over the world, especially in America. There a Polish Arab called Bask won the American National Championship in hand, under saddle and in harness for three years running. The Polish breeders have done very well,

because after the war, in 1945, there were hardly any pure-bred Arabs left in the country.

The Polish Arab stud has, how-ever, been built up very gradually, and only the very best type of animal is used for breeding. Great attention is still paid to keeping the true desert type and tempera-ment.

Britain was the first Western country to bring in Polish Arabs after the war, but that was not until 1958. Since then they have played an important part in pro-viding fresh blood at many studs.

Polish Arabs are much sought after all over the world

France

Another part of Europe where white horses of a completely different nature have been known for centuries is the region known as the Camargue, in Southern France. The Camargue pony is tough and agile, and is used to herd the fierce black bulls that are reared in the area. This caused one writer to describe the Camargue as 'the cowboy country of Southern France'.

John Skeaping, the sculptor and artist, who has bred these ponies in their native surroundings, has

written of how he has seen them in winter walking about with icicles hanging from 'long polar bear-like coats'. Yet in the scorch-ing summers they are often covered in mosquitoes and flies. So ob-viously they have to be tough to survive.

France was also noted at the turn of the century for the beautiful carriage horses bred in Normandy. These were developed from the native Normandy breeds and crossed with English Thorough-breds or other pure-breds. Because there is no longer much of a

Left : **Carmargue ponies are tough and agile**
Below : **The Percheron is popular in France**
Above : **Hanoverian horses make excellent show jumpers**

carriage trade, most of the breeders in that part of France have concentrated on producing saddle horses, some of which have proved to be excellent jumpers.

There are still quite a lot of draught horses in France, and the best known is the Percheron, a large, strong horse, which is still much used in all parts of the world where heavy horses have not been replaced by machines. This breed is not likely to die out, as several countries, including Britain, have formed Percheron Societies.

Germany

Nowadays, horses and ponies are more popular than ever because of show jumping, and Germany has been very successful with its famous Hanoverian horses.

In the 1972 Olympic Games when Germany won the gold medal for show jumping, eight of the nations competing used Hanoverians, or horses bred from Hanoverian. Originally the Hanoverian was a much heavier fellow than he is today, and was used a great deal for drawing coaches and even guns and ploughs; but the introduction of Thoroughbred blood has produced a much lighter and smarter type of saddle horse.

Some of the first cream horses to be introduced into the Royal Mews in London and Windsor to pull the royal coaches and carriages were brought over from Germany in the time of King George I. They were a breed of Holstein who had a mixed ancestry of Neapolitan and Spanish, into which Cleveland Bay and Thoroughbred blood was later introduced. The mother of George I of England is said to have started the cream breed with the Holstein stallion Mignon.

In Bavaria and the Tirol there is a breed of small mountain pack pony called the Haflinger, which is sure-footed and able to carry heavy loads, a task for which it is still used. It is a very ancient breed indeed and is believed to be descended from the Noriker pack pony, which can be traced right back to the ancient Roman province of Noricum. This is where its name comes from. There is also a stud for breeding these ponies in Italy. They are mostly chestnut in colour with pale cream or yellow manes and tails.

Australia

Australia, on the other side of the world, is one of the most horse-minded countries of all. Racing is one of Australia's passions, and the breeding of Thoroughbreds is very important. Most of the Australian studs were originally started with horses brought from Britain, but for many generations now the Australian Thoroughbred has been a type in its own right. Many of them have been exported to the United States where they have done very well, both on the race course and at stud.

The Australians' 'native' breed is the Australian Stockhorse or Waler. This was first bred by the early settlers, and comes from the Cape horses imported from South Africa, along with some Thoroughbred and Cob blood. The Waler is a small hardy horse, about 15 hands high. He has a deep chest, neat head, and a speedy, long stride. He is capable of covering many miles without becoming tired, and is the first choice of the 'ringers', as the Australian cowboys are called, for rounding up fast wild cattle in the bush.

Australia has a wild horse known as a Brumby which roams the bush in herds, and is in fact a descendant of the saddle horses which strayed from the ranches and the cattle stations. It is easy to see how horses can stray in Australia, because it is not uncommon for a single 'horse paddock' to cover as much as 10,000 acres. It is the custom in Australia for a stallion to be turned loose with a group of mares in one of these horse paddocks, and the band is then left to fend for itself.

Spain

Apart from Britain, Spain has probably had the most influence on the horse as we know it today. Centuries ago, when the Spaniards were settling in South America and Mexico, and in the United States, they took horses with them, including the beautiful Andalusian horses whose influence can be seen in many horses in North and South even now.

A typical Australian Waler used by the New South Wales Mounted Police

The famous white Lipizzaner horses of the Spanish Riding School of Vienna are directly descended from the horses of Andalusia. This is why the school is called 'Spanish'. The horses were taken from Spain to Austria in 1562 by the Archduke Maximilian, who founded a stud at Kadrub. Eighteen years later the Archduke Charles founded the stud at Lipizza, and it is from there that the present-day breed takes its name.

With the Hapsburg family ruling Spain, Austria and some of Italy, the transfer of horses was easy, and in time Neapolitan and Arab blood was introduced. But the Lipizzaners are of pure blood, and the horses at the Piber stud can be traced back to six distinct lines, one of which is the original Spanish sire Maestoso.

As often happens, while the Andalusian has flourished in Austria, in Spain, its own country, it has been in danger of dying out through lack of support. Now, however, Don Alvaro Domecq Romero of Jerez has founded the Andalusian School of Equestrian Art, to keep, as he says: 'the famous traditions of *haute d'ecole*,

a high school, which has made Spanish horses famous for over 600 years'.

Don Alvaro Domecq Romero, who won his first riding award at the Seville Fair when he was only five years old, and has since demonstrated the Spanish equestrian art all over the world, was in 1972 presented with Spain's highest equestrian award, 'The Golden Horse'.

The Middle East

It would not be right to talk about the horses which have made their mark in so many countries without mentioning the Middle East, the home of the Arab and the Barb for many centuries. These are horses which, together with the Thoroughbred, have played a bigger part than any other in producing the many beautiful breeds to be found throughout the world today.

In many parts of the Middle East, in spite of the fabulous fortunes which have been gained by oil, there are large groups of people who live by tilling a difficult sandy soil, and they use horses to help cultivate the small fields, which are enclosed and often very steep.

Most of the sheiks own beautiful horses which are used for racing, and many have large studs where the blood lines are carefully studied and preserved.

In Bahrein, the mounted police all ride pure-bred stallions. In Egypt, the state now owns the

Below: **The famous white Lipizzaner stallions**

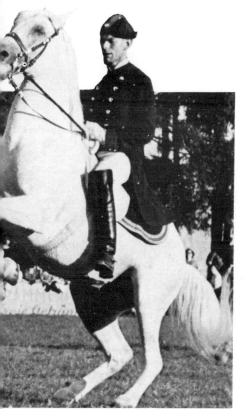

Above: **The Appaloosa**

famous El Azhraa and the centuries-old Ein Sham, two studs which always supplied horses for the Feast of Luxor with its fantastic equestrian displays.

King Hussein of Jordan has also established the Jordanian Royal Stud on the outskirts of Amman, where horses of the true desert type are bred. He built up the stud from a small band of mares carrying the ancient bloodlines of animals which had belonged to his grandfather. There was a stallion belonging to one of the sheiks; others used on the race-track; a plough horse belonging to a farmer. These were brought to the stud to carry on the pure lineage.

In Iran, the Shah is establishing a new breed, the Pahlavan, at the Imperial Stud. This breed, developed mostly from a mixture of Persian Arab, which is larger than the desert Arab and without his dished profile, and the Thoroughbred. The Shah is also trying to make a register of all Persian breeds, including the Darashouli horses from the desert, and the Turkoman from the steppe land of the Caspian Sea.

To learn more about the different breeds and types of horses and ponies you should study some of the excellent books which have been published during recent years. The subject is most fascinating and absorbing.

LOOKS AREN'T EVERYTHING

By John Bullock

The old horse box rumbled along the drive and groaned to a halt in the stable yard. The horses came to the doors of their loose-boxes to watch with interest as a rather pretty middle-aged woman jumped down from the cab and opened a small door at the side.

'You all right in there, Jenny?', she called to someone inside the box. From somewhere inside a voice echoed back, 'Yes, thanks. I'm all right and so is Caesar. I think he quite enjoyed the journey. He hardly stopped eating all the way here.'

Mrs Benton adjusted her red headscarf and poked her head inside before replying, 'You'd better stay there while I go and see whether there is anyone about. I should think it will be all right to unbox him here.'

At that moment a young girl of about twelve years old came running into the yard with a little Jack Russell terrier barking at her heels. 'Hullo, Aunt Marjorie, Mummy is on the telephone. She won't be a minute. Can I give you a hand?'

Peggy Frinton was tall for her age, and her blonde hair flopped round the shoulders of her yellow jumper, which she wore with jeans and an old pair of brown jodhpur boots.

By the time Mrs Frinton arrived, Peggy had helped open up the side of the horse-box, and a brown-haired girl was leading a rather shaggy-looking grey pony down the ramp.

Jenny's and Peggy's mothers were sisters, and Jenny had been invited to stay for a few days during the Christmas holidays.

The grey pony took a long, inquisitive look at the occupants of the yard, and then nuzzled into the pocket of Jenny's coat, where he knew there was usually a peppermint.

'Why do you call him Caesar?' Peggy asked, as she led the way across to one of the loose-boxes. The brown-haired girl stroked the nose of her pony and gave a little chuckle before replying, 'Because he's got a Roman nose. His real name is Caesar Augustus, but we call him Caesar for short.'

Peggy opened the door of the box and watched as Jenny tied him to the big ring in the far corner. Then she helped her to undo the travelling bandages which Caesar had worn to protect his legs during the journey from Wales. 'I think you're going to like it here, aren't you boy?' Jenny said as she slipped off the head-collar, leaving Caesar free to sample the bulging hay net that had been hung ready for him in the corner.

Caesar took a mouthful of hay and walked slowly over to the door to inspect the occupants of the boxes either side. One was a large bay thoroughbred that belonged to Peggy's father, and the other box held Peggy's pride and joy, a rather pretty little chestnut called Playboy. His show name was Playboy Ridgwood Shenton the Third, but he was always called Playboy or 'Boy' for short. He was a pure-bred Arab, and his mother and father were both champions.

Playboy looked across inquisitively at the stocky little grey. Caesar was certainly not a show pony by any stretch of the imagination. Apart from his Roman nose, his head seemed a little too big for his body, and although his shaggy coat had been trace-clipped, it still looked rough compared with the sleek, well-bred appearance of the Arab.

Jenny noticed it too. She loved Caesar, but even she had to admit he was certainly no oil

painting. Her father had bought him at a horse fair in Wales, rather out of pity than anything else.

'When you are ready, come in and have some tea,' Mrs Frinton called across to the two girls. 'I'm sure you must be starving, and Peggy, give Jenny a hand in with her case. You know where she is sleeping.'

By the time they had hung up Caesar's tack, and emptied the horse-box, Jenny's mother and Mrs Frinton were deep in conversation over tea in the large bow-windowed drawing room.

'Jenny must stay as long as she likes,' Mrs Frinton was saying, 'don't worry at all. I'm sure she and Peggy will have a lot of fun together with their ponies. There is so much interesting country for them to explore. We've invited the Saxton twins over tomorrow, so they can all go for a ride together.'

Mrs Benton nodded her head in agreement. 'That really is kind of you, Joan. I know Jenny will love it here. But I must be getting off home now. It's a long drive, and I don't like being out with that old horse-box after dark. I always think it is going to blow up or something awful.'

The following morning, Jenny slipped out of the house early and made her way to the stables. Caesar recognised his young mistress's footsteps, and gave a littly whinny of welcome.

'Hello, old fellow', she said as she stroked Caesar's grey muzzle which he thrust playfully into her ribs, almost knocking her off

balance. 'How do you like it here? It's a bit posh, isn't it? Not quite what we're used to!'

Shenton Manor, where the Frintons had lived for nearly half a century, was certainly rather different from the old farmhouse where Jenny lived in Wales. And the sleek thoroughbreds and show ponies looking out of their boxes at the stocky little grey and his mistress were certainly different from the old Welsh pony belonging to her brother, who was Caesar's usual companion back home. Jenny found a peppermint in the bottom of a crumpled paper bag she pulled from her pocket, 'Never mind, Caesar,' she mumbled in his ear, 'what you lack in beauty you certainly make up for in brains.'

'What was that you said?' Peggy called out as she arrived rather breathlessly in the yard. 'I heard you go past my bedroom, and I thought I'd come and see that everything was all right.'

'Oh nothing really,' said Jenny blushing slightly. She always blushed when anyone caught her talking to her pony. 'I was just having a quiet word with Caesar. Anything I can do to help?'

Peggy chuckled and unlatched the door of Playboy's box. 'It's a good job we are up early this morning. Pam and Wendy Saxton are riding over at 10 o'clock and Mummy has promised to get us a picnic so that we can ride to Branscombe Hill,' Peggy chatted away as she straightened Playboy's rug.

It was half past eight before the ponies and horses had finally been fed, and they heard Mrs Frinton ringing a bell and calling to them from the kitchen. 'That's our call for breakfast,' Peggy said, poking her head into Caesar's box. 'Come on, or we'll be late, and I can smell the bacon and eggs from here.'

The two girls hurried into the house. Breakfast was always a jolly meal at Shenton Manor, and the talk was usually about horses. Jenny found out from the conversation that Branscombe Hill was about ten miles away, and to get there they had to cross Barwell Common and then find their way across country along a series of bridle paths. The Saxtons, she was told, went to school with Peggy and lived at Marlwood House about a mile away.

Jenny was still grooming Caesar when she heard the clatter of hoofs outside. She looked out and saw two smartly dressed girls aged about twelve ride into the stable yard. The taller of the twins, whom she heard Peggy refer to as Wendy, was riding a lovely looking

like a mop. Jenny sighed. Caesar was Caesar and there was nothing she could do about it. However, she did wish that he looked a little more elegant, like the two bays that were prancing along in front, with necks arched, and feet which hardly seemed to touch the ground.

The bridle path wound through woods and then opened up into a long tree-lined glade, and the wind brought tears to Jenny's eyes as the girls urged their ponies into a brisk canter with Peggy leading the way.

Jenny found herself riding alongside Wendy Saxton on her pretty little bay gelding which she learnt was called 'Stardust'. 'Pam's horse is a half-brother, and that's why we call him "Starway",' Wendy explained.

Caesar gave a little squeal and a buck of excitement as Stardust arched his neck and cavorted elegantly alongside. 'Sorry,' Jenny called across, as Wendy tried to calm her pony. 'He does that sometimes when he's enjoying himself. Manners aren't his strong point.'

The wide track narrowed into a path leading through a small thicket, and up on to the common. Peggy turned to the other three. 'We can really let them go here,' she said, 'there's rarely anyone about and there's a riding track all the way round the Common to Swindley Bottom. Come on, let's give them a bit of a pipe opener.'

Caesar didn't need any urging, but hard as he tried, he couldn't keep up with Playboy and the Saxtons' two beautifully bred show ponies. For nearly three miles the track wound through gorse and heather, and Jenny could see the patches of sweat breaking out on her pony's neck.

'Steady up, old boy,' she said, gently reining Caesar back into a canter, 'there is no point in wearing yourself out trying to keep up with those speed merchants. We have a long way to go yet.'

She cantered down a small dell and saw that the Saxtons and Peggy had stopped and were giving their ponies a breather. Jenny jumped off Caesar and loosened his girths. 'You went too fast for old Caesar, I'm afraid,' she said, giving her pony's heaving sides a pat.

'Oh never mind, Jenny,' said Peggy, pulling a tuft of grass and offering it to the little grey, 'at least he's game, I'll say that for him. When we've had a rest we'd better head straight for Branscombe Hill. It's some miles yet and quite a lot of it's uphill from here.'

The girls remounted their ponies and

bay with a white blaze down his face. Her sister Pam's pony had almost identical colouring, and both ponies were about 14 hands.

Gosh, thought Jenny, as she brought Caesar out of the box and got into the saddle, what super looking ponies. 'They always win the pairs,' Peggy explained after the introductions had been done, and they were making their way along the bridle path leading to the common. 'Their mother is very keen on showing, and this year they came second at Wembley. Should have won according to what some people said afterwards.'

'I'm not surprised,' said Jenny. Caesar snorted and shook his head with impatience, making his mane, which Jenny had combed so carefully, fall down on either side of his neck walked them slowly along the path towards a small copse that nestled between a lake on one side and a large field on the other, with an ominous looking notice which said 'Danger – bull, please keep out.'

Pam Saxton turned to Jenny, 'Whatever you do, don't go in there. I wouldn't want to get too near to that bull. He belongs to old Tom Wainwright who has got a farm over the hill there, and he's about the only one who can go near him.'

'Look, there he is,' said Pam, pointing to a big white-faced bull who stood snorting and pawing the ground in the middle of the field. 'Oh, come on,' said Peggy, 'you've got a thing about bulls!'

It was Wendy who heard the noise first. They had just reached the gate leading into the copse when she stopped and held up her hand. 'Ssh! I'm sure I heard something. It sounded like a groan coming from behind that hedge over there.' The girls stood and listened. 'I can't hear anything. You're imagining things,' said Pam, feeling in her pocket for a handkerchief. Peggy jumped off Playboy. 'Here, hold my pony, somebody, we'd better go and look.'

Wendy took the reins, and Peggy scrambled through the hedge into the copse. A few seconds later she gave a shout. 'Hurry! Come quickly! It's Mr Wainwright and he looks as though he's been hurt badly. I think that bull must have attacked him and tossed him over the hedge.'

Tom Wainwright was lying on the ground in a pool of blood which was still pouring from a deep gash in his thigh. 'Anyone got a hand-

kerchief?' said Jenny, taking charge of the situation. 'If you have, give it to Pam, and Wendy, you hold the ponies while Pam goes down to the lake and soaks the handkerchiefs in water.'

Jenny took off the headscarf she had been wearing under her riding hat to keep her hair in place. 'Here you are, Peggy, we'd better try and put on a tourniquet. I remember being taught this at first aid.'

She tied the scarf round the injured man's thigh, and twisted it tight with a piece of branch from a tree. 'There now. Let's hope that will stop the bleeding, but we'd better get help quickly. Where's the nearest house?'

'I suppose it must be the Wainwright farm,' said Pam, sponging Mr Wainwright's face with one of the water-soaked handkerchiefs. 'But that's about three miles by road, and its unlikely that we will meet a car along here at this time of year.'

'How far is it across the fields?' Jenny asked, jumping into Caesar's saddle. 'Tell me again which direction the farm is in.' Wendy shook her head. 'You'll never make it. Old Wainwright always has his gates padlocked, and he's a stickler for keeping his fields drained, which means that all his hedges have got big ditches as well. And to make matters worse, you'd have to go across that field with the bull. You'd never do it!'

'Well, we'll have to try won't we?' said Jenny, taking Caesar round in a wide circle and putting him straight at the hedge. 'Come on now, Caesar,' she said urging him on, 'don't let me down now.' The grey measured the hedge perfectly and, ears pricked, cleared it with inches to spare.

'She's mad,' said Pam, pushing back the brim of her riding hat, 'plain staring bonkers! I wouldn't like to be in your shoes when you get home, Peggy, you're meant to be looking after her!' The girls ran to the hedge as they heard the bull snort, and after giving the ground a final paw, thunder after Jenny and the grey.

Heaven help Jenny if Caesar refuses that fence, and it must be every bit of four feet high. He can't possibly make it!' Peggy stood with fingers crossed and her heart in her mouth. Caesar saw the ditch and the fence, faltered slightly, then lengthening his stride, he gave an enormous leap and landed clear the other side into a ploughed field.

'They're over. They've done it! Good old Caesar!' Peggy found herself jumping up and down with excitement and relief. 'And good

you, we don't want riders on our land!'

Jenny slowed Caesar to a walk. 'Are you Mrs Wainwright?' she said, jumping off and opening the gate into the farmyard. 'Yes, I am. What's all the rush?' the woman replied, still waving her apron. 'It's Mr Wainwright. He's badly hurt. We think he has been gored by a bull. He's in the copse by the lake. Do hurry. My friends are looking after him, but he does need help quickly. I rode here as fast as I could.' Jenny blurted out her story as she tried to get her breath back.

Mrs Wainwright's tone changed. 'Oh bless you, my dear. I'll go and ring the doctor straight away,' she said, adding, 'you put your pony in that stable over there if you like and then come on in the house. You look as though you could do with a nice cup of tea. I always said that darned bull would get him some day.'

Jenny loosened Caesar's saddle and walked him round to cool off. Then she rubbed him down with some straw she found in the barn.

A few minutes later Mrs Wainwright came into the stable. 'I managed to get the doctor just as he was leaving. Another few minutes and we would have missed him,' she said, giving Jenny a friendly smile. 'I don't know how to thank you enough. I'm sorry I was so bad tempered, but it's been a bad year, and the thought of young people galloping over our fields was just too much. Now what about coming into the house?'

'No thanks, Mrs Wainwright, I'd better get back to my friends, if you could just tell me the way round by the road,' Jenny said as she slipped gently into the saddle. 'Caesar and I will be all right.'

She met Peggy and the Saxtons riding along the lane towards the farm. 'The doctor has taken Mr Wainwright off to hospital,' said Wendy, giving Caesar an admiring glance. 'He said he's lost a lot of blood, but thanks to your quick action he's going to be all right.'

A few days later an envelope arrived at Shenton Manor addressed to Jenny, along with a large brown parcel with Caesar's name on it. Jenny opened the envelope. Inside were six tickets to the Christmas circus and a note from Mr Wainwright which just said, 'With thanks to a very brave girl.'

And the parcel? That was full of carrots and a note which said 'To Caesar, a very clever pony. With grateful thanks from Tom Wainwright.'

'You see,' said Jenny to Caesar as he munched contentedly away at a carrot that evening, 'looks aren't everything, are they?'

old Jenny,' said Wendy. 'It's up to them now. There's not much more we can do.'

Jenny let the pony have his head as he galloped on across the plough. He seemed to sense the urgency of the situation. She steadied him slightly as they galloped downhill and headed for a post and rails at the bottom. Caesar cleared the rails, but saw the ditch the other side too late. Pitching forward on to his nose, he shot Jenny out of the saddle.

'Ugh!' said Jenny, spitting out a mouthful of mud. To her surprise she found she was still holding on to the reins. Caesar struggled gamely to his feet, and stood quietly beside her.

Gathering up the reins Jenny sprang back into the saddle. 'Come on Caesar, it can't be far now,' she whispered.

They galloped along the length of the hedge and came across a stile at the other end. This time Caesar made no mistake, and cleared the obstacle by a good nine inches.

At the top of the next rise, Jenny looked down into the dip below them and saw the farmhouse nestling in between some trees. As she set off downhill at a brisk canter, a woman came rushing out of the house. 'What do you think you're doing,' she yelled at Jenny, waving an apron in the air. 'Be off with

The Story of Driving
by Commander Donald Douglas

At most of the major Horse and Agricultural shows in Britain today, the programmes include classes for horses and ponies in harness. These may be Coaching classes, Private Driving classes, classes for Trade Turnouts or Combined Driving Competitions.

It is becoming very obvious that the public interest in harness horses is on the increase, but one wonders whether the spectator at the ringside ever gives a thought as to 'how it all began'.

When horses were first domesticated man either carried his wares on the animal's back, or sat there himself as a means of moving around his land. It did not need much intelligence to work out that the strength of the horse might be put to better use by asking him to drag a load rather than to carry it. So the first conveyance was invented, a kind of sledge on a couple of poles fastened around the horse's neck.

No one knows for sure who first invented the wheel, but the brilliance of the idea and its effect on man's world of transport was incredible. Man now realised that he could make improvements to his horse-drawn transport, although it was still a long way to the horsedrawn carriage as we know it today. The dragging poles could now be raised to the horizontal, so that the load would travel more securely, and this also meant that a man himself could travel on top of his load in reasonable comfort. Even more important was the fact that the horse could draw a much heavier load than before.

The wheel certainly must have been invented many thousands of years before the Christian era, for the Egyptians, on their monuments, show us the complete wheeled chariot used both in war and for sporting races. In the book of Genesis, dated some 1700 years before Christ, Joseph told his brethren to take their waggons out of the land of Egypt.

War chariots and racing chariots have been reproduced by sculptors and artists throughout the ages. More recently they have been shown to us on the cinema screen in such epics as *Ben Hur*, with charioteers challenging each other in the great amphitheatres of Rome. A good example of a war chariot can be seen at Hyde Park Corner in London in a mighty statue of Queen Boadicea driving her pair of fiery steeds. The wicked looking knives protruding from the wheel hubs of her chariot tell us that this vehicle was never built for sporting activities; it was used to fight off the invading Romans.

However, we must not dwell too long in the ancient past, for it is only in the last hundred years that driving horses really came into the public eye, and possibly more so in the small island of Britain than anywhere else in the world.

We will now advance a few thousand years to study the horse-drawn transport in Great Britain, for it is only some 400 years since wheeled vehicles were first used for carrying passengers in Great Britain. Carts were used for goods long before they were used for passengers, because in those early days there were no roads as such

Runaway carriage horses causing an accident (early 19th-century print)

in our country, and what tracks there were were quite impassable in winter.

Over such tracks the crude carriages of our ancestors would be drawn by teams of heavy and powerful horses, whose strength was more necessary than speed. These animals were the 'Great' or Shire horses, which are still valued and carefully bred today.

When roads eventually improved more rapid travel became possible, and this created a demand for lighter and more active harness horses.

Carriages were in use in Europe a long time before they appeared in England. In 1294 when Philip the Fair of France, wishing to suppress luxury, issued an order that wives of citizens were forbidden to use carriages, the wives in England were still travelling in the horse-drawn litter.

A litter was a box-like body on two poles rather like a sedan chair, but instead of being carried by two men, the poles were slung between two horses. The leading horse was generally ridden and

the rear horse followed, carrying his share of the load. Being wheelless vehicles they were able to traverse the countryside on the only tracks available at the time. It was considered unbecoming for men to travel in such conveyances, and horse litters were only used for ladies of rank. History tells us that they fell into disuse in the fourteenth century when Anne of Bohemia, wife of King Richard II, introduced the sidesaddle, and ladies could travel on horseback in elegance.

Although the Europeans were ahead of Britain with their carriages, these were still very basic in design; in fact they were little better than farm waggons, with no springing, and thus uncomfortable.

We now come to the period when the 'coach' proper was first introduced into England, and this gives us a good opportunity to look into the origin of the word itself. I have been unable to discover why a coach is called a coach, but I do have a theory which may have a bearing on the

subject.

During a visit to Hungary, when viewing carriage horses and Hungarian vehicles, I noticed that the Hungarian word for a car is KOCSIT, and this is pronounced 'coachy' in our language. I mentioned this to one of my Hungarian hosts, and he explained that the word came from the village in Hungary of the same name. This village was the birthplace of many of the European coaches; it was there that many of the kings and heads of state in Europe had their carriages built. Many of Napoleon's carriages were made in Kocsit, and some of these can be seen to this day in the famous 'Waggon Museum' in the Palace of Schönbrunn, on the outskirts of Vienna.

The first recorded coach in England was that built by Walter Rippon for the Earl of Rutland in 1555. In 1564, a Dutchman called William Boonen brought from Holland a coach which he presented to Queen Elizabeth I. Walter Rippon, the original coach builder in this country, also built a coach for his Queen and, in fact, later became her head coachman. But the roads were very bad in those days, and the coaches built without any form of springing, so Queen Elizabeth soon went back to riding pillion behind her Master of Horse.

In 1564 the first example of the stage coach made its appearance. These 'Long Waggons', as they were called, are recorded as having travelled between London and Canterbury, Norwich, Ipswich and as far afield as Gloucester. Carrying both goods and passengers, they were known as 'Stages' because they made their long and very slow journeys in stages. They had very broad wheels, almost like garden rollers, and so were able to cover the bad surfaces without sinking too far into the mud.

Transport of this nature continued for some 200 years before steel springs were used on horse-drawn carriages. This great advance enabled the occupants to travel in more comfort and also eased the burden of the horses. In 1750 springs were first used on coaches in England.

Most of our History of Driving is centred in or around London, for it was to and from that great city that the stage coaches ran, and it was London which first saw the forerunner of the modern taxi, the Hackney carriage.

In the year 1605 the first of the Hackney carriages appeared, but they did not roam the streets or 'crawl' about as did their later two-wheeled cousins, the Hansom cabs or 'Crawlers'. They stayed in their yards until called for. Some thirty years later the first Hackney 'stand' was established in London by a retired sea captain, one Captain Bailey. He placed four of his Hackney carriages at the Maypole in the Strand, with his coachman in livery. Soon all the other Hackney owners followed his example. In no time, London was overcrowded with these horse-drawn carriages, and in 1635, King Charles I objected. He proclaimed that the 'general . . . use a Hackney coaches in such numbers caused disturbance to the King and Queen personally

The Four-in-Hand Club at Hyde Park, London

and to others. That these great numbers of carriages "pestered" the streets, broke up the pavements, and caused increases in the price of horsefood.'

He forbade the use of Hackney carriages in London and Westminster and the suburbs altogether, unless the passengers were making a journey of over three miles. Only private carriages were permitted.

At the time of this Royal Proclamation, there were no less than 6000 horse-drawn vehicles cluttering up the streets, but two years later only sixty Hackney carriages were operating. After thirty years the situation had again got out of hand. The number of coaches plying for trade had become so great that they were forbidden to stand in the street for hire.

In 1662 there were some 2500 Hackney carriages in London, and King Charles II passed a law reducing this great number by the granting of licences. Only 400 of these were issued and, originally costing £5, they frequently changed hands for as much as £100, an enormous sum of money in those days!

The Hackney owners who were unable to obtain licences moved out of London to the little towns within some twenty miles of the city, and set themselves up as stage operators. At this time there were only six Long Stage coach services.

It is known that a coach ran between London and York and to Chester and Exeter. Each of these services used forty horses and carried six passengers. They left for their destinations three times

The Hansom cab was once a familiar sight in England

Going in first rate style

each week.

These early 'Flying coaches' travelled faster than their successors, and journeying in them must have been mostly uncomfortable and dangerous. Nimrod, that great authority on all matters concerning the equestrian art, recalls in his book *The Road* details of a journey by coach from London to Oxford in the year 1742. Leaving London at 7 a.m., the coach reached Uxbridge at midday. Arriving at High Wycombe, about half way, at 5 p.m. the same evening, both horses and passengers rested for the night.

The following day the coach made a similar journey completing the next twenty-seven miles in ten hours. The whole journey of fifty-seven miles had taken nearly two days!

What had happened between 1740 and 1840 to make travel so much faster? It was not the horse, although with the coming of stage coaches better carriage horses were bred for the work; nor was it the carriages, although with each year that passed improvements were seen here also. The increase in the speed of travel was made possible by one man, John Macadam. Born in Ayrshire in 1756, he devoted his life to the improvement of Britain's roads. Between 1798 and 1814 he travelled some 30,000 miles of the country's roads, and in 1818 his road-making method was finally approved. Macadamised roads were constructed all over the country. He died in 1836, by which time the 'Golden Age' of coaching had begun.

In the last twenty-five years of the eighteenth century the Long Stages were still slow, but passengers did not mind because life

Cobb's old stage coach on a windy day

itself was slow in those days. Provided one had a comfortable resting place each night, good food and good company, it mattered little how long it took to reach one's destination. However, our leisurely traveller was quickly to be caught up in the world of speed.

In 1783, Mr John Palmer, a theatre manager from Bath, was distressed by the corrupt and extremely slow postal service of the day. He noticed that the stage coach from London to Bristol, a distance of some 114 miles, took 17 hours. The post boys who delivered the mail on ponies still took two days to complete the same journey. He wrote to the Prime Minister, William Pitt, in the following terms: 'The Poste at present, instead of being the swiftest, is almost the slowest conveyance in the country.' He suggested that the Post Office should use his fast coaches, called Diligences, and in 1784 his scheme was adopted.

The postal service now entered a new age, and Palmer's fast mail coaches soon spread throughout Britain. The London to Bristol

A Hackney shows its paces

mail would change their four horses every seven to ten miles. There were no delays at the 'Turnpikes' or tollgates, as the mail did not have to pay tolls. Indeed, by using their posthorns, they warned the turnpike men of the approaching mail coach, and if he failed to give the coach a free and rapid passage through his gate, he was fined quite severely.

The only employee of the Post Office on the mail coach was the guard. This trusted gentleman was armed with many weapons with which to protect his mails and passengers from the numerous highwaymen of the day. He also wielded the 'Yard of Tin', or posthorn, and warned the villages of the arrival of the mail. The postman must be ready to take the mails, and the livery yard must be ready with the change of horses. Nothing was allowed to delay the mail coach, which prided itself on running to the minute!

Because speed and punctuality were so important, better horses were needed, and by 1815 the

A 'Buggy' by Currier and Ives

mail coaches were using some of the finest coach horses in the world. Founded on the famous Cleveland Bay horse, these animals possessed speed, stamina and great courage. Life was hard on them and they received little consideration. Their work on the road seldom lasted more than three years.

The mail coach service set a standard for speed, efficiency and reliability, and soon the example was followed by the private coaches. Coach driving became a favourite occupation among gentlemen, and men from all walks of life devoted themselves to 'horsing' coaches. This did much to promote a spirit of rivalry between coach proprietors, which in turn helped to improve the standard of coachmanship throughout the land.

The best coaches now ran at an average speed of 10 to 10½ miles per hour, though their speed over good stretches of road was, of course, much greater than this. The famous 'Quicksilver' coach which ran the mails from London to Devonport, travelled half a mile per hour faster than any other coach. It completed the fastest section of the journey, the four miles near Hartford bridge, in twelve minutes. This same coach once completed the whole 216-mile journey in 21 hours and 14 minutes including stoppages.

On May Day it was customary for rival coachmen to race each other for the entire day's journey. Little wonder that coaches had few fare-paying passengers on 1st May. This 'sport' became very dangerous, and in 1820 a law was passed putting an end to this 'wanton and furious driving or racing'.

In 1835 there were 700 mail coaches, and some 3000 stage coaches running in Britain, using over 15,000 horses and employing 30,000 men. Private coaching had become a sport amongst the more wealthy members of the community, and some of the smartest of these were to be found on the famous Brighton Road. Brighton, a mere fishing village before it was patronised by King George IV, was

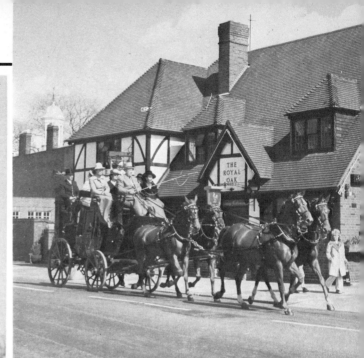

Two scenes from Windsor. *Below* Prince Philip negotiates the Obstacles Driving Test at the European Driving Championships *Right* The Coaching Marathon

by now a famous seaside resort, and in 1819, upwards of seventy coaches visited and left the town every day.

Each year, on the King's birthday, a great procession of mail coaches, built to a strict pattern and gleaming in freshly painted colours of maroon, scarlet, and gold, paraded through London. The procession was always led by the Bristol mail, which was the oldest service, and when it reached its destination, St James's Palace, the King's health was drunk. Sadly, the last parade took place in 1838 and after that changes happened fast. In 1837 fifty-two new mail guards had been appointed, but six years later, there was only one new guard.

This decline in the mail coach service was brought about by that new invention, the railway. Many of the guards and coachmen found other employment with the railways, and this proved to be the end of the Royal Mail coaches.

Private coaching went on for a while, but its days were numbered, and four-in-hand driving became one of the lost arts. Traditions were kept up, however, by Driving Clubs. The earliest of these, the Kensington Driving Club, was formed in 1807, and lasted until 1854. Two years later, the 'Four-in-Hand' club was formed and this kept the memory of coaching alive until 1870, when the Coaching Club was formed in London.

This famous club still exists,

Bozo Prprić of Yugoslavia at Virginia Water in the European Driving Championship Marathon

and its enthusiastic members enable us to see these lovely vehicles today, in the show rings throughout the country.

Although the roads in Britain saw fewer and fewer big coaches with their teams of four horses, there were still many smaller privately owned vehicles about, being driven either by single horses and ponies, or pair turnouts. London was crowded with these, and also with the Hansom cabs, named after their designer John Hansom, a Birmingham architect.

The Gig, the Ralli car, the Phaeton and the Dog Cart are the names given to but a few of these smaller vehicles. With the coming of the motor car, these too found their way on to the scrap heap, or in many cases, more fortunately, into barns, sheds and carriage houses all over the country.

During the second World War when motor cars were forced off the road by lack of fuel, many of these smaller vehicles were brought back into use, and people became interested in driving again.

When the war ended and horse shows started up again, there were classes for driving enthusiasts, but these were poorly supported and the standard was not high. In 1957, Colonel Arthur Main, at that time President of the Coaching Club, and Captain Frank Gilbey found themselves judging a driving class together at the Royal Windsor Horse Show. They were not impressed by what they saw, and decided to call together several members of the Coaching Club who were present on the ground to discuss the possibility of forming a Driving Club which could encourage the sport of Private Driving, and improve the standard of 'Coachmanship'.

It was agreed to hold a conference later in the year, and to call together anyone interested in 'the Driving of Horses or Ponies'. On September 23, this conference was held at the offices of the British Horse Society in London and forty-six people attended. It was agreed that a society should be formed whose object would be to provide help and encouragement to all those interested in the art of driving. At the opening meeting, Mr Sanders Watney was elected President of the newly formed British Driving Society.

At the first meeting, ninety-two members were enrolled, and it was agreed that the official meet of the society should take place at Windsor Horse Show. These few enthusiasts little thought at that time that within a few years the annual Meet would see a hundred turnouts on the show ground.

Today, with membership of the society in the region of 1350 and classes for driving at nearly every horse show throughout the country, driving is established once again as a major equestrian sport and pastime.

Recently yet another harness sport has come into Britain, called combined driving. Rules were drawn up for this new sport in 1969 at a meeting in Switzerland at which Colonel Sir Michael Ansell took the Chair. These rules were mainly designed for international competitions for four horses, but they were not really connected with coaching, and the British Driving Society was asked to look after the sport in Great Britain.

A combined driving event is run on similar lines to a ridden three-day event, and consists of three separate competitions. Firstly, there is 'presentation', a form of show class, which is followed immediately by a dressage test. The second phase, as in the ridden event, includes a cross-country trial, and the final competition involves driving through a set course of obstacles in the show ring.

Great interest has been shown in this sport, and national competitions have been staged for both Teams, Pairs and Single Turnouts at shows. Britain has competed at the European Championships in Budapest in 1971, the World Championships in Germany in 1972, and again at the World Championships in Switzerland in 1974. At both the World Championships, Great Britain won the Team Gold Medal.

Eventing
by Lieutenant Colonel W. S. P. Lithgow

This very popular and exciting sport of eventing originally started in the Cavalry Schools of France. It was meant as a test of the horse's training, ability and fitness for war, and for that reason it was – and sometimes still is – referred to in France as the 'Militaire'.

The officers felt that to be of any real use in war a cavalry horse must, firstly, be obedient to his rider; secondly, have the courage, strength and endurance to carry him long distances across all sorts of country at varying paces; and thirdly, it should be able to come

out again after a rest, fit and sound and well enough for more work. All this, of course, meant that the rider had to have a similar courage, fitness and ability – coupled with sympathy, judgement and a high degree of training.

The test took part over three days and was designed as the complete test – 'Concours Complet' as it is now known in France – of horse and rider. Any weakness in either would certainly be found out. Event riders today face very much the same tests.

On the first day they have to

perform a test of basic training and obedience lasting about ten minutes in an outdoor arena twenty metres wide by sixty metres long. This is called the Dressage Test and consists of a series of simple movements such as moving in a straight line, halting, turning, circling, reining back, at the walk, trot, and canter. The rider has to learn these by heart. They are simple movements, unlike those which high school and circus horses have to perform, but have to be done very accurately and well. For instance, if the horse is

Competing in the Dressage phase at Badminton

moving down a straight line, it has to be absolutely straight, and if told to halt at a certain point, it must do so exactly there.

The test is divided into a series of movements, each marked out of six or ten and judged by two or three judges. Their marks are then converted by simple mathematics to penalty points. If the test is marked out of a hundred and the judges award sixty, that would be the same as forty penalties. In fact of course they don't allow it to be quite as simple as that!

On the second day the test is for speed and endurance, and it is on this that the competition is won or lost. This test is split up into four phases – A, B, C, & D. Usually phase A consists of two or three miles over roads, tracks and ordinary country at an average speed of about eight miles per hour, which is the pace of a fast trot, though it is normally ridden at a mixture of walk, trot and canter.

Phase B is a steeplechase course with up to twelve 'racing type' fences to be ridden at the gallop. The time for this is pretty fast, and if riders take too long they earn penalty points which are added to their dressage penalties.

Having completed this they go straight into Phase C, which is another five to ten miles of Roads and Tracks, as they are called. Once again, as in Phases A and B, competitors have to be careful not to exceed the time allowed and so earn more penalties.

At the end of Phase C there is a ten-minute halt. The rider dismounts and the horse is inspected by experts to make sure that it is neither lame nor unduly distressed. Grooms and helpers do everything they can to freshen their horses up for the next phase by removing the saddle, sponging them down with cold water and facing them into the breeze to help them to catch their breath. It is also a short rest period for the rider, during which his helpers give him any information they have acquired from spectators and riders who have already finished which might assist him in the next phase. Then after the halt, off he goes on Phase D with everything to ride for. Four miles or so across country at a fast canter with up to thirty-five fences of all sorts and shapes, including twists and turns, uphill and downhill, some good going and some not so good. The fences themselves are not particularly large – about 3 ft 9 ins – but are skilfully designed and

placed to set a problem to both horse and rider. To complete this phase in the time allowed is quite difficult, and requires a very fit and willing horse and a bold and capable rider. Taking too long means more penalty points. At the same time in both Phases B and D – steeplechase and cross country – penalties are awarded for refusals and falls. Failure to complete the course or jump each fence after three attempts means elimination.

By the end of the day, each horse will be very tired, and it requires great care and expert attention to make sure that it is fit and ready to come out again and do its best the next day.

On the third day, the horses are first of all led out by their grooms – 'trotted up', as they say – for inspection by a panel of experts to be sure that they are in every way fit to compete. They are then required to complete the Jumping Test which consists of a show-jumping course of about twelve fences with penalties for refusals, falls, knocking down fences or going too slowly. The course is usually pretty twisty and, as I have said, the object of the show jumping is to prove that the horse is still fit and supple enough to do its job after a severe effort the day before. It will inevitably be a bit stiff first thing, and the skill comes in working this off and warming up the horse without doing too much.

After all this the winner is the one who has been given the least number of penalty points over the three days.

That, then, is a Three Day Event, and as I'm sure you will agree, it requires a very fine horse and rider to complete it all – let alone to win it. Those of you who have read your history and more especially seen the films of 'Waterloo' and 'The Charge of the Light Brigade' will realise how essential those qualities of obedience, fitness, endurance and courage were to the war horse and how sensible the French were to devise such a means of training and testing them. The Charge of the Light Brigade must have been

Above: Richard Meade on Laurelston. *Right:* Cornishman being 'warmed-up' before competing at Badminton

alarming enough as it was, but it would have been worse if the soldiers knew they couldn't even steer their horses.

Before the last war, our cross-country horsemen concentrated mostly on hunting and racing and knew little, if anything, of the Three Day Events which took place in Europe. One was included in the Olympic Games in Germany in 1936 and, although we sent over a team of three from the Cavalry School at Weedon, no-body really paid much attention and it created no interest at home. The most notable thing about the competition was the water jump – a fence with a wide stretch of water on the landing side into which the horses had to jump. I have seen a film of it, and horse after horse jumping on the left-hand side found the water too deep and went under. Rumour had it – probably wrongly and unfairly – that only the Germans, who had organised it, knew where the shallow bit was, and all of them jumped it safely! Nowadays, of course, all riders would have made sure that they also knew by wading about in it to test its depth.

There were no more Olympic Games until after the Second World War. In 1948 it was our turn to run the Games in England, and they included, of course, a Three Day Event. A number of our most experienced horsemen and administrators, with representatives from the International Federation, got together to organise it. They decided to hold it in Hampshire with the Steeplechase (Phase B) on Tweseldown Racecourse, and the Cross Country (Phase D) on the training area by the Royal Military Academy, Sandhurst. Not only were these suitable, they were also the right distance apart for the main Roads and Tracks (Phase C).

It was arranged that Britain should enter a team, and though the Cavalry School at Weedon no longer existed, there were people available who had attended the courses there. From among them, officials selected what today we call a 'short list' or in football terms a 'squad'. In due course the numbers were reduced to a team of three.

Though the British riders did their very best, they were totally lacking in experience of that sort of competition and two of them failed to complete the second day. I was instructing at Sandhurst two years later, and we often rode in the area of the Cross Country Course. To our inexperienced eyes, it looked very big indeed, but by modern standards it was both smaller and much more straightforward. But the great thing was that the Olympic Games Three Day Event aroused interest. One of the most enthusiastic was Colonel Moseley, who had been a distinguished amateur steeplechase rider before the war. Later he was to become Chairman of our Selection Committee and of our Junior Team, both of whom have been so successful in International Competitions. After the 1948 Olympics he vowed to do everything in his power to put Britain at the top of the Three Day Event world.

But most important of all, the Duke of Beaufort also saw the possibilities of the sport and generously placed his lovely estate at Badminton in Gloucestershire at the disposal of the British

Above: An excellent jump in the Cross Country phase
Right: **A large and interested crowd watch as a competitor gallops into water**

Horse Society. A Badminton Committee was formed to organise and run a Three Day Event there. A lovelier and more suitable place for such an event could not be imagined, and that, coupled with the excitement of the competition itself, quickly fired people's enthusiasm. The audiences have grown from the few thousand who attended the first Event in 1949 to the almost too vast crowds who now attend every year.

Many other things have helped to create this enthusiasm, not least being the great interest Her Majesty The Queen has taken from the start. She never fails to attend each year, and was present to see the success of Her Royal Highness the Princess Anne. It was partly as a result of this that the sport now gets such excellent

coverage on television.

So in 1949 a successful competition had been held, and a small band of enthusiasts, seeing the possibilities, realised that to put the sport properly on the map, British riders must succeed at International level. Britain in those days was well behind the Europeans, particularly the French, the Swiss and the Italians.

It is, of course, a very big step to go straight from ordinary riding or hunting to a full-scale Three Day Event. As a result, the idea grew of holding One Day and later Two Day Events, using the same main tests of Dressage, Cross Country and Jumping, but on a smaller scale and leaving out, at least in One Day Events, the Roads and Tracks and Steeplechase. This of course is the backbone of 'Eventing'.

It is interesting that, unlike any other sport, Eventing has developed in Britain from the top downwards, rather than the other way round. From the Olympic Games down through adult One and Two Day Events to Pony Club and Riding Club Events, or Horse Trials, as they are often called now, run on the same lines and under the same rules. Even further down we have what are called Combined Competitions consisting of a Dressage Test and a Show Jumping round. These competitions have grown tremendously in popularity and are often sponsored by firms who have qualifying competitions throughout the country working up to a final at the Horse of the Year Show at Wembley each year.

I was lucky enough to be involved through the Army Saddle Clubs Association in the early days of the One Day Events, in particular the one held on Mr Neil Gardiner's estate at Great Auclum in Berkshire. This was later moved to Tweseldown, where it has been held every year since. To me it was very exciting because it was a new sport with comparatively few competitors, and I remember being very proud of having as many as thirty-five starters at Tweseldown. While the rules themselves were complete, there was still plenty of scope for ideas and initiative in the organisation of the event itself.

Mr Gardiner, who was soon to become Chairman of the Combined Training Committee (yet another name for the sport!) was a tremendous enthusiast and full of drive. He lent his land, planned the course and always rode first himself. One year he was very keen to have a jump in his pond, which would have been fine provided the bottom was hard and the water not too deep. For some reason or other he was unwilling to lower the water level until the day of the competition, but he kept insisting that the bottom was of gravel and very hard. As he advanced upon the fence it quickly became clear that the bottom was far from hard. With his horse floundering along and half falling at the fence, he nose-dived into the water, emerging like Neptune from the deep with the immortal words – 'And in my own so-and-so pond too!'

To stand a chance of winning an International Competition Britain had, of course, a long way to go. Traditionally the British riders and horses were vastly experienced at cross-country, but way behind riders from other countries in dressage and the art of jumping a few fairly simple show jumps without fault. As a result, they had to take a lot of risks and go very fast across country in order to offset the penalties they usually earned in the other two tests. If something went wrong, as can so easily happen, all was lost.

To try and overcome these faults for the Olympic Games in Helsinki in 1952, a 'short list' was once again picked. Horses and riders trained together for six months at Porlock Vale in Somerset, under the expert eye of Captain Tony Collings, who had the assistance of foreign dressage trainers and show-jumping experts.

This plan was so successful that Britain should have won, and probably would have if Major Rook had not had a very unlucky fall on the flat after the last fence which so concussed him that he went the wrong side of a flag. But the team was on the right lines, and at the next Olympic Games in Stockholm in 1956, Britain won the Gold Medal. It is nice to know that the three members of that team are still actively engaged in the sport. The Captain, Colonel Frank Weldon, of whom many of you will have heard, runs the Three Day Event at Badminton; Major Rook is Chairman of the Combined Training Committee, and Mr Bertie Hill, who was riding Her Majesty the Queen's horse, Countryman, trained our Gold Medal-winning team for the Mexico Olympics and has been one of Britain's several trainers ever since.

British riders had really arrived, and thanks to the great generosity of landowners in lending their

Right: Richard Meade again. This time on Wayfarer II. Below: Tough going at the Durweston horse trials

land and the hard work and enthusiasm of countless organisers and helpers, the number of events held in the British Isles increased, and with it the number and the standard and quality of competitors and horses.

So far so good but, as is the way of these things, the 'ups' were to be followed by the 'downs', and it was to be ten years or so before Britain was again to win a top International Competition. By that time it was very noticeable how enthusiasm and support had begun to wane. Success, however, came again in 1967 and was followed by five more winning

years including two Olympic Gold Medals, a World and two European Championships. Popular support and interest quickly returned. Since then the British riders have lost twice, and so, as you can imagine, all stops are out to win the European Championship in Germany and the Gold Medal in Montreal.

And so a completely new national sport has grown up in twenty-five years. While international success is, as I have said, vital to its well-being, the meat and blood of the sport are the countless One Day Events at all levels and the many hundreds of

competitors taking part for the sheer love of it, often with little prospect or even hope of winning. All they want is to take part, meet their friends, improve their horses and their own performance; it has become 'their' sport.

The girls nowadays outnumber the men and very good, brave and competent they are. This does not mean that the sport has become any softer. Far from it, indeed I could tell some great tales of the gallantry of the girls, but in these days there are fewer and fewer men who can spare the time for all the training that is involved.

For those of you who are keen to try your hand, and can afford to keep a pony, the opportunities are there with your local Pony Club or Riding Club. Don't be put off by the thought that the dressage is too difficult and that everyone will be watching you make a fool of yourself. It isn't, they won't, and there will be a lot far worse! You'll love the galloping and jumping, and once you have been bitten by the bug, it will give a whole new object and purpose to your riding. The dressage will soon fall into place with the help of your instructors, and the effort involved will seem very worthwhile.

I feel that the popularity of the sport goes much deeper than just the Royal interest, the thrills and spills and the lovely places in which the events are held. I believe it is because it is a really 'good' sport in every sense of the word. As a result of it horses are on the whole much better looked after, and are ridden better and trained better than ever before. It is nice to think that out of all the grisly deeds that were asked of soldiers at Waterloo, Balaclava, and in countless other wars down the ages, something has developed that is also of benefit to the horses.

Some Experiences of a Chef d'Equipe

by Lieutenant Colonel W. S. P. Lithgow

You can imagaine how excited I was, while serving as a soldier in Aden in 1964, to receive a letter asking if I would like to succeed the famous Colonel Frank Weldon as Chef d'Equipe of our Three Day Event Team for the next four years, leading up to the Olympic Games in Mexico in 1968.

Each year there is one International Competition – sometimes in England and sometimes abroad. My job as Chef d'Equipe was to be Manager and Captain of the team which our Selection Committee had chosen for this competition.

Apart from taking charge of the team during the competition, I first of all had to get to know as much as I could about the members of the team and their horses; what they had done in the past;

their strengths and weaknesses, and their likes and dislikes.

In fact, I had to know everything that would help me to help them, and at the same time get the very best out of them. I also had to organise any journeys that were necessary, and make arrangements for the short period of a week or two when everyone got together at Ascot, near Windsor, immediately before the competition. The object of this period was to enable the members of the team to get to know each other better, to exchange ideas, finish off their training, and work up a team spirit in which everyone was going flat out to do their very best, for themselves and for the team.

Ascot is a wonderful place for this. There are splendid stables, and we were allowed by per-

mission of Her Majesty The Queen to train in Windsor Great Park and use Ascot Racecourse for our gallops. This was very exciting, imagining as we did all the great horses and jockeys who have raced on that turf. We ourselves lived in one of the boys' houses at Eton College, as they were away on holiday at the time.

My first competition was to be the European Championships in Moscow, and we were all very excited at the thought of going there. The year before, our team had been beaten in the Olympic Games in Tokyo, when at one stage they had looked like winning the Gold Medal. The last time the British team had won the Gold Medal was in the Stockholm Olympics in 1956, and everyone was naturally keen to make a

really good start towards training a team to win in Mexico.

We were to go to Moscow by air, with the horses and grooms and our vet, Mr Peter Scott-Dunn, in one plane and the rest of us in another.

Horses, on the whole, travel well that way, and don't seem to mind flying any more than they do travelling in a horsebox. But if, as does occasionally happen, one gets frightened and starts to panic, it is a bit alarming for everyone else in the aeroplane! To help keep them quiet, we don't give them a feed on the morning of the journey, so that they will be a bit hungry when they get on board. When the plane starts to take off, the grooms give them bits of carrot, which they love, and before they know where they are, they are airborne, and happily eating a a feed.

In those days the arrangements were pretty old-fashioned. The horses had to walk up a gangway just like ordinary passengers, and the stalls in the plane were not very secure. Nowadays, things are better organised, and we load them into very strong and secure stalls on the ground. These are then lifted into the aeroplane and out again on arrival. The horses much prefer this method of loading and unloading.

When we arrived in Moscow it was dark and pouring with rain, and there was no one to meet us! All we had been sent were six lorries with no covers and no loading ramps for the horses to walk up. I suppose they expected them to jump into the lorries! It took us nearly all night to get our horses unloaded and into the lorries, with the aid of the ramp we took from the aeroplane.

Though it did seem rather strange and unwelcoming at first, things improved considerably once we got used to the Russians and their ways. At one stage I asked them to give us eggs to cook for ourselves for breakfast at the stables, because the breakfast in the hotel was too late for our very carefully planned timetable.

'Yes,' said the interpreter. 'How many would you like?'

'Now let me see,' I replied, 'there are twelve of us, so two eggs each makes twenty-four eggs.'

'Ah,' he said, 'but we are only paying for eight of you!'

'Well then, I replied, 'shall we say eight of us and three eggs each!'

'Oh yes,' he said, beaming, 'that will be quite all right!'

The competition consisted of a dressage test on the first day; an endurance test on the second, and a show-jumping course on the third. The endurance test started with a stretch of two or three miles over roads and tracks at the trot and canter. This was followed by a two-mile steeplechase course done at the gallop; then another five to eight miles of roads and tracks. Finally there was a cross-country course of about four miles, with just over thirty fences, to be ridden at a fast canter.

In Moscow this was all very well arranged, and it was a good competition. Sadly, we only managed to finish third. The Russians won, and they were very good indeed.

The next year the World Championships were held at Burghley, in Lincolnshire, and this time we

Left: **The official British Team and individual riders for Kiev**
Below: **Horst Koehner (GDR) in immaculate style at Munich**

Above: **Bruce Davidson (USA) goes clear with Irish Cap**

Top: **A great partnership – Mary Gordon Watson with Cornishman**

were eliminated as two of our team failed to finish the cross-country course. I felt so ashamed that I wished the ground could have opened up and swallowed me.

The following year the European Championships took place at Punchestown, near Dublin, and this time we won the event. That was pretty exciting in itself, and it also gave us tremendous hopes for Mexico.

We travelled back from Ireland in a cattle boat with 700 fat beasts. Luckily the sea was calm! When we arrived at Holyhead the tide was out. It was dark and the ramp on to the narrow landing stage was very steep. We didn't think the horses would face this as it was also very slippery. We told the Captain, who said: 'All right, I'll unload 300 cattle from the other side of the boat and this will tip it up and make the ramp more level.' And it did!

And so to Mexico and all we had been dreaming and hoping and working for. But this time, not only were we up against the top horses and riders, because it was the Olympic Games, there was another serious problem – our competition was to take place at a height of about six thousand feet. As many of you will know, the higher up you get, the shorter of breath you are, until in time you get used to it and become, as they say, acclimatised.

For this reason we got the horses as fit as they could be, and went out a month before the competition so that they could rest on arrival and get used to the air, before being worked up to peak condition again.

It all went even better than we had hoped. By this time we had gathered a strong team of horses and riders. Major Allhusen and his Lochinvar, and Mr Whiteley's The Poacher remained from the Punchestown team. Sergeant Ben Jones of the King's Troop Royal Horse Artillery was to ride The Poacher, and in addition we had Jane Bullen, a very experienced competitor and past winner of Badminton, with Our Nobby, and Richard Meade on what was to become perhaps the greatest of eventers, Cornishman, who had been kindly lent to the team by Brigadier Gordon-Watson.

The Brigadier's famous daughter. Mary went on to win the European Championship the following year on Cornishman, and the year after that they won the World Championships together.

We also had two spare horses, but they were not quite as good, and so it was very important that our four main team horses should not go lame during our training. We had some anxious moments but in the end all went well.

The competition was to be held in a really lovely place – a golf course about a hundred miles from Mexico City – in a valley surrounded by trees, with a stream running down the middle. We lived in little chalets, and there was a wonderful swimming pool.

Our only worry was that every day at about two o'clock in the

Bottom: Columbus showing his brilliance with Captain Mark Philips at Burghley

Above: After the Dressage and Cross Country events, horse and rider have to show accuracy in the Show Jumping phase. *Right:* HRH Princess Anne and Goodwill going into the Pond during the Cross Country section of the Badminton Horse Trials. *Bottom right:* The Normandy Bank creates no problems for Columbus

afternoon, despite a lovely clear morning, it would pour with rain and parts of the course became flooded. The Mexicans said it would be all right by the time of the competition, but the big day drew nearer and nearer with no change!

On the dressage day, Sergeant Jones had to do his test in a very heavy thunderstorm, with lightning flashing in every direction. But just before The Poacher took his test he was frightened by some clapping from the crowd, and he reared, escaped from his groom and bolted back to the stables.

Luckily the stables were only about 200 yards away, and we got him back in time. At any other event the stables would have been much further away, and he would almost certainly have been disqualified for being late – our first bit of very good luck!

On cross-country day we asked the Mexicans to start early so that everyone would have finished before the rain, but they said this was not possible as there were distinguished visitors coming, and

all the plans had been made.

Lochinvar went first and did a good round with just one refusal. Next to go was Our Nobby, but he had two falls – one at the last fence where Jane's sister Jenny, who was acting as her groom, was fortunately there to help her. At one stage on the roads and tracks, when Jane was running alongside Our Nobby to rest him, she slipped up and let him go. As he started to gallop away she stretched out and caught him by his tail – our second bit of very good luck!

And then came the rains, harder than ever before, and flooding the stream down the middle of the course. Neither Richard Meade nor Sergeant Ben Jones had ridden their horses in a big competition before, and they did wonderfully well in such terrible conditions.

On the steeplechase course Sergeant Jones could not see the fences at all because it was raining so hard, but luckily The Poacher could! The last fence but one was a bank with a stream in front of it, and a rail in front of that to show the horses where to take off. When

Richard went the rail could still be seen, but for a long time afterwards it was underwater and several horses fell. Just before Ben Jones arrived, someone stuck some twigs in along the rail, and so The Poacher saw it in time – our third piece of really good luck!

And so on the last day the British team were still leading over the Americans and Australians, our chief rivals. It was an anxious time, but we held on to the lead, and in fact even managed to increase it. So those four years were over, and thanks to our wonderful horses and riders, we'd won the Gold Medal. You can imagine what excitement we felt and what celebrations we all had after that!

I was asked to go on for another four years, and naturally was delighted to accept. Luck continued to go with us, and we won all the next four competitions including the Gold Medal at the Munich Olympics.

We had all sorts of adventures, including another trip to Ireland and one to Haras du Pin in

Normandy. This was the first time that Captain Mark Phillips, who had been our reserve rider in Mexico, rode in the team. The following year at Burghley, Princess Anne, though not in the team, won the competition to become the European Champion.

Some people had said that the sport was too tough for the girls, especially if they were in the team, when even if hurt, they would have to carry on. At Haras du Pin, Polly Hely Hutchinson finally put paid to this idea, for, having taken a very stiff fall, she rode on, although she said later she would never have thought of continuing if she had not been in the team. Bertie Hill, himself a Gold Medallist at Stockholm, was at the fence, and gave Polly a leg up. 'What should I do Bertie?' she asked. 'sit down and ride like mad,' he replied, and she did!

And so for yet another four years! In 1973 we went to Kiev in Russia where they looked after us very well. The course was a big one, with a very large and difficult second fence of which many of you will have heard.

Princess Anne came with us to defend her Individual Title as European Champion. Unfortunately she had a heavy fall at the second fence and could not continue. The British team eventually finished third, behind the West Germans and the Russians.

Another World Championship Event was held at Burghley in 1974 when luck perhaps was not quite so much with us. Captain Mark Phillips had done a wonderful round on Her Majesty The Queen's Columbus, and would almost certainly have won the Individual Championship, but sadly Columbus became lame, and we could not get him fit in time for the next day.

In the end the British team was second, beaten by a strong American team who well deserved their success.

Throughout my time as Chef d'Equipe I have had tremendous help from riders, trainers, owners, grooms and, above all, our vet – Mr Peter Scott-Dunn. I can never thank these people enough.

Mares and Foals

Polo

Jonathan Alan

Polo is one of the oldest games in the world. There are drawings in the British Museum which show that the game of polo, which flourished in the East as long ago as 525 BC, was in some ways similar to the game which is now played all over the world. Even in those early days it was not only played by men. It is said that the ladies of Persia played polo in the reign of Chosroes, about 600 BC.

A fifteenth-century water-colour shows polo in China

Cachar Polo Club in India is considered to be the oldest polo club. It was founded in 1859 by some British tea planters in Assam, but it was not until some years later, in 1869, that the 10th Hussars introduced the game into Britain. A group of officers heard about the 'hockey on horseback' which was being played in India, and decided to have a go. They found some sticks with crooked ends, and mounted on chargers, they chased a billiards ball from one end of the parade ground to the other, with rather disastrous results. The sport was launched in Britain, however, and its popularity began to grow, particularly as it was thought that it might become a good training sport for young cavalry officers.

In 1869 the 10th Hussars chal-lenged the 9th Lancers to a match on Hounslow Heath, and by all accounts it was a very remarkable match. One of the best descriptions was published in that famous London paper of the time, the 'Morning Post', which said:

'Nearly all fashionable London journeyed from Town to Hounslow on Tuesday to witness a new game called "Hockey on Horse-back" between the Officers of the 9th Lancers and 10th Hussars. The 10th are quartered at Houns-low, and the 9th came up from Aldershot for the match.

'The game took place on Hounslow Heath, and the various equipages quite surrounded the space allotted to the players.

'Four upright posts, some twenty feet apart, marked the goals through which the ball (a small sphere of white bone) had to be driven by the players before either side could claim any ad-vantage. The sticks used were like those for hockey, of ash, and crooked at the end, and with these the ball was often struck a con-siderable distance. The distance between the goals was a little under 200 yards, and the players having taken up their positions in front of their own respective goals, the ball was thrown into the centre of the ground by a Sergeant Major of the 10th Hussars, who then galloped off, when each side immediately galloped for the ball at the best pace of their ponies. The 10th appeared in blue and yellow jerseys, and the 9th in parti-coloured shirts of blue and red, and both sides in mob caps with different coloured tassles attached.

'The game which has been im-ported from India, and which has been for a long time in vogue among the Manipoories, one of the Frontier tribes, was watched with the keenest interest by the numerous and aristocratic com-pany present. The game lasted for an hour and a half, with an interval of ten minutes when half-time had been played.

'The players numbered eight on each side, and were mounted on active, wiry little ponies about $12\frac{1}{2}$ hands high.

'At the end of the prescribed time, the Hussars had gained three goals to two gained by the Lancers; and although the general remarks made it evident that the new game is most fitted for Cavalry soldiers, it was admitted by all who were looking on that it was more remarkable for the strength of the language used by the players than for anything else. Mr Hartopp on the side of the Hussars, and Mr Moore on that of the Lancers were much applauded throughout the game for their activity and the speed of their ponies.'

Although this may have seemed a rather harum-scarum match, it

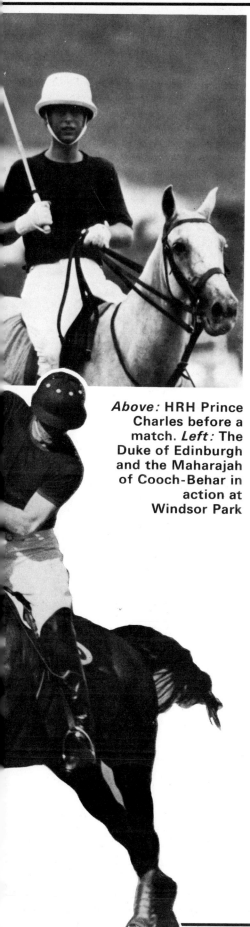

Above: HRH Prince Charles before a match. Left: The Duke of Edinburgh and the Maharajah of Cooch-Behar in action at Windsor Park

did draw attention to the sporting possibilities of polo, and shortly afterwards a set of proper rules were framed which restricted the number of players to four a side.

Until the start of the First World War, the height of polo ponies was limited, but this rule was dropped in 1918, enabling players to use much faster thoroughbreds and part thoroughbreds.

The Army, and the Cavalry officers in particular, kept polo alive in Britain up until 1939, but when many regiments had their horses replaced with motor vehicles, it seemed very likely that the game might die out. Since 1946, however, there has been a really remarkable interest in polo in Britain, and thanks to people like Lord Cowdray, who encouraged top sportsmen from other countries to play in Britain, the standard of play has improved considerably.

In the same way that Princess Anne's brilliance at eventing has done a great deal for that sport, so polo has benefited greatly from the active participation of the Duke of Edinburgh and his son Prince Charles. The Pony Club took an interest in polo in 1959, and decided to encourage young riders by holding an Annual Tournament which has now become a regular feature of the Summer Polo Programme.

Rather similar to the ladies of Persia who showed such interest in the sport all those thousands of years ago, the modern ladies of England and America have also shown tremendous keenness. Since the Ladies' Polo Association was formed in 1939, there have been some very brilliant lady lady players, and the Ladies Champion Cup at Hurlingham is always a very keenly fought game.

International polo is played at a really tremendous speed, and ponies are specially bred for their courage, speed and temperament. Besides the Championship Cup, the Military Tournament, County Polo and other important matches, there is the Westchester International Trophy which is played for in England and America.

Almost all well-bred ponies can

be used for the sport providing they are nimble, well mannered and game. Indeed, polo will improve a pony's manners by teaching it balance, and making it handy and obedient, because it has to be able to perform at all paces and under a wide variety of conditions. The rider must also develop a good seat and hands and cultivate those qualities that go to make up a polished horseman.

Expensive equipment is not necessary when a rider is starting. All that is needed is a child's plastic ball and a walking stick. Before attempting to hit the ball from the back of a pony, however, the rider should be taught the four fundamental strokes which can be developed into the fourteen various strokes necessary for good polo. This can be done either on a wooden horse or a bicycle. A mirror is also very helpful to show a player how well a stroke is being made. In this way the pony will be saved from being struck about its legs, or being jabbed in the mouth as its rider tries to hit the ball. It is also necessary to learn the rules thoroughly so that the finer points of the game can be appreciated from the start.

The pony will need boots and bandages to protect all its four legs against knocks from the stick and the ball; a pelham or double bridle; a standing martingale and a saddle. The rider should have a polo helmet for protection, a left-hand glove, a polo whip, boots and breeches and a suitable polo stick varying in length according to the height of the pony. A beginner may prefer to wear jodhpur boots to start with, but whatever boots are worn, they must have a good heel, because practically all polo players keep their feet well home in the stirrup irons.

As polo is frequently played on hard grounds without much grass it is as well to fit polo studs or calkins to the hind shoes of the pony to give it extra grip, and prevent it from slipping on the turns.

As far as the ground is concerned an ordinary football pitch is quite adequate to begin with, but the goal posts will have to be well padded to prevent damage to the pony and rider. The regulations state that a full-size ground should not be more than 300 yards in length or 200 yards in width, but if the ground is boarded the width should be reduced to 160 yards. There are four players on each side, and the maximum duration of play is limited to sixty minutes, divided into eight periods of seven and a half minutes each.

Two mounted umpires control the play, and there is also a referee who watches the match from a central position at the side of the ground. In all matches there is a half-time interval of at least five minutes after the third or fourth periods. All other intervals between the periods are usually of about three minutes duration to enable the riders to change to fresh ponies. Unlike most other games, there is no off-side rule in polo, and a goal is scored when the ball passes between the goal posts and over the goal line.

All players taking part in matches are given an official handicap by the Hurlingham Polo Club according to their experience and ability. The higher the handicap, the better the player, but the highest handicap anyone can be given is ten. Teams are also handicapped, and the differences in total between the teams goes to the benefit of the opposing team. This enables a less experienced team with a lower total handicap to play a stronger team and still have a chance of winning.

The correct schooling for the polo pony is an absolute essential and ponies that have been introduced too quickly to the game never reach top class. The great majority of intelligent and reasonably trained ponies can be schooled, providing their riders are prepared to have patience and understanding and don't try to play a pony until it understands what it is expected to do.

To begin with a pony must be taught to stop, turn, gallop on and answer quickly to the leg or alteration of its rider's weight. Once a pony has become handy and obedient it can be introduced

A fast chukka in progress at Cowdray Park

to the stick and ball, but before doing so the rider must ensure that he has complete control of the stick and that there is no fear that he might hit the pony by mistake. Again patience will be essential and the rider should spend a long time slowly gaining the pony's confidence by carrying a stick whenever he goes out for a ride, swinging it about gently, and rubbing it on the pony's neck until he has become so used to it that he will ignore its presence. Sometimes a trainer will hang up two or three sticks in the stable or by the door so that the pony will become accustomed to seeing them and will ignore them.

When the time comes to start hitting the ball from the pony, this must always be done at the walk by just tapping the ball steadily in front of the pony. It is also preferable to try and do this in a confined space so that if the pony does become frightened it is less likely to get out of control.

When the pony has become

used to the stick and ball the next and most difficult problem will be to persuade it to ride close to another pony. This can be done in the form of a musical ride with a number of riders each carrying a polo stick riding towards one another and persuading their ponies to keep as close to each other as possible.

When the time comes for the pony to play in its first game, everything should be taken very slowly so that it will gradually understand what is expected of it. Good experienced ponies seem to know almost as much about the game as their riders, and it is always easy to tell one that has been correctly and carefully schooled.

It should be remembered that polo is a team game, just like hockey or football, and individual selfish players can ruin a team. When played properly, and in the right spirit, it is one of the finest games, to be enjoyed by ponies, players and spectators alike.

THE DIDEKAI
by Judith Campbell

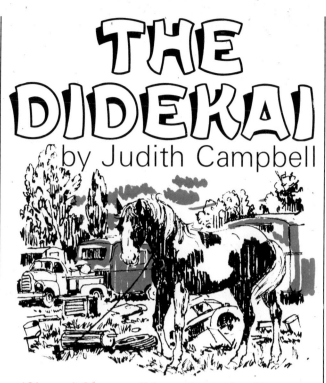

'Simon! Simon, did you hear that?'

Jacky's voice was so full of excitement that her brother, never at his best before breakfast, roused himself sufficiently to mumble 'Hear *what*, for heaven's sake? You do make a racket. . . !'

Jacky ran into his room, her eyes shining. 'It was the man on the radio,' she said, 'He's been talking about how the police moved on all those gypsies that have been camping along the Turnpike, you know, for ages – and then, when all the caravans and lorries had gone the police found they'd left a pony behind . . . all by itself!'

'A pony?' Simon was fully awake now. 'D'you think it's *that* pony. . . ?'

His sister nodded with conviction. 'Must be, the radio man said it was black-and-white.'

For a moment the children fell silent, their thoughts back with that day only a few weeks before when the car had conked out coming home along the Turnpike from a family picnic. It hadn't been a very serious breakdown, their father had fixed it quite quickly, but while he was fiddling about under the bonnet the children had looked at the encampment, across the road from their lay-by. It looked more like a rubbish dump than an encampment. There were big heaps of every kind of junk, rags, empty tin cans, and piles of rusty bits and pieces of what had once been cars. It bore no resemblance to the gypsy camps their mother had described seeing, when she was a girl and the Romanys were on the roads. These people didn't look like the secretive, dark-skinned race from India either, who their mother said had been the traditional horse-dealers – sometimes horse-stealers – of the world. And there was certainly nothing that reminded her of the gaily painted horse-drawn waggons about this selection of trailers pulled by old bangers and lorries not in their first youth. ('Diddies! Drop-outs!' said their father scathingly, glancing up from his tinkering.)

And then, just as the car roared into life once more, the pony had wandered into sight, tethered with a long rope round its neck and grazing amongst all the junk.

Their parents were in a hurry to get home and there had been only a moment to look at it, but it was so exactly the kind of pony that could fill the Twala Club's most pressing need, that as Jacky had remarked: 'It was like having a little bit of a dream coming to life. . . .'

'I expect you're right and its the same pony,' said Simon now, trailing down to breakfast. 'But even if it is, I can't see there's much to get excited about.'

'Oh, but that wasn't all the radio man said – the RSPCA are looking after the pony and are trying to trace its owners, but if they can't find them they'll look for a good home for it. . . .' There was an expression on his sister's face that Simon knew well, it meant she was hatching a plan. But as he started to remark witheringly, 'Well, if you really think . . .' he realised Jacky wasn't listening. She was rummaging in the kitchen for her riding cap and shouting impatiently, 'Come on, do hurry, its our turn for Jobiska and Spot, and if we're late they won't get a decent rest before the others take them out!'

Only two years before, riding and looking after ponies had been as much of an unattainable dream for this brother and sister as for the six other members of the Twala Club. Then Mrs Jameson, who lived on the hill and wrote occasional, odd books about horses, had suddenly decided it was time she came down to earth and did something concrete. And by that she meant something about the little group of local children she was always lecturing for feeding Twala on iced lollies, ham sandwiches and all the other highly unsuitable fare that would have given any other pony acute colic within minutes. She had a plan, she said, and she coerced them into it. After that things had started to happen.

As Mrs Jameson said with truth, the one commodity they all lacked was money, but they could make up for that with enthusiasm

– and the children's matched her own. Before anyone really realised how it came about, those eight children had been sponsored for some riding lessons. Then, with at least the basic facts of correct riding drilled into their eager heads, the Club had been formed and they started out on the big adventure of acquiring their own horse-sense. Mrs Jameson made only one all-embracing rule – that the members of the Twala Club should do all the work, properly, and she would chase them up if they didn't!

For the first few weeks there had been just those eight members, and just Twala to practise on, look after, and fall off. As Simon and Jacky ran down the lane that morning eager for their ride, they stopped to have a word with him. Twala, always enchanted to see 'his people', whinnied and strolled over to eat a carrot and have his ears scratched. Mrs Jameson said Twala had taught more children to ride than she could remember, and he had won innumerable rosettes for jumping and gymkhana races, but now he was old. For a while after Aunt Jobiska and Spot came on the scene, Twala still did his share, but now, although still gay and willing, his elderly joints did not allow much work. He only came out of retirement for special occasions, and here lay THE PROBLEM – that eight keen riders don't divide into two ponies all that satisfactorily.

Of course the Club had a rota, for riding in turn, just as they had other rotas for watering, feeding and tack cleaning; of course both Spot and Jobiska had a minimum of twenty-four hours off work every week, and their feed was always stepped up so that they could cope easily with the work in hand. And in the beginning, when no one was good enough to ride very far or do very much, it had been all right. Even now, when dark evenings restricted riding in the winter to holidays and weekends, weather permitting, lack of a third pony wasn't too noticeable. But from Easter through the summer, now they could all jump and wanted to go in for gymkhanas, now they were capable of galloping down by the sea, taking breakwaters and salty pools in their stride, now they would all love to ride for hours – if only there weren't always two more riders to have a turn that day, and consideration for the ponies was of course number one priority – one more pony would just make all the difference.

'Which is why,' said Jacky suddenly and apropos of nothing in particular, 'I'm writing to the RSPCA and offering that pony, just the sort of pony we want, a good home with the Twala Club!'

Simon was riding Aunt Jobiska, the grey cob with the kind eyes that Mrs Jameson had managed to acquire as a rescue operation. She was still not exactly a beauty, but she was round and plump in the right places, and was hardly recognisable as the poor wreck of eighteen months before, with a pitifully thin neck and ribs standing out like a toast-rack. In all the world there was no pony better at taking on timid young riders totally lacking in horse-sense, and teaching them how to go for a hack, how to pop over an 18-inch pole, how to come to the understanding and companionship that should make life with a pony a constant joy. Even so Jobiska had her reservations. When Simon gave a hoot of laughter and dug her unnecessarily hard with his heels, she whisked her tail indignantly and shot straight from her up-and-down walk into her own, rather odd version of a gallop.

This was altogether too much for Spotty, the splendid 13-hand Welsh pony that the Club were lucky enough to have been loaned 'indefinitely'. He was beautifully schooled and jumped like a rocket, but he was not above 'taking the mickey' out of an inattentive rider. Now he caught Jacky out with a buck that left her temporarily out of control, and set off in pursuit of Jobiska at a speed that caught and passed the mare before they were half-way across the next field.

'You might have warned me . . .' shouted Jacky as the ponies, fun over for the time being, condescended to slow down to a more manageable canter, but Simon only grinned. 'Didn't know myself, Jobiska caught me out, too – I was busy laughing! Just think,' he chanted, 'just think of your poor little letter arriving, one little letter amongst all the thousands and thousands and thousands of others, from every pony-mad girl in the country!'

A reply from the RSPCA arrived three weeks later. They thanked Jacky for her offer (her letter was one 'of a great number' received) . . . they noted the Twala Club's good efforts at doing everything for themselves, but under supervision . . . and appreciated that though everything possible was done to raise funds, there was nothing left over for buying a pony . . . under the circumstances the Society took pleasure in 'short-listing' the Twala Club as a possible future home for the pony in question . . . BUT, it must be stressed

did seem a bit unlikely they'd just abandon something they'd actually bought, but then it could have been exchanged – and there was always this rising cost of hay.

Mrs Jameson reported back to the Club. Simon listened and then took himself off to see the local police sergeant. Could he possibly tell him where the gypsies were now? Well, yes, he could – they were twelve miles away in a spinney where they had no right to be, just off the road between Coltsby and Witham.

Simon got up early, wrote a note to say he'd gone for a bike ride – a one-time favourite occupation – cut some sandwiches and found a road map. As he set off the sun was just coming up, the sky was full of small, fluffy, pink-tipped clouds, there was a blackbird singing fit to bust in the sycamore tree by the gate. It would have been a marvellous morning to take a pony out, but this jaunt was much too far for Jobiska or Spot. By the time he was toiling through Coltsby High Street in the heat of the day, Simon was beginning to wonder if perhaps it wasn't rather a long haul for a thirteen-year old boy.

The spinney was about two miles outside the town, and you couldn't miss it because it seemed already to be overflowing with exactly the same collection of junk they'd noticed at the Turnpike, only of course this time there was no pony grazing amongst it.

It was difficult to know how to begin. Simon stood leaning on his bike and gazing into the camp while a clutch of very small and very dirty children gazed back at him in total silence. Then a lurcher, one of the many different varieties of dog wandering around, decided to object to the silent stranger and began to bark at him. Other dogs rushed to join the fun until there was a bristling chorus, snarling and yelping within a few yards of his bicycle.

Simon was used to a dog, if not dogs, but he couldn't pretend he wasn't frightened. However, he knew better than to turn away quickly and invite an attack, and suddenly there was a man's voice cursing the dogs, and a boy, some years older than himself, cuffing them off back into the camp. Still Simon didn't move, and the boy said, 'You better be off!' It was now or never, and Simon found his voice. 'Did you ever have a pony?' he asked.

The boy was swarthy as a real Romany. He drew his thick brows together over dark eyes that were suddenly watchful and threatening. 'What do you mean?' he demanded roughly. 'What pony? Why should I have a pony?' This boy was big, and he was angry, and

that there was no question of placing the pony anywhere until its previous owners had been traced.

If the letter scarcely fulfilled Jacky's wildest hopes, even Simon had to admit it was better than it might have been. They told Mrs Jameson the story. They called a special meeting of the Club. 'Somehow we've got to find out that pony's history,' they told the members, and everyone pledged themselves to try.

Mrs Jameson went to the police. They were sympathetic but their information was not very helpful. To begin with no one had reported even losing a nice-looking, 14-hand piebald gelding aged about nine years. The gypsies insisted they'd bought it at Appleby Fair, that a friend had dropped it off for them at the Turnpike, that there was no transport when they were 'moved on', so they left it behind. The story could be true, there were still horses enough at the Fair, the gypsies' great annual gathering, and all transactions were still 'done by hand' – no written contracts, no records. It

obviously he liked Simon as little as the dogs. Nothing for it but to give him the whole story, and out it came, non-stop, about seeing the lovely piebald, the Twala Club, oh, everything.

Curiously, the boy stopped looking angry quite quickly, but he didn't smile. Maybe he didn't smile much anyway. 'Yes,' he interrupted suddenly, 'That was my pony – I found it!' 'Found it?' repeated Simon a little doubtfully, with a thought for Appleby Fair. 'We was on Shaghill Common, I was getting a hare and there was this pony, not tethered nor nothing, just wandering and grazing, looked kind of lost. I rode 'im in – he's a good 'un!' 'Without a head-collar?' inquired the practical-minded Simon. The boy looked scornful. 'We're horse folk – not like some . . .' with a glance behind him to the camp. 'My Uncle Jem, he'd been up Appleby and got a lorry load of horses, he brought the pony to Turnpike for me . . . but there was no way for him when we left.'

As Simon headed for home the boy called after him: 'Don't you forget, he's a good 'un!'

The Twala Club were delighted, they were getting somewhere, even if they still didn't know how the pony came to be on Shaghill Common in the first place.

Mrs Jameson rang the RSPCA, realising as she did so that their address was only a few miles from that same Common. The Society were impressed. They had also decided, although still unable to do anything permanent, to loan the pony to one of the three applicants now on the short list – final selection of the lucky one to go to the rider who got on best with the pony. Would Mrs Jameson like to bring a Twala Club member over, and ride out with the pony? A borrowed horse for herself was available.

The amiable chestnut of uncertain vintage suited Mrs Jameson very well. For once words had failed Jacky. The piebald was even more lovely than she had remembered and, trotting along the lanes to Shaghill Common, she was finding that his comfortable paces and willing good manners matched his looks. Once on the common, the merest touch and he slipped into a canter as smooth as silk, yet he was willing to remain quite happily behind the solid quarters of Mrs Jameson's chestnut. Until, that is, without the slightest warning, the piebald pony flipped right-handed while the chestnut went straight on, and without any increase in pace, or the slightest regard for his rider, continued on down the track towards a distant cottage.

By the time a flustered Mrs Jameson had discovered their absence and tracked them down, the piebald pony was standing with his head over a gate looking into a little garden. 'What *are* you doing, Jacky?' demanded Mrs Jameson crossly. 'I've no idea!' said Jacky cheerfully, 'We'll have to ask him!'

At that moment a grey-haired woman wearing very colourful jeans came out of the cottage and advanced upon them, cooing; 'Good morning, can I do . . . ?', when her eye took in the pony leaning over her gate, and she gave a little scream. 'Oh! It's darling boy – it must be darling boy! Wherever have you been, my pet? Oh, what a clever little girl to find my darling boy!'

It was all very bewildering and rather muddled, and it took quite a while to sort out, but they managed it in the end. This was the pony's original owner, and when her husband had taken a job in America 'all in a rush', she had yielded to the persuasions of a girl she knew vaguely and who lived a few miles away, to 'give darling boy a home'. It had never occurred to her that the girl's undoubted 'love' for ponies went along with almost total ignorance of how to care for them. She had now just got back for a flying visit to arrange the sale of the cottage, and was still suffering from the shock and horror of discovering, only that morning, that 'darling boy' was missing; that when the price of hay had rocketed those people had actually brought the pony along to the Common and turned him loose to fend for himself – and seemed not to care what happened next!

There was a lot of this story and it took a long time to tell, but it resulted in the only possible solution – of *course* the Twala Club should have 'darling boy'.

So, a few days later, a kind of a reception committee met down the lane from Jacky's home. There was Twala leaning over the fence with his ears so pricked they were nearly meeting; there was Jobiska, looking coy and inclined to squeal; and Spotty, his intelligent little face wearing a thoughtful expression as though he was wondering just who might be going to be boss now? One close look at the piebald pony and all the Club members had been reduced to 'ooing' and 'aahing'. Then someone asked his name. '*She* called him "darling boy" . . .' volunteered Jacky dubiously.

Simon broke the stunned silence. 'We're going to call him The Didekai,' he announced. 'My Dad says it means a half-bred Romany.'

Training the Royal Horses
by Alison Oliver

As a young girl I used to spend all my spare time at the local riding stable, doing odd jobs and trying to make myself useful in return for rides. I never even in my wildest dreams thought that one day I would have the Queen's horses in my care, and help her daughter, Princess Anne, to be the first Princess to become the European Ladies Champion.

Every evening, when I walk round the stables and look in at horses like Arthur of Troy, Columbus, his first sister Candlewick, and the other Royal horses, I can still hardly believe my good fortune.

It doesn't seem so long ago that I had my first pony, a very flighty little six-year-old mare called Minnie, who was much too big and strong for me. As my parents knew nothing about horses and ponies, they had bought her because they thought she looked nice.

Top: **The West Lancashire Branch of the Pony Club Event team. Alison Oliver is on the left.** *Above:* **Nick and Minnie who were always very game**

I was seven years old and had been spending all my spare time hanging around the stables near my home at Aughton in Lancashire, where I lived with my parents, an elder brother and two younger sisters.

The stables were owned by a wonderfully kind and clever horseman called Harry Monks, and

although I used to save up two weeks' pocket money for an occasional lesson, he encouraged me by allowing me to exercise some of his ponies in return for help, mucking out, filling hay nets, feeding, grooming, carrying water buckets, cleaning tack and any other job that a horse-mad seven-year-old was able to do.

I often think now that I was probably more of a nuisance than a help, but Mr Monks never made me feel that that was the case.

The ponies he kept were all sorts of shapes and sizes and temperaments, and I soon learnt that there was more to riding than just sitting on a saddle and holding the reins.

By the time my parents bought me Minnie I was beginning to realise that horses and ponies, like humans, have likes and dislikes, frustrations and fears, and that no two are the same, and each requires some special extra understanding.

Apart from being a brilliant horseman, Mr Monks was also a sort of horse psychiatrist, and he persuaded me to try to learn, not only how ponies thought, but how they reacted to either a word of encouragement or a word of reprimand.

Not many young hopefuls can have had such a wise and helpful teacher, and I was always grateful to him for making me aware of the need to size up and assess each horse or pony, and to study their own special ways, in order to get the maximum co-operation from them.

Alison Oliver with Candy who used to bolt when people clapped

Mr Monks was my hero, and whenever I could, I tried to persuade my parents to take me to the local ballroom, not because I wanted to dance, but because Mr Monks used to take along his favourite horse, Golden Jay, a big 16.2-hands chestnut, which he fitted with special shoes and gave

dancing displays on! Sometimes as a treat I was allowed to sit on him and walk round the yard.

When I was nine, I joined the West Lancashire Branch of the Pony Club, and had a great deal of fun at shows and rallies, although I didn't always cover myself in glory. At one gymkhana, when I was riding a pony belonging to a friend, I remember being bucked off in all the races and having to walk ignominiously back to the collecting ring, where someone had caught the pony ready for me to have another go. There was quite a cheer when I managed to stick on for the final race.

With help and encouragement from the instructors, I finally got into the Pony Club event team with a wonderful grey pony called Nick which my parents bought as a four-year-old from Mr Monks. Nick really had a very posh name, but no one ever used it. He was 14.2 hands and part Welsh, and he meant a great deal to me, because I was the one that backed him when he was broken in at the local riding school. He turned out to be a super ride.

I had a lot of jumping successes with him. I remember one Pony Club Show when I won the 14.2-hand class on Nick; my sister Judy won the 13.2-hand class on Minnie, and my youngest sister Mary won the 12.2-hand class on Robin, the first pony I ever rode at Mr Monks' stable.

It was quite a day for us, and I remember the pride with which we all took home our cups and put them on the sideboard for my father to see when he got home that evening.

Soon afterwards I was sent away to school at Tenby in Wales, and although I still managed to ride while I was there, I hated it most of the time, and couldn't wait for the holidays when I could get back to my beloved Nick.

Nick was sold when I was away at school, because my parents felt there was a limit to the amount of money they could spend keeping the ponies during term time. I remember crying myself to sleep at night and hoping that he was being well looked after.

I needn't have worried, because he went to a very charming family, and although I never rode him again I often used to go and see him during the holidays.

My first experience with horses was very short lived. My father bought me a horse called Country Life which we nicknamed Tommy, and soon after having him I had a fall and broke my leg. My parents decided they couldn't keep Tommy while I was hobbling around with my leg in plaster, and he was very soon sold.

When I was seventeen I left school, and although my parents did not encourage me to go and work with horses, they realised that that was all I really wanted to do, and that I would never be happy doing anything else.

I passed the Assistant Instructors Certificate of the British Horse Society while I was studying with Mr Monks, but I had to look for new opportunities to further my career.

We were lucky that Mrs Hilary Booth had a stable of very fine show horses in Aughton, and I was able to go and work for her. I had already ridden some of her horses at various shows. Although she never rode herself, she was tremendously interested in the reasons why horses behaved differently, and we used to stay up together until the early hours of the morning, discussing various horses and wondering how we could learn to understand them better.

When I went to shows to compete with Mrs Booth's sister, Kay, I used to come out of the ring and spend hours watching the horses and ponies, not just the riders and their performances, but also trying to work out why a particular horse or pony behaved in the way it did. There was so much I didn't understand, and so much I wanted to learn.

After my taste of eventing in the West Lancashire Pony Club, I was anxious to spend more of my time competing in this fascinating sport. I have always found eventing one of the most interesting ways there is to learn about horses and ponies, and to develop mutual trust and

Marley Password at Harewood in 1958

confidence between horse and rider.

I gradually persuaded Mrs Booth to extend her interest from showing to eventing, and before long I started eventing horses for her, and had my first real success with a horse called Marley Password. This was a part-bred Irish mare who was highly strung, temperamental, bad in traffic and a thorough menace,

She belonged to some neighbours of Mrs Booth, and one day after she had thrown her rider, we were asked to keep her at Mrs Booth's stables to see whether we could do anything with her while her owner recovered from her injury.

She was the sort of horse who had to be handled with tremendous understanding and patience, and all the early training and advice I had had from Mr Monks proved invaluable.

I would spend hours persuading her to jump a ditch, and then when we got back to the stables she would refuse to go into her box!

She really was a most frustrating and antagonising animal, but we realised her possibilities, and Mrs Booth was able to buy her quite cheaply from her owner who was by then anxious to get rid of her.

I owe a lot to 'Marley', who not only taught me more about the mind of a horse, but also gave me my first exciting rides across the great event courses of Harwood and Badminton.

Luck plays an important part in everyone's career, and it was certainly lucky for me when I was introduced to Mrs Joan Gold, who asked me to come and work for her at the stables she owned at Warfield, a little village in Berkshire.

All sorts and types of horses were sent to the stables for special schooling, and apart from helping with their training, I was able to ride many of them in competitions. Some of these horses I remember with great affection, but there were others who are perhaps best forgotten!

But even horses like Touchwood had their good points. He was an unbelievably difficult horse, and would even run away on the lunge rein, pulling whoever was trying to school him along behind!

But although he was a problem, he was very honest and courageous once he decided to get on with the job.

I eventually bought Touchwood, and then sold him to buy another grey called Fairplay, who was afterwards jumped with considerable success by my husband, Alan.

We weren't married at the time, and it was Alan's father who saw me jumping him, and asked whether he could buy him for his son, who had an extremely good string of Grade A horses, and was making quite a name for himself as an international rider.

Fairplay was a very sensitive horse, but like all sons of Colonist II, that brilliant race horse once owned by Sir Winston Churchill, he was very temperamental.

My husband Alan still had him when we were married.

Another of my favourite horses was Freeman, a stocky little chestnut that I also rode at Badminton. He was part-bred Irish and very bold, and gave me a lot of fun before I finally sold him.

I have always hated selling horses that have given me so much pleasure, but over the years I have realised that providing you find the right home for them, and they have been well schooled, they will also be able to give their new owners a great deal of enjoyment.

Soon after I sold Freeman, the Olympic Committee bought a horse called Foxdor, which they sent to me to school and to ride in competitions. His record was not particularly good, and he had certainly ended up on the floor more times than I cared to think about!

I took him over to Ireland and rode him at Punchestown. It was the first three-day event they had ever held there, and the course was absolutely enormous. We were going well until we reached the water, which had a big post and rails in front. Unfortunately Foxdor tipped up, and we both ended up in the water. He slightly injured his shoulder, which meant we were unable to finish the course.

Alison Oliver riding Foxdor in the 1966 World Championships

very important that she should do so, because however well trained a horse might become, it is essential for the rider to school with the horse.

She proved to be an excellent pupil. She always tries to get the best out of any horse, and she is very lucky to have fantastic balance, which is not only a great asset when riding over the big fences to be found on international event courses, but it also enables her to have a good firm seat, and excellent, sympathetic hands.

Purple Star soon had a number of other horses from the Royal stables to keep him company, such as Doublet, the horse Princess Anne rode to become European Champion. Like most of the royal horses, he had been bred by the Queen, and he proved to be very much an individual – but then all

He went well with me at the horse trials at Tidworth, and then in 1966 I rode him in the World Championships at Burghley. After giving me a brilliant ride, he stopped at the Coffin, which had always been a bogey fence with him, and I fell off. The fence consists of a post and rails and a ditch, and he managed to get his legs through the rails so that I had little chance of staying on. I managed to hold on to the reins, however, and after remounting we finished the rest of the course successfully, and ended up in eighth place.

Soon after that the Olympic Committee passed him over to Sergeant Ben Jones to train for the Mexico Olympics, and they had a number of hair-raising falls together.

I was really fond of that little horse because we developed a trust in each other, and I learnt to understand his problems.

By that time I had proved that I could produce and train horses to international standards and I was prepared to take on the awkward horses as well as the good ones.

One day the phone rang at home, and I was thrilled to hear Colonel Miller's voice on the other end of the line.

Colonel Miller is the Crown Equerry, and he asked if I would train a horse called Purple Star for Princess Anne. He was a five-year-old bay gelding about 16 hands high, who had been bred by Colonel Miller out of his old Olympic mare, Stella. Purple Star is still a great favourite with Princess Anne, who hunts him whenever she has the time.

I told Colonel Miller that I would be delighted, and it was arranged that I should drive over to Windsor to meet Princess Anne, who was then about sixteen years old and still at school.

Although she had ridden for many years, and was a keen member of the Pony Club, she had never done any eventing or really competitive riding.

After Colonel Miller had shown me round the Royal stables, Princess Anne and I went for a hack in Windsor Great Park, and that was the first time that I rode the famous Doublet, who was then four years old, and had just been broken. Princess Anne rode Blue Star, Purple Star's elder brother.

I was very impressed with her enthusiasm and keenness to learn, and it was agreed that I would take Purple Star home with me to Warfield, and that Princess Anne would come over whenever she could to ride him there. It was

horses are individuals! He was rather aloof and somewhat shy, but always generous in anything that he did, and always tried so hard to please, the real proof of what we call 'a good 'un'.

He would give of his best in the indoor school, or when we were out at exercise, but if he became bored and wanted to do something different, he would somehow show it, and then we would vary his training or exercise periods. This is something you can only do with an honest or obedient horse or pony, because it is never a good thing to change a routine or exercise, just because a horse is being naughty. In the case of Doublet we were anxious to keep his interest. During the early days that we had him we tried hunting him, but that only made him unsettled, and we never hunted him again.

How different he was to Columbus, the horse which Captain Mark Phillips rode to so many victories with such wonderful understanding. Princess Anne had ridden Columbus on a number of occasions, but he is really more of a man's horse, being a big 17.1-hands grey, by the famous Colonist II, the sire of so many of the Queen's horses.

Columbus has always been quite a character. Apart from being highly strung, he absolutely hates being looked at, and when he is in the stable he seems much happier being left completely alone. Although this reaction is not unknown, most horses and ponies are only too pleased when someone comes to the door of the stable and shows an interest in them. In fact it is far better if a rider can spend a reasonable amount of time each day with their horse or pony. Doing so makes them more responsive and, like most animals, they are usually

Left: **Purple Star being ridden by Alison Oliver at Tweesledown**
Above: **Doublet at the start of his eventing career**

glad to see you.

However, Columbus is different, and has to be treated with a lot of sympathy and calmness. Like most animals, he can't stand being teased. He is, however, a very honest horse, and will invariably do what is asked of him without being too difficult. Certainly with Captain Mark Phillips in the saddle he usually behaves impeccably.

Being a big horse he finds the dressage phase of a three-day event very difficult, but as he is so honest he tries hard, and still manages good marks. He is without question a horse who needs understanding, but he has a mind and brain which can be put to advantage with careful training and sympathetic riding.

I was particularly sad when

Columbus had to be withdrawn at the Championships at Burghley in 1974 after the cross-country phase, when he and Captain Mark Phillips were in the lead, and were almost sure to win the Gold Medal for Britain. As they neared the end of the testing course, Captain Phillips realised that something was wrong, and when they pulled up, it was found that Columbus had injured his hock, and had to be withdrawn from the final show-jumping phase.

Princess Anne had a number of successes on a 16-hand grey gelding called Collingwood, who was also sired by Colonist II. The horse was never one of the Princess's favourites, however, and after she had competed with him in several shows he was eventually sold to Mr John Smart, who has since evented him successfully.

A more popular horse with Princess Anne is Candlewick, a half sister of Columbus. She is a very beautiful dark brown mare who looks almost black on occasions. She was also bred by the Queen, but unlike Columbus, she has a wonderful temperament, being calm and kind, and we are hoping that, like Arthur of Troy, she will develop into a really fine international eventer.

Princess Anne is very lucky in having parents who encourage her riding ambitions, and she is now also fortunate to have a husband who loves eventing and all forms of equestrian sport as much as she does.

I first met Her Majesty the Queen at a Horse Trials when Princess Anne was competing, and it was obvious from the start how thrilled she was with her daughter's success. Although he prefers polo, Prince Philip also goes along to watch Princess Anne whenever he can and their enthusiasm and interest has become infectious. They are such a wonderfully natural and relaxed family to be with.

There cannot be any other country in the world, or perhaps any other sport, where the Royal Family can take such an active part, and meet other competitors

Setting off to walk the course with Princess Anne. *Opposite:* Princess Anne during the European Championships at Burghley. After entering the Trout Hatch Doublet slips but manages to find some firmer ground and with an encouraging pat from Princess Anne they are on their way again

Above: **Princess Anne receives the European Championship from the Queen and Prince Philip**
Right: **After their brilliant performance Princess Anne and Doublet receive a tremendous ovation from the crowd**

Patience is essential; understanding and sympathy are vital. I find the day-to-day challenge of each horse and pony, with their various characters and temperaments, to be absolutely fascinating. I have grown to realise that horses and ponies are never just 'made'; they all require making, and I am glad that I have devoted my life to doing just that. It is the job I love, and I am sure that, had my earlier circumstances been different, I would still have found my life and fulfilment in the equestrian world.

My advice to any young horse lover who wants to make a life with horses is to watch, read, and ride as much as they can. Have patience and never give in, despite the problems they are bound to come up against from time to time.

Alison Oliver is the wife of Alan Oliver, one of Britain's best-known International show-jumping riders. They have a young son, Philip, and live in a large country house near Windsor, surrounded by the horses they help to make famous.

and their families with complete freedom of movement and in such a happy atmosphere.

Captain Mark Phillips leads a very busy army life, but in his free time he frequently joins Princess Anne in schooling sessions over the cross-country course adjoining my home near Windsor.

In the careful training programme needed to prepare a horse for a big international event, we have to treat each horse quite separately and as an individual. We have to make use of all the facilities we have available, including the indoor schools; manèges; open country; quiet roads; show-jumping courses; and cross-country fences.

If we find a horse is losing concentration we vary his training programme, and as soon as he has learnt the lesson we are trying to teach him, we either put him back into the stable or give him something fresh to do, so that he never loses interest. Repeating the same thing over and over again never does much good in the long run.

Treating a Sick Pony

by Alan Britton

Ponies, unlike more highly-strung thoroughbreds, are remarkably tough and resilient, but even so the sight of a favourite pony sick or lame is something every owner dreads.

If you ensure that your pony is looked after properly, and is given the necessary care and consideration, the likelihood of it becoming unsound is very much reduced.

A healthy pony feeds up well, and is alert and interested in its surroundings. Its ears are pricked and the linings of the eyes and nostrils are salmon-pink in colour. It will stand evenly on all four feet, and although it is quite common for a pony to rest a hind foot, it is a sure sign of trouble if it tries to rest a fore foot.

Droppings should be passed about eight times a day, and be firm enough to break on hitting the ground. The pony should 'stale' easily, several times a day, and the urine should be light yellow in colour. Unlike its owner, a pony would be said to have a normal temperature of about 100.5 degrees fahrenheit, and respirations of ten to twelve a minute.

If a pony becomes sick or lame it should immediately be made as comfortable as possible, and kept away from other animals, although not necessarily out of sight of them. A loose-box or a separate paddock should be provided, and the pony should be handled with extra gentleness and understanding.

Lameness is the commonest form of unsoundness in a pony, and may be caused either by sprains or strains or by bony enlargements. Sprains affecting nerves or muscles are of less importance than those affecting tendons, ligaments or joints which can be far more serious. A bony enlargement or swelling, providing it is clear of the joint, need not necessarily cause concern.

An all too frequent illness in ponies is known as laminitis, or fever of the feet. This is extremely painful, and the pony will find difficulty in walking. It is usually caused by the pony being turned out in a field where the grass is far too rich. Rest and very careful feeding will be essential as well as an immediate visit from the veterinary surgeon.

If your pony becomes lame, you will have to find out where the trouble is and in which leg. By trotting your pony gently along the road you will see that if it is lame in the foreleg it will nod its head each time the sound leg comes to the ground. If the lameness is in one of the hind legs, the weight will be seen to be on the sound leg when it is put to the ground.

About ninety per cent of all lameness is centred in the foot, and so that is where you should start. As you feel your way gradually along the pony's leg, compare the one you are examining with the other leg, not only for size and shape, but also to see if any unusual heat is present.

There are some very common reasons for lameness. Perhaps a stone has become lodged between the shoe and the frog. The pony's sole may have become bruised by a sharp object like a flint, and be tender to pressure and show a red mark where the bruising has occurred. If the pony has been shod recently, one of the nails may be pressing on a sensitive area of the foot, or it may have actually entered the sensitive part. Ponies can also get corns through badly fitting shoes, and in severe cases these may even cause festering.

Ringbones, which are bony enlargements of the pastern bone either above or below the coronet, can be more serious, and if they interfere with the joint more permanent lameness may result. Side-bones, which occur in the region of the heel, are also serious because the flexibility of the heel may be lost.

Thrush, however, is a much more common complaint. It is a foul condition of the frog of the foot due to neglect which will need daily cleaning and dusting with a dry dressing.

If your pony has put its foot in a rabbit hole it may well develop a sprained fetlock, which is not as serious as it sounds, providing the injury is treated without delay, but the joint will become swollen and painful to the pony.

Another form of fetlock strain is known as a windgall, which is a swelling of the joint sacs which can again be painful when first formed. However, a windgall usually responds quickly to treatment and causes little real trouble.

Sprained tendons are a far more formidable problem. They are caused by strain and are particularly common among jumpers. Your pony may, however, suffer

Above: Prevention is better than cure and so always make sure your pony is properly bandaged and rugged when travelling
Left: Loose boxes allow the pony a greater measure of freedom
Above right: Regular visits from the blacksmith are essential
Far right above: The hoof pick is used for cleaning out the feet
Below right: To check for lameness trot the pony along an even surface
Far right below: The bridle must fit comfortably or a sore mouth will result

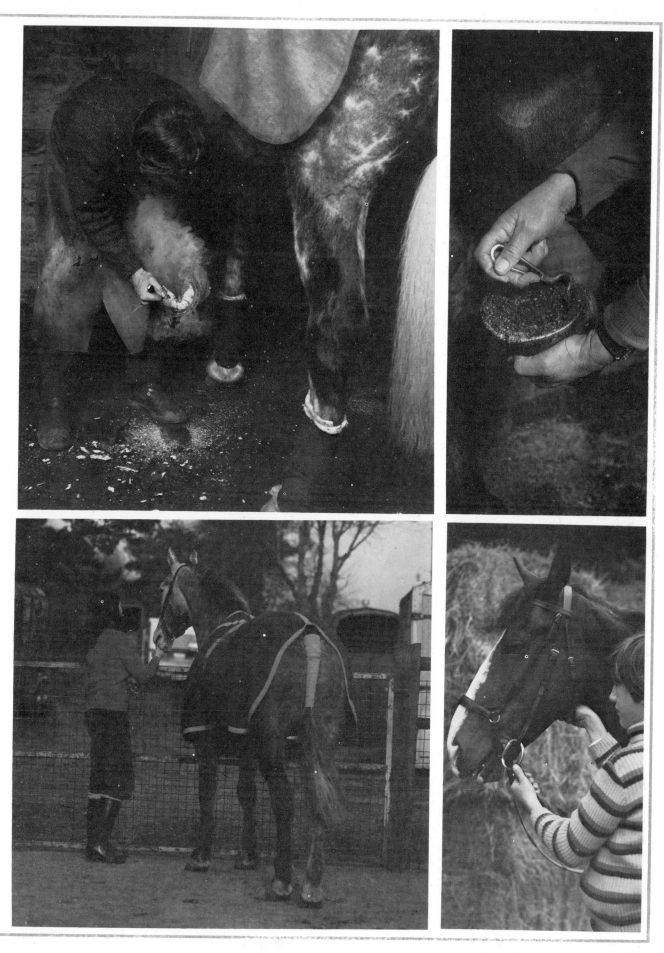

from a fever or a cold, or plain tummy ache, known as colic. Once you have seen a pony with colic you will never forget the symptoms. Apart from being restless and off its feed, it will look intermittently around at its flanks and try to kick itself in the tummy. It will also get up and down and roll at frequent intervals.

The usual cause of colic is irregular feeding, sudden changes of diet, chronic indigestion from poor quality hay, or taking sand into its intestines through drinking water from shallow, sandy bottomed streams or rivers.

The pony must be kept warm and given a colic drink. By walking it slowly round you will also be able to prevent it from doing injury to itself and rolling.

Contagious diseases, such as strangles, spread very quickly, but fortunately this is an illness which affects younger ponies more than older animals. It is worrying, but rarely dangerous.

Coughs and influenza are, of course, common complaints, and like us, ponies can also suffer from these diseases and cuts and bruises caused by jagged bits of metal, flints, barbed wire.

Very often it is the small wound which seems to cause the problem. A horse in my stable tore a great gash in its side by galloping through a gap which had a large nail protruding from one of the posts. When the vet came to stitch it I wondered whether it would be the same horse again, but a month later it was being ridden, and within six weeks it was almost impossible to see the scar.

Small wounds, unless they are properly treated, however, can cause considerable trouble, and may mean that you will be unable to ride your pony for weeks.

Ringworm and sweetich are common complaints in ponies. You will not be very popular if your pony gets ringworm because this can be transferred from ponies to humans, and you should call a vet immediately. Sweetich, when a pony rubs sore patches on its tail, is very annoying. You can get lotions from your vet to rub in to the mane and tail, but it is always best to keep a pony stabled between the hours of four in the afternoon and ten in the morning when the midges which cause the irritation are most active.

Mineral or vitamin deficiences can quickly cause lack of condition and make your pony look off colour. If it starts gnawing wood or bark, or trying to lick the soil when it is turned out, you should make sure that the diet is not lacking in minerals.

Ponies need to have regular dental checks to see whether their teeth are giving trouble. The grinding process carried out by the back teeth, or molar teeth, can cause the teeth to become very sharp, and when that happens the cheek or tongue can become lacerated. The teeth must be rasped even to prevent any further damage being done.

All ponies harbour worms, but a healthy and well-conditioned pony will have sufficient resistance to overcome them. They will be most harmful in a pony which is unfit and lacking a proper diet. Many worms infest ponies, but the most dangerous, and probably the best known, is the little Red Worm which can cause serious damage if it is not removed by a safe method of deworming as recommended by the veterinary surgeon.

A peculiar disease which ponies may suffer from at any season of the year is called Azoturia, or 'Monday morning disease'. It is a sudden breakdown of the fibres in the big muscles of the loins and quarters and usually occurs when a pony takes part in some form of strong muscular exertion after it has had a period of rest on a full working diet. The real cause is unknown, but it is sometimes called 'Monday morning disease' because it often used to happen to working horses when they had been rested on Sunday while still being kept on full rations. The old grooms and ostlers used to try to prevent this by giving their charges a bran mash when they finished work on Saturday night to 'let them down' during their rest period.

A pony with Azoturia is a very unhappy sight, and in bad cases it may even sway or fall. Blowing, considerable distress and sweating will also be in evidence, and the muscles of the quarters will be hard and tense with muscular tremors.

The pony should be kept as warm as possible, and be allowed to rest in some sheltered place. It will need plenty of drinking water and bran mashes, and the affected muscles should be massaged and hot packs applied as quickly as possible. If the pony is stabled and you can safely rig up an electric radiator for him to stand under, the heat will be very good for him. An electric blanket can also be useful in providing warmth to the affected region. A veterinary surgeon must be called as quickly as possible or permanent damage may occur. If ponies have had Azoturia once they may well get it again unless care is taken.

Like their owners, ponies can get lockjaw or tetanus, a serious disease which is caused by a germ living in the soil which gets into the body through a scratch or cut. The disease develops after about ten days and immediate and drastic treatment is essential if the pony's life is to be saved.

If you love and care for your pony you will always want to make sure that it is as well and comfortable as possible. You must constantly be on the look out for less serious but unpleasant ailments like saddle galls, girth galls, brushing wounds, caused by the pony striking one leg against another; over reaches, caused when a pony is jumping or galloping and a hind shoe strikes a foreleg; cracked heels, when the skin behind the pastern becomes chapped; injuries to the mouth or tongue from bits which have become worn or do not fit properly, or perhaps thorns or barbs which get into a pony's legs either out in the field or when it is being ridden across country.

If your pony is off colour and you are not sure of the cause, there is only one sensible thing to do. Call the veterinary surgeon. It will be less expensive in the long run.

Circus Horses

The glamour and excitement of the circus really provides a sparkling background for the tricks and skills of the highly trained circus horses — Plumes swaying and livery glistening, they execute their routines with precision and perfect timing at their masters' commands.

Perfect Combinations

by Alan Oliver

In the world of show jumping there are several well-known riders and horses who are so perfectly matched that they seem to 'go' together in every way.

Because show jumping is covered so well on television nowadays these equestrian combinations are known to all enthusiasts. But even before television became so commonplace, and when the sport of jumping was not nearly so widespread or popular, there still must have been such combinations.

Even the youngest of readers will, I am sure, have heard of the famous Colonel Llewellyn and Foxhunter, the horse that gave his name to the greatest jumping competition in the world. Without any doubt, they were truly a perfect combination.

But even when we call something perfect we are almost certain to find one or two small faults, especially in the case of human beings and horses. A perfect rider and horse combination may sometimes be perfect only on very special occasions. After all, they were both at one time novices!

And they are sure to have their 'off' days, like everyone else!

My idea of a 'perfect' combination is those riders and horses who perform as one creature, seeming to be able to read each other's minds. These are the 'teams' that give such pleasure and excitement to the millions who watch show jumping, either on television, or at the show ring itself.

Obviously in a short book I can only mention a few of the combinations I have known, and I apologise now to those I have not included.

Alison Dawes and The Maverick (Mr Banbury)

The Maverick, who later jumped under a change of name as Mr Banbury, was bought in 1963 by Alison Westwood, as she then was, from Mr Douglas Bunn. This was the horse, soon to be so well-

known and well-loved, who brought Alison into the international jumping scene.

The Maverick was one of those horses that had a will of his own! It took two or three years of intensive schooling and training before he was completely at one

with Alison, but by 1965–66 he was considered one of the best international horses around.

He would jump consistently — and jump big fences — and he was always fast when going against the clock.

When the training period was over, Alison very quickly managed to come to an almost perfect understanding with The Maverick, and always rode with great precision and accuracy. They never performed quite as well at indoor shows; it seemed that they found it hard to adapt to the closed arenas. Outdoors, however, on the big spaces to be found at Hickstead and elsewhere, they were magnificent.

Alison is always hard to beat. I always felt if I could beat her I should win the competition!

Twice Alison and The Maverick have won the very demanding British Jumping Derby – the major competition that brings in the enormous bank at Hickstead. They have also won the Queen Elizabeth Cup and a great many of the top competitions in the world.

Both Alison and Marion, with their skill and determination, will, I am certain, be back at the top during the coming year or two. With both The Maverick and Stroller now retired, they each are bringing along their new strings of horses. I wish them both every success in the future.

Marion Mould and Stroller

Stroller, perhaps the most famous of all ponies, was brought to his state of perfection by the skill, patience and dedication of his world-famous rider, Marion Mould.

Stroller was owned as a youngster by Len Carter, who eventually sold him to Ted Cripps for his daughter, Sally, to ride. Sadly, they did not suit each other and, as Sally grew older, it was decided to part with him. He was then sold to Ralph Coakes – Marion's father – and immediately an understanding developed between this soon-to-be-famous pair. Marion rode in many junior competitions in the south of England, and had much success, although in fact they were never doing anything very extraordinary. Perhaps the fences in those competitions were not big enough!

Then Marion came into adult classes, and her record soon began to speak for itself. It is now almost impossible to discuss horses and riders or certain competitions without mentioning Marion's name. After all, when she was only eighteen, she won the Ladies World Championship at Hickstead with Stroller, and then they went on to win practically everything in sight, including the Queen Elizabeth Cup (twice), a Silver medal at the Mexico Olympic Games, the British Jumping Derby, and the Leading Show Jumper of the Year at Wembley. They helped Great Britain to win three Nations Cups, and Marion herself was voted Sportswoman of the Year in 1965.

I don't believe I will ever see another like Stroller. He was simply fantastic. And always jumped his heart out. They can truly both be called legends in their own lifetime.

Caroline Bradley

Another girl rider, one of the hardest-working in all in the world of show jumping, is Caroline Bradley.

Here is a rider who has always been in or around the top flight, and is a very tough one to beat. Caroline is dedicated to the sport, in spite of the fact that she has never managed to jump what I call an outstanding horse. What would happen if she did is anybody's guess. She would be a world beater.

Of course, in saying that I do not mean she has never ridden some very good horses. I remember the successes she had on Franco, and it is that combination I think of as 'perfect'. More recently she has set up a partnership with True Lass. But she brings her horses on slowly and rides a lot of good novices, most of which she has broken herself.

She has won an incredible number of competitions, and is immensely popular with her fellow-riders.

Harvey Smith

Now what can I say about that most controversial person who has ever jumped? And you know I can be talking about none other than the Yorkshireman, Harvey Smith.

I first saw Harvey many years ago jumping a horse called Farmer's Boy at the British Timpkin Show. It was in the puissance competition – the event in which the fences get fewer and the heights go up until a winner is found. At the trial fence (the one that doesn't count in the competition) Harvey's girth broke. Did that stop him? Of course not. He simply took the entire saddle off and jumped the course, which included a very high wall, bareback! This great personality was as determined then as he is today!

With so many different horses he is without doubt one of the greatest riders in the world. Harvey has a reputation for jumping the sort of horses others can't ride – horses like Mattie Brown, Salvador, O'Malley and Sea Hawk.

For a man with such determina-

tion and skill, Harvey has immense patience. He may upset some, but his hands and strong legs do get an awful lot out of the horse he is riding. And that is the measure of a master.

It is difficult to pick the best horse he has ridden. I always feel Harvey and Harvester were the ideal combination. In fact, they were almost perfect!

Through the years he has won so many competitions that the record of his wins would take up too much space to list. But in any case it is not necessary – Harvey Smith is so obviously a man with a will to win.

David Broome

Quite the opposite of Harvey is David Broome, his close friend and rival. David is a cool, calm and brilliant horseman and is perhaps at his best when mounted on a well-schooled and well-trained horse.

I can remember David many years ago, when he was quite a slight boy and an active member of his local branch of the Pony Club. Long before he was sixteen he had gained considerable competitive experience and, just as today, he always seemed to have something special going for him. His ponies and horses respond so quickly to his quiet riding style. He seldom seems to be doing anything, but he gets results. That is the mark of the brilliant horseman he is.

David has ridden so many top-flight horses that it is almost impossible to single out any one. Although he won the World Championship on Beethoven, considered by many as not the greatest horse of all, David's combination with Mr Softee was outstanding. Softee, as we all knew him, was really a world-beater, and it was on his back that David won his second Men's European title.

Today, I think he has the best string of anyone riding, with Philco, Sportsman, Jaegermeister and Ballywillwill. But he will always be remembered for his partnerships with Sunslave, Mr Softee, Beethoven and Manhattan.

Ted Edgar and Uncle Max

When two 'mad' things come together we had the greatest combination of all – Ted Edgar and Uncle Max. They *were* perfect!

Ted, who is David Broome's brother-in-law, is a brilliant horseman. But with Uncle Max both he and the public found something extra. Max was honest as the day is long, courageous to an extreme, and a showman's dream come true.

This ex-circus horse very quickly established himself with the crowds. Seeming to love the atmosphere of Wembley, he always put on a most spectacular display of jumping. At least, it was spectacular for the public – and quite hair-raising for Ted! And, as the crowds roared their approval, so Max seemed to jump with extra vigour and display.

Ted started riding when he was very young on show ponies, and it was through his Pony Club that he became interested in show jumping. In his younger days he was a great gymkhana expert – a

part of the sport which can do much to promote riding ability if handled properly and skilfully.

Ted has been through it all – not only show jumping of the highest order, but also point-to-point racing, and the hunting field is perhaps one of his greatest loves. He is a man with a genuine ability for all things equestrian.

Peter Robeson

Peter Robeson seems to have been around a long time. In fact, he has. Though not nearly as long as me!

Peter is a perfectionist of style. He is a cool, skilful rider who never gets excited, and an absolutely brilliant horseman.

Ever since his junior days he has kept up a really amazing record of success. Some of his greatest riding was on a fine horse called Craven A, a home-bred mare that he rode with much care and skill. For my money these were another perfect combination.

Peter won a Bronze Medal in the 1956 Olympic Games when riding Scorchin, and he has represented his country dozens of times since then. Two of his better-known horses are Grebe and Firecrest, both consistently good winners.

Peter spends hours and hours getting his horses to go his way, and gives a great deal of time, trouble and patience to his schooling sessions. He is a rider who would rather have a horse compete in the way he feels is correct, than to have a horse that wins in the way the horse would like.

Among younger riders today there are many 'perfect' combinations. I like to think of Tony Newbury on Warwick; Graham Fletcher on Buttevant Boy; Derek Ricketts on Tyrolean Holiday; Pip Nicholls on Timmie, and Nick Skelton on Everest Orchid.

I have dealt here only with the show jumpers. Think who I might have included had I been writing about eventing, dressage or polo.

The magnificent Gold State Coach

The Royal Mews

by Judith Campbell

For centuries, horses were not only an indispensable part of the royal household, they were also an important symbol of the might of the Crown. And even after monarchs of old, riding magnificent chargers, ceased to lead their armies into battle, they still appeared in public mounted on equally magnificent coursers, carefully chosen to increase the prestige of the King in the eyes of his people.

Today the horses ridden by the Queen in the royal parks at Windsor, and which inhabit the mews close by the castle, are her private property, used for the recreation she most enjoys. But the carriage horses kept in the Royal Mews at Buckingham Palace are state horses, still with important rôles. For instance, they help

to preserve the 'touch of magic' that surrounds the throne, as well as adding so much to the splendours of many royal and state occasions.

When Henry VIII's royal stables in the area which is now called Bloomsbury were destroyed by fire, he ordered the re-housing of his stud in quarters near Charing Cross in the 'King's Mewes'. Up till then this place had been inhabited, not by horses, but by the royal falcons during their 'mewing' or moult. Many reigns later, when George III bought the mansion called Buckingham House (only ready for occupation as a palace in time for Queen Victoria) the stables there were used in addition to those at Charing Cross, and in 1764 the architect, John Nash, designed the

present beautiful royal riding house (school). The stables and coachhouses at the palace were redesigned by the same famous man four years after George IV came to the throne, and in 1825 they became the official royal mews.

Through the years, a wonderful collection of saddles, bridles and other equipment presented by Heads of State, and of carriages and harness, has been built up, but part of the fascination of the mews is that it is not only a museum of historic treasures but also a very busy working unit. It is run by the Department of the Royal Mews under the executive command of the Crown Equerry. The Department is concerned with all royal travel by road, and since the day-to-day transport of modern monarchs is nowadays usually by car, the Crown Equerry must be responsible for cars as well as for horses and carriages.

Thus limousines and luggage brakes, the buses and Land Rovers that convey the royal household, the Royal family's private cars, and

The Cleveland Bays with the State Landau Leaving the Royal Mews for a state occasion

A pair of Windsor Greys with the Royal Postilion Scarlet livery for the royal coachman

the four beautiful state Rolls Royces frequently used by the Queen on official occasions, are all kept in the mews, in converted coach-houses beyond the main quadrangle. But although these motorised vehicles, and their maintenance, are an indispensable part of the Mews and of the work that goes on there, this does not mean that the coaches and carriages, still housed as they have always been on the east side of the quadrangle, are only for show. Nor does it mean that the horses kept in the original stables, still considered some of the finest in existence, are show-pieces retained only for their appearance.

On the two afternoons a week when the public are admitted to the mews, they are able to walk down the broad corridor dividing the long rows of roomy stalls, now mostly converted into loose-boxes, and admire the horses, each one of which has its name adorning the wall above the manger. At different times since the reign of George II, the royal carriage horses have been duns, creams or blacks. Now many are bay, a few still of Dutch, German or Irish origin, but mostly pure or half-bred Cleveland Bays. The breed is descended from sturdy pack ponies, but now resembles the handsome York-

Below Cleaning the Irish State Coach

shire Coach Horses popular in Edwardian times. The remainder of the horses are the famous Windsor Greys. They are not a breed — some of them hale from Ireland, others are German Oldenburgs. There has also been an occasional half-bred Percheron not the heavy horses discussed in another chapter, these take their name from the small grey horses, not much larger than ponies, that were kept at Windsor for drawing Queen Victoria's private carriages around the Parks.

But whatever their colour, the state horses with their gleaming coats, wearing rugs that bear the royal cipher and with their tails done up in attractive blue bandages, have considerably more to do in life than to spend their time peacefully dreaming amongst the graceful arches and decorative architecture of by-gone days.

For wherever there are horses there are specific daily chores to be done at specific times. At the mews, the days start early with the usual routine of watering, feeding, mucking out and grooming. By normal standards the tack cleaning is a monumental task, for in addition to the workaday harness and exercise saddlery, there is all the priceless ceremonial harness to deal with, some of it so old that only care can preserve it. It takes two men all their time to keep the eight different sets of state harness oiled and polished, and as soon as they finish it all it is time to start again!

All the horses are exercised daily except for Sunday. Those without a special duty on hand are either driven out and about the London streets before the traffic builds up, or are ridden under saddle. A branch of the Disabled Riders' Association have been given permission by the Queen to hold some of their sessions in the big riding house, and both the size and convenience of this building are also fully used for exercising the royal horses. There are always young horses being 'brought on', and much of their training, too, takes place on the soft tan of the school. And an added convenience is that this training is carried out to the accompaniment of an ampli-

Above: **The Queen passing Horse Guards Parade to the delight of the crowds**

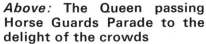

Left: **The Tritons on the State Coach**

fied recording of most of the sounds, very strange to a young horse's ears, that accompany ceremonial occasions.

Just like a police horse, any royal carriage horse has to be very dependable before being used for work like this. The older animals also receive frequent 'refresher courses' in the clamour produced by brass bands and rolling drums, by the tramp of marching feet and shouts of military orders, or the sudden shrill notes of a fanfare and the swelling roar of cheering. The one element that cannot be reproduced in the training is the actual atmosphere of tension and excitement built up by vast crowds, which can have a big effect on animals as sensitive as horses. And, as we have already seen in the chapter on training police horses, the best way to overcome this obstacle lies in long and patient

training.

Six days a week, soon after breakfast and again after lunch, a royal coachman wearing the everyday livery of a black jacket and top hat with the customary cockade up the side drives out from the mews under the entrance archway with its distinctive clock tower, and turns left into Buckingham Palace Road. The vehicle is always that single horse small, four-wheeled closed carriage called a Brougham, of which the Clarence, drawn by a pair, is a larger version. Although the same horse is on 'duty' for a day at a time, most of them are used in turn so that they become accustomed to being driven singly in traffic. The destination is the palace, with a stop at the royal post office and another at the Privy Purse door, to pick up the royal mail that goes by hand. After collection, the conveyance trots off down the Mall to Clarence House or any other required destination.

Many royal guests, and all new ambassadors calling to present their credentials to the Queen, are conveyed to and from the palace by carriage and pair. Sometimes the chosen vehicle is the handsome, maroon-coloured King Edward VII's town coach. Occasionally it may be the fairy-tale glass coach that, with its wide windows and interior lighting, is a favourite with royal brides. This is the coach, drawn by a pair of Windsor Greys driven from the box, that brought Princess Anne and Prince Philip to Westminster Abbey for her wedding, and conveyed bride and groom back to the palace afterwards. Together with all the other pageantry the lovely coach increased the splendour and entrancement of that exciting day.

New High Commissioners of republics within the Commonwealth have the honour of going to the palace in one of the five historic semi-state Landaus, Queen Victoria's favourite carriages for ceremonial occasions. The one built in 1866 that she used a year later for the Jubilee Thanksgiving Service at Westminster Abbey, was drawn by six cream stallions. Stallions are not suitable for modern conditions, and nowadays the state Landaus (that can also be drawn with a pair) semi-state Landaus, and the lighter, even more elegant Ascot Landaus used for the Queen's procession at Royal Ascot, are usually drawn by teams of four geldings. The horses are controlled by two postilions, who wear for state occasions a scarlet and gold jacket, wig and cap, and have a dark blue jacket with gilt buttons and gold laced top hat as their semi-state livery. For Ascot, their scarlet, purple and gold jackets are in the Queen's racing colours. Whatever the livery, postilions always wear buckskin breeches and top boots with a guard on the outside of the right leg, as protection from the harness. They always ride the near-side horse, and control the off-side animal as well.

The coachmen, who take precedence over postilions, with a head coachman over all, drive pairs or teams of four from the box. Their liveries are even more splendid; the full State livery consists of a magnificent and weighty scarlet and gold frock coat, scarlet plush knee breeches, pink silk stockings, gold buckled shoes, and a tricorne hat with ostrich feathers, to top the customary wig.

Except when the Queen visited the City of York and made a point of using Cleveland Bays, the local breed, a team of Windsor Greys, either driven or postilion controlled, always draws the Queen's carriage, and, usually those of other members of the Royal Family.

When there are great ceremonial processions, like the state opening of Parliament to which the Queen drives in the gilded, crown-sur-mounted Irish State Coach, every suitable coach, carriage and horse in the mews is pressed into service, including attractive barouche in which the Queen Mother drives to the Trooping the Colour, and the elegant Scottish State Coach that was renovated quite recently. Some of the other exhibits, the Balmoral Sociable in which Queen Victoria was driven over a pass in the Swiss Alps, or the unique Ivory Phaeton, are used occasion-ally at Windsor or Balmoral, or

appear on some occasion like the Royal Windsor Show. Even the French charabanc, with its striped and fringed top that was used for Victorian picnics and shooting parties, makes the occasional appearance for the press. It seems a pity that modern winters no longer often provide the snow, necessary for Queen Victoria's 'quite charming' drive out from Brighton, in the sleigh known as the State Sledge.

There are also some fine private vehicles in the mews, wagonettes, governess carts, pony carriages — little used since the two younger Princes outgrew their Shetland pony — and the dog carts that Prince Philip often uses for his new sport of competitive driving.

He began this sport when he gave up polo, and starting with a single harness horse, with charac-teristic determination has now arrived at the point where he competes with a four-in-hand of the pure or half-bred Cleveland Bays. He drives them with verve in all three phases, particularly in the cross-country section, giving his team work that is very unlike their normal routine of trotting sedately around the London streets!

In the early morning of the first Saturday in June, the Mews sees an unfamiliar sight — policemen in shirt-sleeves, busily grooming a number of police horses to an even greater state of perfection than usual. Later, they accoutre the animals in ceremonial saddlery, ready for the service chiefs and high ranking members of the Royal household who will ride them to the Trooping the Colour, the ceremony to celebrate the Sovereign's official Birthday, held on Horse Guards Parade. And before long a very special horse (for many years now the black mare, Burmese, presented by the Royal Canadian Mounted Police) is seen being led around wearing a beautiful ceremonial bridle and the side-saddle, with one gilt-gold stirrup and blue saddlecloth em-broidered in gold, that the Queen uses for the one and only occasion when she appears in public on horseback.

Amongst this wonderful collection in the Royal Mews, there is only one vehicle with which the horses must go no faster than a walk. That is the most famous and valuable of all — the superbly carved and decorated coach that was built for King George III, and first arrived at the Mews on the 24th November 1762. It is 24 ft long, 12 ft high and weighs four tons. It has been used for every coronation since that of George IV, and the last time this magnificent gilded vehicle was out on the road was on the 2nd June 1953. On that day the Gold State Coach controlled by postilions and attendants on foot and drawn by eight of the Windsor Greys, decked out in the sets of crimson morocco-leather harness that are ornamented with gilt ormolu and weigh more than 100 pounds each, took Queen Elizabeth II out from the palace, through Admiralty Arch and so to Westminster Abbey for her Crowning.

Above left:
The Royal coachman and the Gold State coach
Above:
Royal postilions in full State livery
Left:
Scarlet and gold pageantry

A Glossary of Terms used in Riding

Aids
The signals given by the rider to a horse to tell him what to do. There are two types of aids – the natural, which are the voice, body, legs and hands; and the artificial, which include spurs, whips, martingales.

Backing
Mounting a young horse for the first time when breaking it in.

Bits
The metal, rubber or vulcanite bar worn in the horse's mouth and attached to the bridle and reins. Several different types of bits are in use, the simplest being called a snaffle.

Braiding
An American word for plaiting.

Bridle
The leather headpiece worn by a horse. The bit and the reins are fitted to the bridle.

Browband
The band which crosses the forehead under the forelock.

Brushing
This is caused when the edge of the shoe on the inner side of the hoof catches the opposite leg, usually near the fetlock joint. Brushing is common with horses that jump and, when it occurs, brushing boots are fitted as protection.

Chestnut
The natural horn-like growth on a horse's legs.

Cheek-pieces
Part of a bridle, comprising two straight pieces, each with a buckle at either end, to which the bit is fitted.

Colt
A young unbroken male horse.

Conformation
The build of a horse.

Dam
A mother horse.

Ergot
A horn-like substance found on the point of the fetlock joint.

Farrier
Another name for a blacksmith.

Filly
A female foal.

Flash
A broad white stripe running down a horse's face.

Forehand
The part of a horse in front of the saddle.

Forelock
Part of the mane which falls down a horse's forehead.

Frog
Found on the sole of a horse's hoof. It is shaped like a triangle.

Gelding
A male horse which, after an operation, cannot be used for breeding purposes.

Girth
The strap that goes under the horse's belly and secures the saddle.

Hackamore
A bitless bridle.

Halter
A form of headcollar made from webbing and rope. Used for leading and tying-up.

Hand
Horses are measured in hands – each hand being 4 inches. Therefore, a horse standing at 15 hands would stand 60 inches, or five feet, from the highest point of his withers to the ground.

Headpiece
That part of the bridle which passes behind the ears and which is buckled to the cheek-pieces.

Impulsion
A word used to denote the impetus to move forward that is built up in a horse by correct use of the hands, seat and body weight of the rider.

Irons
Another word for stirrups.

Leathers
The leather straps, running from the saddle, which hold the stirrups or irons.

Martingale
One of the artificial aids. It is a strap that is fixed from the noseband or reins to the girth to prevent a horse from throwing up its head. There are several kinds, including the Standing, Running and Fixed martingale.

Near-side
A horse's left-hand side, the side from which mounting usually takes place.

Numdah, Numnah
A saddle cloth, made from either lambswool, nylon or cotton.

Poll
That part of a horse's head between the ears.

Pommel
The front and highest part of the saddle.

Roller
A form of girth, usually made from leather or webbing, which fits round a horse's body to keep rugs in position.

Run-out
A term used when a horse avoids a jump or leaves the ring without being asked.

Schedule
The programme prepared for a show. This will show the types of competitions and the heights of the fences, together with any special local rules and conditions.

Sircingle
A form of roller.

Skip
Used when mucking-out a stable.

Stallion
A male horse that can be bred from.

Star
A white patch, sometimes in the shape of a star or diamond, found on a horse's forehead.

Stirrups
The metal fittings, frequently referred to as the 'irons', in which the rider's feet are placed.

Stud
The place or establishment at which horses are bred.

Tack
Another name for saddlery.

Throatlash
A strap which passes under a horse's throat from the bridle.

Tree
The frame around which a saddle is built.

Withers
Highest part of a horse's back, from which all measurements of height are taken.

Yearling
A horse which is more than one year old, but which has not reached two years.